PUBLISHED ON THE LOUIS STERN
MEMORIAL FUND

GEORGE ELIOT

GEORGE ELIOT

&

JOHN CHAPMAN

WITH CHAPMAN'S DIARIES

BY

GORDON S. HAIGHT

NEW HAVEN · YALE UNIVERSITY PRESS

LONDON · HUMPHREY MILFORD · OXFORD UNIVERSITY PRESS

1940

To M. N. H.

PREFACE

IN 1842 when Marian Evans became acquainted with Charles Bray of Coventry, he was absorbed in the study of phrenology, the new "science" that was to solve all the old problems of the world through a proper understanding of human character as revealed by the contour of the skull. His enthusiasm was quickly communicated to her, and she went with him to Deville's shop in the Strand to have a cast made of her head. It was still in Bray's possession in 1885, when in his autobiography he described his remarkable young friend. Whatever one may think of phrenology, his account deserves serious consideration as the opinion of one who had known her intimately for nearly forty years. Her head was

a very large one [he wrote], 22¼ inches round; George Combe, on first seeing the cast, took it for a man's. . . . In her brain-development the Intellect greatly predominates. . . . In the Feelings, the Animal and Moral regions are about equal; the moral being quite sufficient to keep the animal in order and in due subservience, but would not be spontaneously active. The social feelings were very active, particularly the adhesiveness. She was of a most affectionate disposition, always requiring some one to lean upon, preferring what has hitherto been considered the stronger sex, to the other and more impressible. She was not fitted to stand alone.[1]

"She was not fitted to stand alone." In that phrase lies the key to an understanding of her extraordinary life. All the strange contradictions in her career, from the passionate childish dependence on her brother, reflected in Maggie Tulliver, to her marriage with John W. Cross a few months before her death are explained by her "always requiring some one to lean upon."

In the official biography of George Eliot, Mr. Cross perpetuated the Victorian Sibyl, who spoke all the modern European languages, read her Sophocles in the Greek, translated Spinoza's *Ethics* as a hobby, and turned for recreation to lectures on experimental physics. It has struck more than one reader as curious that this

1. Charles Bray, *Phases of Opinion and Experience during a Long Life: An Autobiography*, 2d ed., London [1885], pp. 74–75.

solemn Wise Woman who smiles so rarely in the pages of her biography should be the creator of Mrs. Poyser and Jane Glegg. And it has seemed even more paradoxical that her characters are destined to suffer relentlessly for any deviation from the moral code, while for twenty-four years their author lived openly in London with a married man whose lawful wife dwelt only a few squares away.

Mr. Cross knew her only in her Sibylline years. In treating the earlier periods of her life he deliberately sought evidence of a later sententiousness. Her letters contain many passages that would have relieved his too somber portrait had he published them; but as he explains, "no single letter is printed entire from the beginning to the end"; he has "pruned" them "of everything that I thought my wife would have wished to be omitted."[2] When she wrote, "It is raining horribly here—raining blue devils," the last three words were pruned; her description of German ballet girls as "Greek shades looking like butchers in *chemises*" disappeared altogether; and when she exclaimed over some misplaced proofs, "I would rather have lost one of my toes," Cross silently changed the word *toes* to *fingers*.[3]

From such treatment it is small wonder that George Eliot emerges as a rather chilly goddess, with little trace of the humor and common sympathy that her novels show her to have possessed in abundance. Fortunately, the letters are now in the Yale University Library, where I am editing them for publication. When the complete text is available the real George Eliot will appear, not less worthy of admiration, it is hoped, but far more plausible than the marmoreal image her fond husband presented to the world.

None of Cross's prunings did more violence to the portrait of George Eliot than his virtual elimination of John Chapman from the *Life*. He is mentioned only a few times and in a casual manner suggesting a remoteness that was far from the truth; the index omits his name altogether.[4] And yet for two years George Eliot

2. J. W. Cross, *George Eliot's Life,* 3 vols., Edinburgh and London, 1885, I, 38 and vii.
3. 11 October 1849; 9 January 1855; Sunday [February 1846].
4. The Yale collection includes about 70 letters that George Eliot wrote in

lived under the same roof with Chapman, regarding herself as his
"helpmate"; he was an important link in the chain of circumstances that transformed the country girl from Warwickshire into
the most famous Englishwoman of her day. With so many of her
letters before him Cross can hardly have failed to see the signifi-
cance of her first years in London. Had he wished, he might have
made inquiries of Chapman, who survived George Eliot fourteen
years. More than one contemporary remarked it as curious that
Chapman had contributed nothing to her biography.

In my opinion the omission was intentional. Cross had doubtless
heard some unsavory gossip about Chapman, who was a notorious
philanderer. A preposterous myth was current that he had had a
son by George Eliot who was secretly educated in Edinburgh.[5]
Needless to say, there was no basis of fact for such scandal, and
Cross's effort to minimize the friendship merely cast an air of mystery about it that encouraged absurd speculation.

Fortunately, there has survived the Diary that Chapman kept
in 1851, when Miss Evans came to live at his house in the Strand.
Found about 1913 on a bookstall in Sneinton Market, Nottingham,
it passed successively through the hands of Sir W. Robertson Nicoll
and of Mr. Clement Shorter, who seems to have contemplated
writing a life of Chapman. Thanks to the Altschul Fund, the Yale
Library Associates acquired it in 1930 from Mr. Gabriel Wells. It
is now published for the first time. Miss Evans is mentioned frequently in this closely written little book, for she played a leading
role in the extraordinary drama of love and jealousy revolving
about Chapman in 1851. Some leaves have been cut out, and many
of the more intimate references to her are heavily overscored, apparently by Chapman himself. With photographic enlargements
contrived by Mr. Frederic G. Ludwig, and other devices, it has
been possible to recover most of these passages. They are indicated
in the text by angular brackets, $< >$.

Together with this volume Chapman's Diaries for 1860 and
1863 were also found. Though not lacking in human interest, supplied in this case by a young German opera singer, the 1860 Diary,
which is likewise in the Yale University Library, deals mainly with

1852; of the 31 containing references to Chapman, Cross prints excerpts from
25, but Chapman is mentioned only twice: I, 278, 298.
5. Anne Fremantle, *George Eliot*, New York, 1933, p. 105.

the *Westminster Review* and Chapman's perennial business difficulties. Miss Evans—or Mrs. Lewes, as she is now called—is referred
to only a few times. The 1863 Diary never came into Mr. Wells's
possession; my efforts to find it have been frustrated by the war in
Europe. From existing descriptions of its contents, however, it
seems unlikely to add anything to the story of George Eliot.

The Diaries are of a common type published in London by
Letts, Son and Steer. They measure 7¾ by 4⅞ inches and are
bound in black cloth with the date prominently stamped in gilt
upon the cover. The title page for 1851 is reproduced on page 122,
the cover for 1860, facing page 221. The prefatory section contains directories of provincial bankers, government officials, and
members of Parliament, calendars, interest tables, and other miscellaneous information. In the Diary proper, printed headings
give the day of the week, the day of the month, and the day of the
year, with the number of days remaining, the phase of the moon,
and the number of the month:

15 Thursday [*135–230*] ○

15 May ⌒   ⌒ *5th Month 1851.*

This form has been simplified in the present volume to:

Thursday 15 May 1851.

If the page where an entry appears differs from the date when it
was written, the latter is given in square brackets:

Wednesday 15 [*19*] *January 1851.*

The present text of the Diaries reproduces the original closely,
without attempting to make a page-by-page facsimile of the
manuscript. For the reader's convenience letters or words inadvertently omitted by Chapman have occasionally been inserted in
square brackets. His spelling and punctuation have been kept in
all their glory, without intrusion of the admonitory *sic*. Some words
like *controul* and *benifit* he misspells consistently; but usually he
seeks variety, particularly in proper names. He writes both *Evans'*

and *Evan's, Dickens'* and *Dicken's* as well as *Dickins,* while his son's name appears on the same page as *Ernest* and *Earnest.* In the text such eccentricities have been retained. In passages quoted elsewhere, however, I have corrected them, expanded habitual contractions, and normalized the punctuation. The same editorial method has been followed in quoting from manuscripts of George Eliot, though her spelling has been changed only in the word *surprise,* in which she habitually employs a *z.* The symbol GE in the notes signifies George Eliot.

Unless otherwise specified, all manuscripts cited are in the Yale University Library, to the staff of which I acknowledge my gratitude for constant assistance. Miss Emily H. Hall, Supervisor of the Rare Book Room, helped especially in reading deleted passages. To Professor Chauncey Brewster Tinker, the Keeper of Rare Books, I am deeply indebted, both for his acquisitive zeal, through which the Yale Collection of George Eliot has become the greatest in the world, and for permission to use the books and manuscripts in his private library. Mr. Morris L. Parrish, with the generosity that has endeared him to scholars, opened to me his famous collection at Dormy House, Pine Valley, New Jersey; through his kindness some of the most remarkable letters in this book are published here for the first time.

The Library of Congress, the Huntington Library, the Morgan Library, the New York Public Library, the New York Academy of Medicine, and the Reference Library of the Bank of England have all contributed in various ways. The National Youth Administration provided clerical assistance for transcribing the Diaries, and Mr. Robert J. Fitzwilliam, who held a Bursary Appointment in Berkeley College, Yale University, typed the manuscript. Professors Anna T. Kitchel, Richard L. Purdy, Carl F. Schreiber, and Townsend Scudder helped with special problems. Professor George H. Nettleton read the entire manuscript and made many valuable suggestions. To all of these my hearty thanks.

GORDON S. HAIGHT

Calhoun College,
14 July 1940.

CONTENTS

ILLUSTRATIONS

GEORGE ELIOT AND JOHN CHAPMAN

GEORGE ELIOT AND JOHN CHAPMAN

CHAPTER I

John Chapman, Publisher

IN the autumn of 1843 a fine-looking young man of twenty-two entered the shop of John Green, the publisher, at 121 Newgate Street, and offered him the manuscript of a little book he had written. It was called *Human Nature: A Philosophical Exposition of the Divine Institution of Reward and Punishment which Obtains in the Physical, Intellectual, and Moral Constitutions of Man: with an Introductory Essay. To which is Added a Series of Ethical Observations Written during the Perusal of the Rev. James Martineau's Recent Work Entitled "Endeavours after the Christian Life."* Having published a good many similar books from both sides of the Atlantic, Green was not in the least appalled by this title. But he explained to the young man, who was named John Chapman, that it would be unfair for him to undertake the work, since he had decided to dispose of his business and was at that very moment looking for someone to buy it. The outcome was that Chapman himself became the purchaser, and *Human Nature* appeared with his own imprint in February 1844.

Little is known of his early life. He was born at Ruddington, near Nottingham, June 21, 1821,[1] the third son of William Chapman, a druggist,[2] and his first wife (1789–1824). At the customary age he was apprenticed to a watchmaker named Robert Mason at Worksop. A handsome youth of striking appearance, Chapman was "so much like the portraits of Lord Byron that amongst his companions he was always called 'Byron.'"[3] In these new surroundings his extraordinary faculty for making friends at once asserted itself, though the

1. In a letter to Barbara Leigh Smith, 24 August 1855, Chapman writes, "I was born in 1821." The commonly accepted date as given in *The Dictionary of National Biography* is 1822.
2. He is so listed in Francis White, *History, Gazetteer, and Directory of Nottinghamshire*, Sheffield, 1853. John Chapman's marriage registration describes him as a "chemist." William Chapman was born in 1792 and married for the third time in 1851. See Diary, 20 June 1851.
3. *Athenæum*, 15 December 1894, p. 828.

more conservative stood aloof, considering him something of a radical. He had an original, speculative mind, eager to welcome phrenology or coöperatives or any new idea that promised to improve the lot of mankind. At the Pestalozzian Institution, which brought scientific and literary men to lecture at Worksop, Chapman occasionally met "advanced thinkers" like John Bowring, John Minter Morgan, and Robert Owen, imbibing some of their opinions. Such interests consort ill with the character of the Industrious Apprentice; one learns without surprise that Chapman was far from contented with his lot. According to Robert White of Worksop, "a most intimate friend of his during this period,"

Chapman, having grave complaints against his master's treatment, determined to run away. At this time his brother was studying medicine in Edinburgh, and as this was before there was any railway communication between that city and this town he had to get to the nearest seaport from which he could take steamer to Leith. The writer well remembers assisting to get his box to the coach by which he went to Gainsborough and thence to Hull. When his master got to know where he was, he sent a man after him to Edinburgh, and Chapman, on hearing he was pursued, went a few miles into the country until his pursuer was tired of waiting. On his return, and after staying with his brother a short time, the latter purchased him a stock of watches, chronometers, sextants, &c., and he went to Adelaide, S. A., where he commenced business. I possess a copy of his engraved business card done in Edinburgh before he left. After staying a few years in Adelaide, he returned, and a few days after his arrival I received a letter from him in which he stated that he had made a fortune, but had been shipwrecked and had lost it.[4]

Some of these details smack of the romancer making a good story of his travels for a gullible friend. White adds that the next stage in Chapman's eventful life was to go to London to study medicine at St. Bartholomew's. Of this there is no record. We learn from his Diary,[5] however, that he was in Paris in 1842; he always insisted that part of his medical training

---

4. *Ibid.* White was the author and publisher of *Worksop, "The Dukery," and Sherwood Forest*, Worksop, 1875.

5. 4 January 1851.

was obtained there, and one of his letters refers to the French chemist Gay-Lussac as "my old teacher."[6]

The period allotted to each of these ventures must have been brief, for he was just twenty-two at the time of his marriage June 27, 1843, when he described himself in the register as a "surgeon," dwelling in the parish of St. Werbergh's Derby.[7] His bride was Susanna Brewitt, also "of full age," daughter of Thomas Brewitt, a lace manufacturer at Basford, Nottingham, who made a generous settlement on her.[8] After the marriage, which was performed according to the rites of the Established Church, the young couple went to London, where Chapman relinquished his unlicensed career as surgeon for that of author and publisher. The only account of him at this time is an oblique one supplied by his Diary,[9] where Chapman remarks that he saw in Herbert Spencer, "in all his views, his zeal, his idealism, and confidence that there is no absolute evil, etc. the mirror of what I was in 1843-4 and 5." No doubt there were differences between them that the author of Human Nature did not discern.

The Chapmans settled down in Clapton, where their first child Beatrice was born December 28, 1844. Here they began giving the evening parties that made so pleasant a feature of their life in later years. At one that Herbert Spencer attended in January 1846 he met William Howitt,[10] whose Popular History of Priestcraft Chapman had just reprinted.[11] At another he was introduced to Miss Sara Hennell, a sister of Mrs. Charles Bray of Coventry. There were boarders living with the family, too, among them Miss Eliza Lynn, the author of a learned historical novel called Azeth the Egyptian. "Very

6. Chapman to Johanna von Heyligenstaedt, 24 October 1861.

7. From a certified copy of the entry at Somerset House, London. The officiating minister was R. W. Almond, M.A., and the witnesses Thomas Strover, Lieut. R.N., and Maria Wayre.

8. She had £60 apart from her husband, but probably a larger sum over which he had control. See Chapman to Barbara Leigh Smith, 4 September 1855.

9. 27 April 1851.

10. Herbert Spencer, An Autobiography, 2 vols., London, 1904, I, 294, 347.

11. The seventh edition of a book written in 1833, when, like Chapman's father, Howitt was a chemist at Nottingham.

peculiar of Miss Sennacherib to take lodgings at Mr. Chapman's; how many more young ladies is he going to have?" Mrs. Bray inquired of her sister.[12]

Among other things inherited from Green was the English agency for the *Dial;* Chapman's name appeared on the cover of the final number in April 1844. Having long felt a great admiration for Emerson, he was eager now as a publisher to add him to his list of authors. He secured a letter of introduction from Henry G. Wright, just back from a disillusioning experience in Alcott's Fruitlands community. On the same sheet with this letter (which described his good and increasing connection among the best of our modern thinkers, "especially among the Unitarians") Chapman wrote Emerson August 3, 1844. In due course a friendly understanding was reached, by which he was to publish Emerson's books in London on a basis of half profits.[13] The first to appear was *Emancipation of the Negroes in the British West Indies,* in October 1844, followed in November by the *Essays, Second Series* with Carlyle's Introduction.

A quarterly magazine called the *Christian Teacher,* edited by the Reverend J. H. Thom, was also among the assets acquired from Green—or liabilities, rather, in this case, for its circulation had declined until it no longer paid expenses. Though the magazine was liberal in its way, representing the more advanced group of Unitarians, it was too narrow for its new publisher. He dreamed of transforming it into an international periodical that would attract the most enlightened minds in England as well as America. Writing Theodore Parker to enlist his support, Chapman begged him to sound out Emerson, to whom Parker accordingly wrote:

12. Bray–Hennell Extracts, 12 November 1846. For the use of Mr. Cross these extracts relating to Marian Evans were copied by Sara Hennell from correspondence with Mr. Bray and other members of her family. They are in the collection of Professor Chauncey Brewster Tinker.

Miss Lynn says that Chapman was called the "Raffaelle bookseller." (Eliza Lynn Linton, *My Literary Life,* London, 1899, p. 92.)

13. R. L. Rusk, ed., *The Letters of Ralph Waldo Emerson,* 6 vols., New York, 1939, III, 265 n. 93; 297. By permission of the Columbia University Press.

Mr. Chapman—a transcendental bookseller (121, Newgate Street London)—successor to Mr J. H. Greene the Unitarian & Transcendental Bibliopole for all England hitherto—wishes to start a *new* Dial i.e. a monthly Magazine—to be printed in London—to be written for by *yourself*—Mr *Carlyle, Tennyson, Hamden—Bailey* & such others as may be—not excepting *Jas. Martineau* & Mr *Thom.* He is sanguine of writers,—& readers none the less—I am sanguine of neither, & think the thing will never go—But he requested me to see if you would 'coöperate,' with him & his in case such a thing was started.[14]

Since Parker's lack of enthusiasm was shared by most of the others, nothing resulted from the appeal to Emerson. In 1845 a triumvirate of Unitarian ministers—Martineau, J. J. Tayler, and Charles Wicksteed—joined the editorial board; the *Christian Teacher* then became the *Prospective Review,* appearing quarterly until 1855, when it was merged with the newly founded *National.* The *Prospective* differed little in tone from its predecessor, and though Chapman remained as its publisher, it was far from satisfying his ideal of a review.

During 1846 his publications bore the imprint *Chapman Brothers.* Which of his brothers had joined the firm I do not know. The arrangement was short-lived, terminating at the end of the year, when the imprint once again became *John Chapman.* The most important book published during the partnership was Emerson's *Poems.* To its author this edition proved "a magazine of vexations" on account of the careless proofreading. By the time Emerson set out for England in 1847 no profit whatever had accrued to him from any of his London editions, so that his opinion of Chapman as a publisher was, to say the least, equivocal.[15]

Chapman had just leased a house at 142 Strand and moved his publishing business into the ground floor, while he and his family (now including two children—Beatrice, aged three, and Ernest, a year and a half) occupied the floors above. It was a very large house with ample room for boarders, who seem to have followed the Chapmans wherever they went. The evening gatherings that had begun at Clapton now be-

14. *Ibid.,* III, 287 n. 30.   15. *Ibid.,* III, 356, 378; IV, 14.

came something of an institution. Many literary people found the house a convenient place to stay in London. Americans, too, made it their headquarters—Greeley, Jarves, Putnam, Noah Porter, and Bryant, for example—and recommended it to friends who were going abroad. Here on his arrival in town at the end of October 1847 Emerson called to meet his publisher, to whom he was soon referring in letters as "my London friend, John Chapman the bookseller."

The following March, when he returned from his lecture tour, Emerson became a boarder at 142 Strand, with a good sitting room and chamber to himself, which he occupied for nearly three months. Chapman made himself very busy about lecture engagements for his distinguished guest, and talked to him a good deal about the plan for an international review to be "published simultaneously in London & Boston, and as he constantly affirms, substantially on the plan of the Dial." In April Emerson wrote his wife:

I find Chapman very anxious to establish a journal common to Old & New England, as was long ago proposed—Froude & Clough & other Oxonians & others would gladly conspire. Let the Mass. Q. [*Massachusetts Quarterly Review*] give place to this, & we should have two legs, & bestride the sea.

The earlier doubts had been completely dissipated on acquaintance, for Emerson added: "In Chapman's plan of a common Journal, we should really secure a phœnix of a publisher a man of integrity & of talent in his trade with the liveliest interest in the project itself."[16]

At the end of his visit Emerson was sent on his way with a large party at the Chapmans', attended, according to one perhaps excessive estimate, by two or three hundred persons.[17] On the way to Liverpool he stopped at Coventry to see Charles Bray, author of *The Philosophy of Necessity*, who was waiting on the station platform when the train pulled in at midnight. Next morning the Brays presented their friend Miss Mary Ann Evans. Emerson fell at once into earnest conversation with her. Suddenly Mrs. Bray saw him start as if

16. *Ibid.*, IV, 60, 56, 61.
17. Townsend Scudder, *The Lonely Wayfaring Man*, New York, 1936, p. 144.

some remark of the low-voiced girl had shocked him. He had been surprised on asking what her favorite book was, to hear her reply, "Rousseau's *Confessions.*" "It is mine, too," he said. Soon Edward Flower, the wealthy brewer from Stratford, who had learned that Emerson was at the Brays', came and persuaded them all to go over to "see Shakespeare" and lunch at his house. Having paid their respects to Stratford past and present, the Brays and Miss Evans drove home with Emerson in an open carriage. Years after, she recalled that mild face that smiled so beneficently on her as they rode through the lanes of Warwickshire.[18] "He was much struck with Mary Ann," Mrs. Bray wrote her sister; "expressed his admiration many times to Charles.—'That young lady has a calm, serious soul.' "[19]

The phœnix of a publisher and the lady with the calm, serious soul were not strangers to each other. In 1843 when Mrs. Bray's brother Charles C. Hennell married Miss Elizabeth Rebecca Brabant, he interrupted an arduous labor that she had undertaken—the translation of David Friedrich Strauss's *Das Leben Jesu.* Mrs. Hennell—Rufa, her friends called her—suggested that Miss Evans should complete the work, which had progressed only part way through the first of three volumes. She began in January 1844; by the end of November the first volume was finished; the second was ready in April 1845; proof began to come in November; and by April 1846 the manuscript was complete. Mr. Hennell, who attended to all the business arrangements, had agreed with Chapman to publish it for half profits. At the end of May, just before the book came out, Miss Evans went to London to stay with Miss Sara Hennell, who had helped her with the translation, criticizing it, "correcting" the style, and reading proof. Sara lived with her mother not far from the Chapmans and often called on them.

Although no record of a meeting survives, there is little doubt that the translator of Strauss and her publisher became acquainted at this time. They stood in curious contrast—

18. GE to Sara Hennell, 27 August 1860.
19. Bray–Hennell Extracts, 16 July 1848.

Chapman only twenty-five years old, handsome, confident, magnetic, brimming over with enthusiasm for his ambitious projects, and the homely country girl two years his senior, but diffident of her powers, with hair unbecomingly curled over her ears, "badly dressed," having "an unwashed, unbrushed, unkempt look altogether,"[20] and an awkwardness of manner that bespoke her provincial background. Did he try to dazzle her calm, serious soul? Later, when some question arose about the agreement for publishing Strauss, Miss Evans wrote Sara Hennell: "I hope Mr. Chapman will not misbehave, but he was always too much of the *interesting* gentleman to please me. Men must not attempt to be interesting on any lower terms than a fine poetical genius."[21] She too, it seems, had noticed the Byron in him.

During the next three years she was increasingly occupied with her father, whose health had long been precarious. In September 1848 when the doctor said that Mr. Evans might die suddenly at any time, the anxiety became intense for Mary Ann, who was always alone with him. She struggled to resign herself to the inevitable loss, turning for consolation to Spinoza and Thomas à Kempis.[22] She had first read Spinoza in 1843;[23] now during the months of waiting she began to translate the *Tractatus Theologico-Politicus,* of which there was no English version. At Mrs. Bray's suggestion she wrote Chapman to propose that he publish it,[24] and receiving a tentative consent went at the tightly packed Latin with renewed vigor. "Mary Ann is happy now with this Spinoza to do," Mrs. Bray wrote her sister; "she says it is such a rest to her mind."[25] She was desperately in need of something to lean

20. Eliza Lynn Linton, *My Literary Life,* London, 1899, p. 95.
21. Sunday [28 February 1847].
22. Her copy of *De Imitatione Christi,* inscribed "Mary Anne Evans, Feb. 1849," is in the Gulson Library, Coventry.
Recording her birth in his diary, Robert Evans spells the name *Mary Ann.* The Chilvers Coton parish register gives it as *Mary Anne.* Since Mrs. Bray always wrote *Mary Ann,* I have used that form consistently in this chapter. The name is also spelled without an *e* in Lewes's will; see B. C. Williams, *George Eliot,* New York, 1936, facing p. 168.
23. Bray–Hennell Extracts, 4 January 1843.
24. *Ibid.,* 10 March 1849.   25. *Ibid.,* 19 April 1849.

upon. "What shall I be without my Father?" she asked the Brays. "It will seem as if a part of my moral nature were gone. I had a heroic vision of myself last night becoming earthly, sensual, and devilish for want of that purifying, restraining influence."[26]

After her father's death, she put the translation aside and went abroad with the Brays. For a month they traveled together, and then she settled down alone to spend the winter in Geneva. When Chapman, who had had another translation offered him, made inquiries through Mrs. Bray, Miss Evans replied: "Spinoza and I have been divorced for several months. My want of health has obliged me to renounce all application. . . . Therefore I am by no means eager to supersede any other person's labours, and Mr. Chapman is absolved from observing any delicacy towards me about Spinoza or his translators."[27] The publisher was probably relieved; as he told Herbert Spencer, from past experience of philosophical books it was probable that the more highly he thought of a work the less hopeful he should be of its success. Spencer was urging him to publish *Demostatics,* a title he changed at Chapman's suggestion to *Social Statics;* but Chapman would undertake it only with the understanding that he was to be reimbursed for any loss.[28] His business had been expanded far beyond the limits of his capital, and he could not afford to speculate. He was not always so cautious.

In March 1850 when Miss Evans returned to London after a stormy crossing, she was too ill to stir from the hotel. Her principal regret, aside from not seeing Sara Hennell, was at missing the chance of going to the Chapmans' for the evening.[29] She had been considering the feasibility of settling in London to earn her living as a writer. A round of family visits reinforced the attractiveness of the prospect. "It was some envious demon that drove me across the Jura to come and see people who don't want me," she wrote from her

26. GE to the Brays, Wednesday Morning [30 May 1849].
27. GE to the Brays, 4 December 1849.
28. Herbert Spencer, *An Autobiography,* 2 vols., London, 1904, I, 357, 359.
29. GE to Sara Hennell [end of March, 1850].

brother Isaac's in April. In the same letter she asked Sara to tell her "Mr. Chapman's prices for lodgers."[30]

Meanwhile, the Brays' home was hers without any suspicion that she was not wanted. She accepted their invitation to stay at Rosehill while she pondered the next step. The income from the £2,000 left in trust by her father was not enough to support her, and, though her thirtieth birthday was past, no one else had evinced much desire to assume the responsibility.[31] The revolution in her religious beliefs since she came to Coventry would have made it very difficult for her to find a place as schoolmistress, almost the only occupation open to women.

She knew that she could write. The years of laborious struggle to find exact words to translate Strauss had proved a valuable discipline. Since the book appeared she had contributed a good deal to the Coventry *Herald,* which Mr. Bray bought in 1846 to edit in the interest of much-needed reforms. Some of her articles, like "Comic History" or "Vice and Sausages," were in a light, satirical vein; others were quite serious. There was a "masterly review" of Quinet and Michelet that Mrs. Bray advised Sara to look out for.[32]

On March 16, 1849, the *Herald* printed a review of James A. Froude's *The Nemesis of Faith,* which brought a pleasant sequel. Froude had sent the book through Chapman to "the translator of Strauss," and in writing to thank him Miss Evans signed herself in the same way. When the review was published, Froude wrote—again through Chapman, who still refused to give her name—declaring that he had recognized her hand in the Coventry *Herald,* and begging her to reveal herself. She had remarked that the author of *The Nemesis* was "a bright particular star, though he sometimes leaves us in doubt whether he be not a fallen 'son of the morning' "; Froude urged that "if she thinks him a fallen star, she might help him to rise, 'but he believes he has only been dipped in the Styx, and is not much the worse for the bathing.' Poor

30. GE to Sara Hennell, Thursday [April 1850].
31. For a brief period in March 1845 she was engaged to marry, but broke it off voluntarily.
32. Bray–Hennell Extracts, 11 October 1846.

girl!" Mrs. Bray adds in her letter to Sara, "I am so pleased she should have this little episode in her dull life, but I suppose she won't continue the correspondence."[33]

Miss Evans did not reply, but Froude was persistent and when he came to Coventry to visit the Brays in June, just a week after her father's death, she drove over to Rosehill to meet him. Froude was charmed with his new Coventry friends, and it was agreed that he and Chapman should cross the Channel with them when they set out for the Continent the next week.[34] Just before they were to sail, however, Froude sent word that he was going to be married, which, said Mr. Bray, "we thought a sufficient excuse."

Whether Chapman went with them or not is uncertain, but he visited at Rosehill in the summer of 1850 after Miss Evans's return. He came again in October with Robert William Mackay, the author of a book he had just published called *The Progress of the Intellect as Exemplified in the Religious Development of the Greeks and Hebrews.* They proposed that Miss Evans should write an article on this work for the *Westminster Review,* one of the leading English quarterlies. It was a subject that she was well qualified to discuss, and she acquitted herself brilliantly. Before the article appeared her decision was taken to go to London and make her living as a free-lance writer.

During the last two weeks of November she made a trial visit at the Chapmans' house in the Strand, where she particularly enjoyed the evening gatherings of literary celebrities. Eliza Lynn, no longer a boarder, came to one. At the age of twenty-eight Miss Lynn was already a conspicuous example of the Literary Lady. Her novels had evoked comment mainly on the tremendous burden of ancient history that weighted their pages; now, having turned from Egypt and Greece to modern times, she had just finished *Realities,* a story of London theatrical life, which Mr. Chapman was about to publish. The proofs had just begun to come in. "She says she was

33. Bray–Hennell Extracts, 23 March 1849.
34. Mrs. Bray's Commonplace Book; see B. C. Williams, *George Eliot,* New York, 1936, p. 60.

'never so attracted to a woman before as to me,' " Miss Evans wrote; "—I am 'such a loveable person.' . . . .[35] I have enjoyed my visit very much," the letter added, "and am to come again in January."

Her return is recorded in Chapman's Diary, January 8, 1851, along with an astronomical observation that was to prove ominous: "Rose at 6.40. Saw for the first time Venus and Jupiter through a telescope. The crescent form of Venus was distinctly visible. Miss Evans arrived at Euston Square at 3 P.M. where I met her; her manner was friendly but formal and studied." In a room at the end of a long passage, very dark but far enough from the street to be quiet, Mary Ann, or Marian, as she now began to sign herself, took up her residence as a permanent member of the household.

35. GE to the Brays [30 November 1850]. It is illuminating to compare this with Miss Lynn's subsequent harsh description of Miss Evans at this time; see Eliza Lynn Linton, *My Literary Life*, London, 1899, pp. 94–103.

CHAPTER II

142 Strand

A N extraordinary household it was! On the ground floor, in the shop and office, two or three clerks were kept busy with Chapman's publishing and bookselling business. The rest of the house was occupied by the family and the boarders, of whom there were always a number, for it was the year of the Great Exhibition, when the whole world was coming to London to gaze at its wonders. The Americans, in particular, were much gratified when the Strand was illuminated at vast expense by a loyal City, and the Queen passed in state beneath their windows on her way to a ball at Guildhall. But on other occasions they had to be shown about by Mr. Chapman or by his wife Susanna, who had, in addition, to superintend the housekeeping—no easy task where there were regularly about twenty at table and a constant coming and going of boarders.

Chapman had married her in that period of youthful enthusiasm when he wrote his book on Human Nature. Her dowry, which had enabled him to buy Green's publishing business, may partly have motivated the marriage. One imagines that Susanna was not very attractive to look at, and suffered the more in contrast with her handsome husband. When family cares began to absorb her time, she seems to have grown a bit careless about her appearance. She had inconvenient ailments that interfered with his plans—a cough, a sciatica, a headache. "Susanna's incapability of walking far or fast, and general debility presses upon me how much she has aged latterly, and makes the future look sad," he wrote August 10, 1851, when she was about thirty. She was always charging him with extravagance if he had a new dressing case made, bought a barometer, or suggested an iron safe for the office; yet her housekeeping was never systematic enough to suit Chapman—meals never appeared on time, the accounts were always in confusion, and "while the fuss and bustle of her management is a continual disturbance, all is orderly and quiet in her absence."[1]

The truth is that Susanna was not temperamentally suited to her methodical "Byron." For one thing her opinions were far too conventional. While she believed that "there is something in the Church system to be desired, that the most enlightened consciences of the few should be the rule of the many," Chapman disliked all organized religion and needed chiefly solitude for his moral culture.[2] When Darwin's *Origin of Species* appeared, he embraced its implications eagerly; but his discussion of the book of Genesis reduced Susanna to tears.[3]

Though making pretensions to literary judgment, and the discussion of theological and social questions, she simply puts forth her crude opinions with a confidence as if they were really sustained by evidence or careful reasoning, and attempts to silence objectors by the most intolerant and unjust denunciations: on social topics especially, all are immoral who dissent from her doctrines. Her chief reading is novels. Real study of any kind she has never applied herself to since her marriage.[1]

No reader of the Diaries is likely to sympathize with these petulant complaints about Susanna; since the time of Griselda few women have endured their lot more patiently.

Not the least of Chapman's fancied resemblances to Lord Byron lay in his utter contempt for monogamy. There lived in the Strand, as a permanent member of the household, a woman named Elisabeth Tilley who, ostensibly acting as governess and helping with the housekeeping, in reality occupied the more intimate position of Chapman's mistress. How long this arrangement had continued one cannot say. Since most of her friends lived in the north of London not far from Chapman's former home, it is quite possible that she entered the family before they moved to the Strand. "Alas, my love for her is no longer as dazzling as it once was," Chapman wrote in 1851; "hence I discern her faults more (perhaps *too*)

1. Diary, 24 July 1860.   2. Diary, 21 April 1851.
3. Diary, 16 January 1860.

plainly."[4] But he was still perturbed at her threats to leave him, and nothing in his Diary for that year suggests the end of their relationship.

Elisabeth Tilley's origins are obscure. Her family was a humble one, living in the country, probably in Berkshire. Nothing is known of her father; her mother, who appears briefly in the 1851 Diary, seems to have been dependent on her children. One brother had emigrated to Australia, and another was soon to follow him there; a third brother was a lieutenant in the army. There were at least two sisters, Anna who was at school in Greenwich, and Sofia, a milliner, who went out to Australia in 1853 to join her brothers. This record of emigration suggests a general lack of prosperity in the Tilley family. Another indication of the sort is perhaps found in Elisabeth's rather limited education. Chapman is teaching her arithmetic and urging her to improve her mind by attending lectures at the newly established "Ladies College." But her charms were clearly more physical than intellectual. Though she was a year older[5] than Chapman and impresses the reader of the Diary as a thoroughly difficult person, she was unquestionably the center of his affections.

Mrs. Chapman betrays so little jealousy of Elisabeth that it is hard to believe that she knew the true state of their relations at this time. There were momentary disagreements, unhappily too justified, but they passed quickly.

Susanna and I had a serious altercation about going on Sundays, an old subject: She said how much she should like to spend the whole of the Sundays out. I said "Yes, so should I, but you prevented it," meaning that she would not recognize my right to take her or E. as I might think best something like alternately. Her remarks were one tissue of exaggeration, misrepresentation, prevarication, and passion. I bore it calmly, with one or two exceptions, when I could not help stopping her by saying she was a liar, for which I afterwards apologized.[6]

4. Diary, 3 May 1851.
5. She was born 28 July 1820; see Diary, 28 July 1851.
6. Diary, 30 July 1851.

Aside from an occasional outburst of this sort the Chapmans, when they did walk together in the parks with Ernest and Beatrice—now five and seven respectively—beside them, seemed as domestic a couple as one could wish. Chapman was devoted to the children, and, as he was to explain to Miss Evans, "loved both Susanna and Elisabeth, though each in a different way." The Diary gives no clue as to how he reconciled this curious arrangement with the lofty morality he seemed quite sincerely to profess. He gave up the publication of Eliza Lynn's *Realities* because of the warm description of a love scene. "I said that such passages were addressed to and excited the sensual nature and were therefore injurious; and that as I am the publisher of works notable for their intellectual freedom, it behoves me to be exceedingly careful of the *moral* tendency of all I issue."[7]

This was the household Miss Evans entered in January 1851. Though she was certainly ignorant of Elisabeth's position there, her "formal and studied" manner was perhaps the consequence of two letters Elisabeth had written to Coventry, which "occasioned much painful conversation" the week before. "I have endured much suffering today," Chapman wrote in his Diary the day Marian came. The day after, in an entry he deleted in part:

<Had a very painful altercation with Elisabeth, the result of her groundless suspicions; hence I have been in a state of unhealthy excitement all day. She gave notice at the dinner table that she intended to leave in the autumn.

Miss Evans is very poorly; sat with her a short time and talked about Miss Lynn and her book.>[8]

Chapman went with Miss Evans to choose a piano for her own use, and on the following Sunday rose late and sat in her room "while she played one of Mosart's Masses with much expression." His sudden enthusiasm for "Mosart" may explain Susanna's prompt acquiescence in the purchase of a

7. Diary, 12 January 1851.
8. Diary, 9 January 1851. Passages enclosed in < > have been deleted. See p. ix.

piano for the drawing room; thereafter Marian performed more publicly, while Susanna herself sometimes played duets of sacred music with Sara Hennell or another visitor. At this point Chapman developed an interest in German and took lessons every day from the translator of Strauss. When Elisabeth evinced a sudden interest in the language, he became her teacher in turn. There can be no doubt that she was thoroughly jealous of the new boarder, and made Chapman's life miserable with her suspicions and recriminations.

The first open hostilities occurred January 22:

Invited Miss Evans to go out after breakfast; did not get a decisive answer. E. afterwards said if I did go, she should be glad to go. I then invited Miss Evans again telling her E. would go, whereupon she declined rather rudely. Susanna being willing to go out, and neither E. nor S. wishing to walk far, I proposed they should go a short distance without me, which E. considered an insult from me and reproached me in no measured terms accordingly, and heaped upon me suspicions and accusations I do not in any way deserve. I was very severe and harsh, said things I was sorry for afterwards, and we became reconciled in the Park.

Miss Evans apologized for her rudeness tonight, which roused all E.'s jealousy again, and consequent bitterness.

Nevertheless, all three of the ladies went out together to spend the evening with Mr. and Mrs. Holland. But the next morning the quarrel broke out again, and the following day Chapman writes: "Elisabeth has not spoken kindly to me since Thursday evening—on account of Miss Evans." A week later when she began to talk of leaving, Susanna told Chapman that she thought Elisabeth "had some foolish jealousy of Miss Evans, and instanced her bitter remarks." Miss Evans, too, began to talk of returning to Coventry.

Chapman felt that he could not part with either of them. If Elisabeth, his "first love," was essential to his happiness in a physical way, Marian answered a need he felt for intellectual companionship that was almost as strong. Moreover, she was very useful to him in his publishing business. Susanna had been supervising a three-volume historical novel by

James Nisbet called *The Siege of Damascus,* but her correspondence with the author had grown so sarcastic that Chapman asked Marian to take over the task of revision. Miss Evans had also begun a more important work, an Analytical Catalogue of Chapman's publications. Novels were a new and relatively trivial part of Chapman's trade; the bulk of his list consisted of books like Greg's *The Creed of Christendom,* Spencer's *Social Statics,* Newman's *Lectures on Political Economy,* and Vericour's *Historical Analysis of Christian Civilization.* A catalogue containing careful outlines of all his publications would serve as a sort of index to liberal studies in religion and philosophy, and, at the same time, it was hoped, help to sell them. No one was so well qualified to compile such a work as Miss Evans.

She had other projects in hand, too. In order to earn her living she wanted to establish herself as a writer of serious articles for the quarterly reviews, which paid very well. She intended to keep her anonymity, at least until she had made a place for herself; her reputation as the translator of Strauss, however highly it recommended her in liberal circles, would prove a distinct drawback in approaching the editors of the more conservative periodicals. Chapman sent her article on Mackay's *The Progress of the Intellect* to Empson, the editor of the *Edinburgh Review,* proposing a similar article for him, or one on Slavery, or on any subject he would name if it were within her province. But the editor was not interested. Marian sent Mr. Bray the letters of rejection as evidence that she had been trying to work. "You will be pleased to see," she added, "that Mr. C. spoke of me to Empson as a man,"[9]—a significant fact in view of her later assumption of the pseudonym *George Eliot.*

Consultation on these matters naturally threw Chapman and Miss Evans together a good deal, until on February 18 an unfortunate episode occurred. After recording it in the Diary, Chapman carefully deleted the latter part of his entry:

9. Diary, 9 February 1851; GE to the Brays [15 February 1851].

I presume with the view of arriving at a more friendly understanding S. and E. had a long talk this morning which resulted in their comparing notes on the subject of my intimacy with Miss Evans, and their arrival at the conclusion <that we are completely in love with each other. E. being intensely jealous herself said all she could to cause S. to look from the same point of view, which a little incident (her finding me with my hand in M.'s) had quite prepared her for. E. betrayed my trust and her own promise. S. said to me that if ever I went to M.'s room again she will write to Mr. Bray and say that she dislikes her>.

The next morning Chapman sat in the dining room to write,

where M. joined me. We talked, of course, of the excited feelings of S. and E. I gave her an account of what had passed and urged her to talk with S. on the subject to give her an opportunity of dissipating her uncalled-for hatred by expression. E. made some bitter remarks on account of our being in the dining room (i.e. together), and I therefore passed the afternoon in S.'s room without a fire. S. had a long talk with M. before dinner, unsatisfactory to S. from the high tone M. took. Conversation renewed after dinner in my presence, when M. confessed S. had reason to complain, and a reconciliation was effected.

The following evening Chapman had to escort some visitors from Nottingham to a concert. Elisabeth, he wrote,

was kind to me before I went and kissed me several times. At parting she kissed me saying, "God bless thee, thou frail bark!" But, alas, this morning she is all bitterness and icy coldness, the result I believe of conversation she had last night with M., who was very severe and unjust to me yesterday.

Though Susanna had made it "a condition of our renewed treaties of amity" that he should recommence his German lessons with Miss Evans, Chapman knew that it was sure to pain Elisabeth. Happily at this juncture Miss Kate Martineau carried Marian off to Highbury for two nights, and the ruffled feelings gradually grew calm.

I have had a good deal of intercourse with E. today, which has resulted in our becoming friends again, with (I fear) a vain hope of continuing so. Alas, it is so much easier in the absence of the offending cause (M.), and when she returns and I resume my lessons, I dare say she will feel and express herself as bitterly as ever. Bless her, I wish she would be a little more charitable and generous. Unhappily she lives so entirely in her affections that, if they are disturbed, her whole being is in Chaos.[10]

What happened when Miss Evans returned to the Strand no one can tell, for the leaves containing the entries for February 25 to March 3 have been cut from the Diary. The antagonism among the ladies certainly reached some sort of climax. The fact that the long-suffering Susanna is thereafter as hard to placate as Elisabeth leads one to suspect another incident like the one when she found Marian holding her husband's hand. One thing, however, is clear: Susanna and Elisabeth joined forces against their rival and drove her back to Coventry. The succeeding pages of the Diary shed little light on the episode. After nine days without any entry (March 3–12) there is a farewell round of the theaters; then on Monday, March 24 Chapman writes and later deletes in part:

M. departed today. I accompanied her to the railway. She was very sad, and hence made me feel so. She pressed me for some intimation of the state of my feelings. <I told her that I felt great affection for her, but that I loved E. and S. also, though each in a different way.> At this avowal she burst into tears. I tried to comfort her, and reminded [her] of the dear friends and pleasant home she was returning to, but the train whirled her away, very, very sad.

Susanna was much excited today and perplexed with her packing; she reproached me, and spoke very bitterly about M.

Without more evidence it is hazardous to try to reconstruct the events preceding Miss Evans's departure or to assign responsibility for them. There is little question that she was guilty of some indiscretion, which was probably magnified by the exacerbated feelings of the other ladies. Whatever it was, I feel sure that Chapman provoked it. Realizing how useful she could be to him in his publishing business, he

10. Diary, 22 February 1851.

doubtless flattered her with attention. Whether she was conscious of it or not, his pervading physical charm must have fed a yearning for affection that was only the stronger for being hidden behind an unattractive exterior. Then, too, he offered her what so many of her heroines were to seek: an opportunity to devote herself wholly to the service of someone she loved. The harsh awakening from the dream left her bewildered and humiliated.

It was not the first experience of this sort in Marian Evans's life. Eight years before, when she was a bridesmaid at Rufa Brabant's marriage to Charles Hennell, Dr. Brabant had invited her to visit him at Devizes "to fill the place of his daughter." The best one can say for Dr. Brabant is that he was a pompous and rather foolish person who at the age of sixty-two, thanks to an adequate fortune, found leisure from the practice of medicine to impress young ladies with his learning. In his early days he had known Coleridge, who corresponded with him in 1815–16 on the effects of calomel, gin, and laudanum, as well as on questions of German metaphysics.[11] He was acquainted with both Paulus and Strauss, whom he saw frequently in Germany, sharing their rationalistic theological opinions. For years he had been engaged upon a great work that was to dispose once for all of the supernatural elements in Christianity.

Naturally, Miss Evans was gratified to have him recognize her intellectual powers. She arrived at Devizes November 14, 1843, eager to serve the learned physician and metaphysician in any capacity. According to Miss Lynn, "she knelt at his feet and offered to devote her life to his service."[12] The next morning he showed her his library, which she was to consider *her* room, and punningly baptized her *Deutera* because she was to be a second daughter to him.[13] "I am in a little heaven here," she wrote Sara Hennell, "Dr. Brabant being its archangel; . . . time would fail me to tell of all his charming

11. E. L. Griggs, ed., *Unpublished Letters of Samuel Taylor Coleridge*, 2 vols., New Haven, 1933, II, 159, 180.
12. Eliza Lynn Linton, *My Literary Life*, London, 1899, p. 44.
13. GE to Mrs. Bray, Wednesday [15 November 1843].

qualities. We read, walk, and talk together, and I am never weary of his company."[14] Within a few days she wrote her father for permission to prolong the visit to a month. Mrs. Bray, one gathers, did not share her young friend's enthusiasm for the Doctor, and tried to put her on her guard; but Marian insisted that he was really "a finer character than you think—beautifully sincere, conscientious, and benevolent, and everything besides that one would have one's friends to be." They were now reading Greek together, reading *de omnibus rebus et quibusdam aliis,* she added. It was all very exciting. After reading German for two hours to the Doctor, she often felt so faint as to be obliged to lie on the sofa until walking time—when, however, she summoned strength to go to call on a local literary celebrity, "we having agreed in defiance of all the moralists to defer every expedition until my next visit."[15]

But there was a *Mrs.* Brabant, too, in this little heaven, a rather precise lady and less expansive than the Doctor, though meticulously polite to his *Deutera.* And there was a rather formidable sister-in-law, Miss Susan Hughes, who within a week of Marian's arrival had begun to give unsolicited advice about the best routes back to Coventry. As Rufa told Chapman in the summer of 1851, Miss Evans,

in the simplicity of her heart and her ignorance of (or incapability of practising) the required conventionalisms, gave the Doctor the utmost attention; they became very intimate; his Sister-in-law, Miss S. Hughes, became alarmed, made a great stir, excited the jealousy of Mrs. Brabant. Miss Evans left. Mrs. B. vowed she should never enter the house again, or that if she did, she, Mrs. Brabant, would instantly leave it. Mrs. Hennell says Dr. B. acted ungenerously and worse towards Miss E., for though he was the chief cause of all that passed, he acted towards her as though the fault lay with her alone. His unmanliness in the affair was condemned more by Mrs. Hennell than by Miss E. herself when she (a year ago) related the circumstances to me.[16]

14. GE to Sara Hennell, Monday, 20 November [1843].
15. GE to Mrs. Bray, Friday [24 November 1843] and 30 November 1843.
16. Diary, 27 June 1851.

Eliza Lynn, who visited Dr. Brabant under much the same circumstances in 1847, was convinced that he was the original of Mr. Casaubon in *Middlemarch*. She describes him as

a learned man who used up his literary energies in thought and desire to do rather than in actual doing, and whose fastidiousness made his work something like Penelope's web. Ever writing and rewriting, correcting and destroying, he never got farther than the introductory chapter of a book which he intended to be epoch-making, and the final destroyer of superstition and theological dogma.

There are interesting parallels here with Casaubon, whose soul "went on fluttering in the swampy ground where it was hatched, thinking of its wings and never flying," as he strove to make his *Key to All Mythologies* unimpeachable.[17]

When George Eliot was pressed by a friend to tell from whom she had drawn the character, "with a humorous solemnity, which was quite in earnest, she pointed to her own heart."[18] The facts are not incompatible. There in her pain and humiliation lay the venom that was to give Casaubon his horrible vividness years later. This earlier episode illuminates the tempest in March 1851. Chapman, who was a notorious flirt, undoubtedly deserves most of the blame. Still, Rufa's phrase, "in the simplicity of her heart and her ignorance of (or incapability of practising) the required conventionalisms," sticks in the mind as one looks ahead to the career of George Eliot.

As soon as she had gone, calm settled over 142 Strand. Susanna departed for a visit at Truro, and Elisabeth was left in undisputed possession of the field. On returning home, Chapman records, he found the house quite empty and felt a sense of extreme loneliness. He read aloud to Elisabeth out of Mackay's *The Progress of the Intellect* and took her to the

17. G. S. Layard, *Mrs. Lynn Linton*, London, 1901, p. 67 n.; Eliza Lynn Linton, *My Literary Life*, London, 1899, p. 43; *Middlemarch* (Cabinet ed.), II, 11.

18. Mathilde Blind, *George Eliot*, Boston, 1883, p. 244.

Lyceum to see *Cool as a Cucumber*. The mere sight of a letter from Coventry, even when he offered to let her read it, threw her into a passion.

The letters that Susanna wrote him from Truro Chapman forwarded to Marian. They were so bitter in their references to her that she declined to do the Analytical Catalogue—though she wrote again the same day to say that she would consent to continue on condition that he

restate to Mrs. Chapman the fact that I am doing it not because I "like," but in compliance with your request. You are aware that I never had the slightest wish to undertake the thing on my own account. If I continue it, it will be with the utmost repugnance and only on the understanding that I shall accept no remuneration.[19]

The same day he received from Susanna another letter "which gave me great pain (about Miss Evans); answered it in tears (and I fear bitterness) and enclosed her Miss Evans' notes."[20] Once more he wrote Marian.

I begged her to be calm and not to let recent circumstances agitate and needlessly pain her. I told her that I feel even in the midst of the tumult of grief and in the very moment of excitement the most intimate essence of my being, or some element of it, is still no sharer in the enacted scene, but continues a serene spectator, experiencing only shame and regret that any part of my nature with which it is allied should be so moved and agitated by events and affections or the selfish personalities of today and yesterday.[21]

He began now to devote more attention to his business, which had suffered during these turbulent weeks, and to his own self-culture, "especially the moral side," which he felt had been mournfully neglected. He adopted a vegetarian diet, living entirely without meat—for a week. In his Diary he copied a passage from Schefer's *The Artist's Married Life;*

19. From B. C. Williams, *George Eliot*, New York, 1936, pp. 69–70. By permission of the Macmillan Company.
20. Diary, 4 April 1851.   21. Diary, 5 April 1851.

Being That of Albert Dürer: "He who has long known a deep and bitter Grief, need no longer strive after Happiness, but only after Peace. . . . Therefore lifelong Meekness must be the Portion of him whose Heart is broken!"[22]

22. Diary, 19 April 1851.

CHAPTER III

The *Westminster Review*

ON May 1, 1851, W. E. Hickson, the proprietor of the *Westminster Review*, with whom Chapman had previously discussed the matter, called to ask if he still wished to buy the magazine. Here was an opportunity to realize his old dream of a liberal review to be read on both sides of the Atlantic. Although Hickson asked £350, Chapman thought £300 would be accepted. He felt confident of finding support. Only a fortnight past he had received a letter from Mr. Edward Lombe, an English gentleman with an income of £14,000 a year, who occupied himself by supporting liberal enterprises. Lombe wanted to pay for a reprint of Theodore Parker's *A Discourse on Religion* and an abridgment of Strauss's *Das Leben Jesu;* he would pay £50 for an essay on "The Incompatibility of Christian Ethics with Modern Civilization." He assured Chapman that he would also assist in establishing a quarterly review if its policy went far enough in this direction. He was already contributing £200 a year toward the *Westminster,* Chapman learned, but for special articles he wished to have written.

With wealthy men like Lombe, Robert Mackay, and Dr. Brabant backing him, Chapman knew he could collect funds enough to launch the *Review*. But who would help him edit it? His bookselling and publishing business already demanded more time than he could give. And besides, in spite of his buoyant optimism, he was astute enough to recognize that the task was one for which his education hardly fitted him. He knew one person with intellect quite keen enough to conduct a first-rate quarterly, one who would be content to remain in the background while he basked in editorial glory. But this was the plain-looking spinster in Coventry, who had been banished forever from the Strand and was still smarting under a mortification that she felt sure she did not deserve.

Her feelings were hardly more cordial toward the *Westminster Review*. In February when she had proposed to write an article on Greg's *The Creed of Christendom,* "not for money, but for love of the subject," Mr. Hickson and his editor Mr. Slack had rejected her proposal on grounds of "no room" and "subject doesn't suit." It was a blow to her pride that her articles could not even be given away! To propitiate her, Chapman, when he submitted the offer in form to buy the *Review,* made Hickson promise to insert the article, and immediately wrote to tell her so. Perhaps the editors shied off once more, or the sanguine Chapman may have misunderstood their promise; at any rate he records in his Diary a fortnight later that he has got Thornton Hunt to publish it in the *Leader,*[1] where it appeared September 20, 1851.

The *Westminster Review* had a distinguished history as the organ of philosophical radicalism. It was founded by James Mill in 1824 with money furnished by his friend Jeremy Bentham. Mill's position as a civil servant in India House forbade his serving openly as editor; but, while John Bowring and Henry Southern publicly shared the responsibility, Mill in reality determined what articles should appear. He contributed the brilliant attacks on the *Edinburgh Review* and the *Quarterly* that launched the new journal. In 1828 he sold it to Col. Thomas Perronet Thompson, who edited it until 1836, when Sir William Molesworth amalgamated it with the *London Review,* founded only the year before. Under Molesworth's management the *Westminster,* never a profitable investment, is said to have lost £100 an issue, and he was glad to dispose of it in 1837 to John Stuart Mill, under whom it reached its greatest distinction. Seldom have so many brilliant writers been brought together as in the *Westminster* under the younger Mill's management.

In June 1840 Mill transferred it to William Edward Hickson, a retired shoe manufacturer, who could afford to indulge a taste for literature and reform. His first reform was in the budget of the *Review,* reducing the rate of payment to authors until, it is said, the name of the *Westminster* became a

1. Diary, 20 May 1851.

word of terror in literary ears, and many of its best contributors dropped away. So did its subscribers. In 1850 for a single number it was in the hands of Slack, who was glad to return it immediately.[2] Perhaps at this juncture Hickson first discussed the sale with Chapman.

Chapman's offer was accepted within a few days, though the deed of sale was not signed until October 8. He now set about trying to convince his wife and Elisabeth that Miss Evans's presence in the Strand was essential to the success of the venture. When he told Elisabeth that Mr. Bray had urgently invited him to Coventry—that he "could not refuse without great difficulty," that he "had promised almost to go," she immediately became haughty and indignant and left the room, remaining in the same state of sullen anger for three days.[3] Susanna was more amenable to reason, trusting, no doubt, to Mrs. Bray's watchful eye to insure her husband's good behavior.

He arrived in Coventry May 27, 1851, where he "<found Miss Evans shy, calm, and affectionate>." Next morning she was "M." once more in his Diary. They walked together before breakfast, and in the evening left an amateur concert when it was half over to walk home, discussing plans for the new review. Chapman found her still susceptible and resolved to lay his dilemma frankly before her. The following day, he writes:

Walked with M. before breakfast; told her the exact condition of things in regard to E., whom on every account I wish to stay at the Strand. She was much grieved and expressed herself prepared to atone in any way she could for the pain she has caused, and put herself in my hands prepared to accept any arrangement I may make, either for her return to the Strand or to any house in London I may think suitable in October. She agreed to write the article on foreign literature for each number of the Westminster, which I am very glad of. Wrote the greater part of the Prospectus today, and then gave it to M. to finish.[4]

2. See the article on the *Westminster Review* by "Herodotus Smith" in the *Critic*, 15 August 1851, p. 372.
3. Diary, 15–18 May 1851.   4. Diary, 29 May 1851.

With what mingled feelings did she set about the task? Now she understood many things that had puzzled her in Chapman. She longed to put herself completely at his disposal, to write his Analytical Catalogue, his Prospectus for the *Review;* it was as if she had been created to complement him in these projects. She loved him more than he knew. What did he find in Elisabeth that she was not prepared to give? Why could he not realize that Elisabeth, in spite of her pretty face, was not worthy of him? The blind rage that George Eliot could never conceal at man's folly in preferring beauty to more substantial qualities surged up in her heart.

The next day they went together to Leamington, stopping on the way back to see Kenilworth Castle.

As we rested on the grass, I remarked on the wonderful and mysterious embodiment of all the elements, characteristics, and beauties of nature which man and woman jointly present. I dwelt also on the incomprehensible mystery and witchery of beauty. My words jarred upon her and put an end to her enjoyment. Was it from a consciousness of her own want of beauty? She wept bitterly.

"She was not fitted to stand alone," but it was all too plain that Chapman was not the man she could lean upon. Still, to be in London helping him with the *Review* was better than never seeing him. Chapman was wondering how to arrange it.

I find it a matter of great difficulty to determine what can be done in regard to M.'s return to Town. Both Susanna and Elisabeth oppose her return to the Strand, and I suspect they would be equally opposed to her residence elsewhere in London, and yet as an active cooperator with me in editing the Westminster Review she must be in London much of her time. Oh, how deeply I regret that any cause for distrust should ever have been given. I must and will recover the confidence I once possessed. I will act consistently with my own fairer thought and thus raise my own self respect and diffuse peace.

The ensuing five lines are so heavily deleted as to defy all efforts to read more than an occasional word, but the entry concludes:

For my own part I do not feel in raptures with any woman now, and my passionate moods are exceptional and transient and are rather *permitted* as a means of according the strongest evidence of *affection* than storms which I cannot control. The beneficent affection and pleasure of social intercourse which I experience seems to be equally distributed towards Susanna, E., and M., but in regard to *passionate enthusiasm,* my "first love" will, I believe, also be my last. I wish I could make her happy![5]

Marian was calm now, resigning herself to "beneficent affection," though her heart cried out for "passionate enthusiasm." In the drawing room she "sang exquisitely" with the Brays' week-end guests, Mr. and Mrs. Thornton Hunt, whose destinies were to mingle so curiously with hers. Alone in her room she took up the *De Imitatione Christi* that had helped her to learn renunciation during her father's last illness, the same volume that taught Maggie Tulliver to renounce the hope that flattered. She gave it to Chapman to read too; he copied into his Diary a sentence that touched him: "Oh, if thou didst but consider how much inward peace unto thyself and joy unto others thou wouldst procure by demeaning thyself well, I suppose thou wouldst be more careful of thy spiritual progress."[6] Marian set an example of sacrifice, "going without dinner in order to progress rapidly with the Prospectus." She finished it the same evening and read it to Chapman, who sent it off to Mr. Bray's printer the next morning.

The Prospectus of the new *Westminster Review* was a strangely wooden document to have evolved in so highly charged an atmosphere. Like all such instruments it promised more than it could perform. Advocating "organic change" according to the Law of Progress, it recognized at the same time that man's institutions develop very gradually. But that should not prevent scrutiny.

In contradistinction to the practical infidelity and essentially destructive policy which would ignore the existence of wide-spread doubts in relation to established creeds and systems, and would stifle all inquiry dangerous to prescriptive claims, the Review will exhibit that untemporizing expression of opinion, and that fear-

5. Diary, 31 May 1851.   6. Diary, 2 June 1851.

lessness of investigation and criticism which are the results of a consistent faith in the ultimate prevalence of truth. Convinced that the same fundamental truths are apprehended under a variety of forms, and that, therefore, opposing systems may in the end prove complements of each other, the Editors will endeavour to institute such a radical and comprehensive treatment of those controverted questions which are practically momentous, as may aid in the conciliation of divergent views.

An "Independent Section" was to be made available, in which writers who differed widely from the editors might freely express their opinions. Vital political questions and diverse social theories were to be considered, not for their bearing on party or class, but for their relation to the public good.

Since the *Review* was designed to be "an exponent of growing thought," the Editors could not indicate fully the course they would pursue in politics. The trend might be inferred from certain reforms they intended to support, which included progressive extension of the suffrage with a view to its ultimate universality; the extension of constitutional government to all the colonies, with increased influence in Parliament; free trade in every department of commerce; a radical reform of the judiciary, especially in the Court of Chancery; the revision of ecclesiastical revenues; and a system of national education, with modifications of the Universities to admit dissenters to degrees.

In the treatment of Religious Questions the Review will unite a spirit of reverential sympathy for the cherished associations of pure and elevated minds with an uncompromising pursuit of truth. The elements of ecclesiastical authority and of dogma will be fearlessly examined, and the results of the most advanced Biblical criticism will be discussed without reservation, under the conviction that religion has its foundation in man's nature, and will only discard an old form to assume and vitalize one more expressive of its essence. While, however, the Editors will not shrink from the expression of what they believe to be sound negative views, they will bear in mind the pre-eminent importance of a constructive religious philosophy, as connected with the development and activity of the moral nature, and of those poetic and emotional elements, out of which proceed our noblest aspirations and the essential beauty of life.

This version of the Prospectus is the one finally adopted and printed at the beginning of Chapman's first number of the *Westminster*, January 1852. It reached this form only after many compromises. John Stuart Mill, to whom he sent the first draft from Coventry, declared in "a long, half-sarcastic letter" that it was too conservative.[7] On the other hand, James Martineau "in a half-sneering, cold letter" complained that they were stooping to appeal to the mob instead of the intellectual and scholarly readers of the *Quarterly* and *Edinburgh,* a course which, he admitted disdainfully, had commercial wisdom on its side.[8] Dr. Hodgson thought it was too vague on the suffrage question.[9] Hickson, who was still the proprietor, was

much annoyed that I should have taken any steps about the Prospectus; I find the chief reason is a personal and *small* one; to use his own words he does not like to be regarded for so long a time before he actually relinquishes the Review as the "setting sun" and from whom therefore men anxious about the "Westminster" may transfer their interest in order to give it to the "rising man" before the time of actual change arrives! I have consented to be quiet for the present.[10]

While the new Editors debated these matters, the principal question was still unanswered: How was Miss Evans to assist with the *Review* unless Susanna and Elisabeth would tolerate her presence in London? While still at Coventry, Chapman received

an unkind letter from Susanna regarding M., whom I told, and enquired of her whether she would prefer living here or in Town. She became extremely excited and indignant, and finally calm and regretful. . . . <During our walk we made a solemn and holy vow which henceforth will bind us to the right. She is a noble being. Wrote a chiding letter to Susanna>.[11]

7. Diary, 9 June 1851.   8. Diary, 10 June 1851.
9. GE to Chapman, 15 June 1851; see p. 36.
10. Diary, 13 June 1851.   11. Diary, 5 June 1851.

A few days later Susanna evinced "a changed and kinder tone <in regard to Marian>," so that before he left Coventry June 9 he was able to discuss with Mr. Bray the "pecuniary arrangement with Marian E." Though he does not record the details in his Diary, it appears that she was to be paid only for the articles she contributed to the *Review*, receiving no regular salary as assistant editor.

Elisabeth burst into tears when Chapman returned to the Strand after his ten-day absence, tears of joy this time. Susanna also welcomed him affectionately, "but soon got into disagreeable talk about M." All summer long the mere suggestion of Marian's return to London was enough to provoke an outburst of passion from one lady or the other. Elisabeth made his birthday wretched by her "positive assurance that she will not live in the Strand after Miss Evans comes to London," a determination she repeated frequently.

Under these circumstances plans for the new *Westminster Review* had to go on as best they could by post. Chapman wrote an answer to Mill's letter with its "severe animadversions on the Prospectus" and sent it to Miss Evans for approval. Her reply is dated Rosehill, June 15:

My dear Friend:

If, as I suppose, you intend to write the letter to Mill, would it not be better if the first paragraph read thus—"joint aims, so as best to further the main purpose of the future proprietor, which is, to make the Review the organ of the ablest and most liberal thinkers of the time." (For "organ" in the second paragraph read "medium.") I wish, too, you would leave out the dashes, which weaken instead of strengthening the impression on the reader. In the 3rd paragraph for "I am convinced *that*" read "that, I am convinced," for "gratefully received," which sounds too much like a craving for alms, read "duly valued." "Securing air" is an absurd expression and is of course a slip of the pen. I should like the 4th paragraph better if it began thus—"In the sketch submitted to you there is perhaps an unnecessary air of conservatism." I think Mr. Lombe is a capital man, who knows what he means and will not pay for what he does not mean. I do not see that he wants "smoothing down," or that he is a person on whom the process should be tried. Hickson's method with him seems not to have answered, since according to Mr. Lombe's account there had been letters of remonstrance from him, threatening to remove his support unless his views were more fully represented. Why should you shirk the direct fulfilment of his proposition?—the obtaining as good articles as possible on his chosen subjects—since he seems to choose well. I thoroughly agree with him about the "hereditary legislators—" I suppose when he wrote this letter he had not received your last.

I was disappointed not to have fuller details in your letter about your conversations with Johnson, Spencer, and the rest, but do not forget that you have told me nothing. Combe's letter is pleasant and gentlemanly—Dr. Hodgson's friendly, but surprisingly uncritical for him. He is right about the clause on the suffrage—it is as vague as "Render unto Caesar the things that are Caesar's"—what things are Caesar's being left undetermined.

Good Mrs. Hunt has left behind a very pleasant impression. I think she is the most thoroughly unaffected being I ever saw. I am afraid the Leader is not prospering. The names of Thornton Hunt, Lewes, Linton and several more were specified last week in the papers as withdrawing from partnership in the concern—which seems to imply a presentiment of failure. We are all amused at Thornton Hunt's illustration in yesterday's Leader of "boiled mutton chops"—that must be a peculiarly Hammersmith dish.[12]

Mr. Noel has written to say he is just coming to England. He is invited here with his three children and servant, so we shall probably soon have a house full again. He speaks of returning to Greece.

I shall be awfully poor this half year, more than £12 legacy duty being subtracted from my interest.

Have you fixed on "Independent Section" as a title?

I am sorry to hear of your having headache—but it is something to find that you do not complain of a recurrence of toothache. I am dreadfully afraid of those fangs left behind. Mrs. Bray was talking of them sympathetically yesterday.

I want to get out into the air, so goodbye.

Yours faithfully,
MARIAN EVANS.[13]

12. *Leader*, 14 June 1851, p. 549.
13. From B. C. Williams, *George Eliot*, New York, 1936, pp. 72–74. By permission of the Macmillan Company.

Marian's old room had been occupied ever since her departure by a Mr. and Mrs. Hayward, who boarded in the Strand until June 13. As soon as they left, Chapman took the room for a study, moving his table and books thither. He sat down and wrote Marian a gossipy letter to enclose with some analyses for the Catalogue by Ebenezer Syme, a former Unitarian minister whom he had hired to help with the publishing business. She replied:

Rosehill,
June 20 [1851].

My dear Friend,

Your last letter was just what I wanted—it paid up your arrears of news.

I have read Mr. Syme's articles, and think them very well done, at least the one on Toulmin Smith.[14] That on Chapman[15] is more careless and wants revisal. See p. 5, where he is speaking of the relative amount of our Indian and South American exports. He has not said what he means, or rather, what he has said means nothing. I wish you would ask him to do the articles on Ierson,[16] Greenwood,[17] Langford,[18] and Smith's Social Aspects,[19] for all which I have no appetite.

Pray when are we to hear any more of the Strauss abridgment? I have been looking through the work in writing on it for the Catalogue and have been all the time thinking what a capital abridgment I could make.

I congratulate you on your migration, but I hope the room has been duly exorcised since I left it. I pity you, poor soul, with those dismal windows before you instead of chestnut trees and turf. This gold pen is a bad scribbling pen. You see it obstinately refuses to mark every now and then, but I like it exceedingly when I am writing rather slowly. I have delicious walks before breakfast these fine mornings and have said good bye to headache. Mr. Bray is out, Mr. Noel not yet come, so we are having a charmingly quiet interval.

14. Joshua Toulmin Smith, *Local Self-Government and Centralization*, 1851.
15. John Chapman (1801–54), *The Cotton and Commerce of India*, 1851. This Chapman was a cousin of the publisher. See Diary, 29 April 1851.
16. Henry Ierson, *An Introduction to the Religion of Nature*, 1850.
17. F. W. P. Greenwood, *Sermons of Consolation*, 1849, and other works.
18. John Alfred Langford, *Religious Scepticism and Infidelity*, 1850.
19. John Stores Smith, *Social Aspects*, 1850.

There would be the same objection to Miss Bronty as to Thackeray with regard to the article on Modern Novelists. She would have to leave out Currer Bell, who is perhaps the best of them all.

It appears James Martineau was rather apologetic. I shall be glad to know the purport of your second interview with him.

I had left myself hardly time to write before tea, that is, before post time, but I reflected that it would be of no use to write to-morrow.

Yours in haste,

MARIAN EVANS.[20]

There was nothing in this letter that jealous eyes could object to. But with it she enclosed another, apparently more personal in tone. "<Miss Evans' little note is inexpressibly charming, so quick, intelligent, and overflowing with love and sweetness! I feel her to be the living torment to my soul>," Chapman wrote in his Diary. Then he carefully deleted the entry.

By the middle of July he had won from Elisabeth her consent "to meet Miss Evans as a visitor to the Strand. I hereby vow," he added, "that so far as lies in my power she shall never regret her decision." Susanna had apparently concluded that if Marian were to be in town it would be much better to have her living in the house. On August 13, when she came with the Brays to see the Exhibition, a reluctant truce was arranged. Mr. and Mrs. Chapman called on the whole party at Miss Mary Marshall's in Kensington, and the next day, after seeing the Exhibition, Miss Evans and Miss Hennell came home with Chapman

in order that Miss E. might "make a call" on Susanna, and afford the opportunity of a long editorial conference, in which after coffee we accomplished much. Susanna is very poorly with bad headache, and Elisabeth is far from well. She was sad and in tears this evening.

How much Chapman depended on his assistant editor may be gathered from the fact that within the next six weeks he

20. This letter is in the collection of Mr. Morris L. Parrish.

made at least two trips to Coventry to confer with her. At her suggestion he had invited James Martineau to write the article that Mr. Lombe had requested on "Christian Ethics and Modern Civilization." When Martineau asked what "mode of treatment" was to be adopted, Chapman was at a loss to answer his letter without consulting her. On Saturday, August 23, he went to Coventry and

fully discussed the subject with Miss Evans, after which I noted down the topics and mode of treatment to be adopted in the article, which she embodied in a sketch for a letter with such modifications as she thought necessary, and from this material I shall write him our views on the subject, but I fear they will not be acceptable. (See copy book.)

Spent much of my time at Coventry in determining on the final form of the Prospectus, (which is now much improved on the first draft), and on the contents of the January number.

Reached home at 11 on Monday night 25th inst.

The second trip, a month later, caused a minor domestic upheaval. Having business in Birmingham for Monday, September 22, Chapman resolved to go by way of Coventry, spending the week-end with the Brays. When he broke the news to Susanna, she reproached him for not having asked her to accompany him—a matter Chapman had considered and decided against. Having no cogent objection, he was constrained to take her. Susanna soon had reason to regret her triumph. On reaching Rosehill they found Edward Noel and his three children expected, Mrs. Bray very ill, "and all painfully concerned by our arrival." However, the Noels did not arrive after all, and Sunday was a lovely day, "which we all enjoyed fairly, but with the heavy drawback of Mrs. Bray's illness and the consciousness that we ought not to have troubled our friends with our presence at such a time."

During this visit Miss Evans gave Chapman a bit of sound advice. Not content with editing the *Review,* he also aspired to be one of its principal contributors, a function for which neither his ideas nor his literary style properly qualified him. He had already begun an article on suffrage reform for the January number. Miss Evans urged him to confine his efforts

to editorial work, arguing that he would "lose power and influence by becoming a writer in the Westminster Review, and
could not then maintain that dignified relation with the various contributors that she thinks I may do otherwise."[21]

Though Elisabeth had yielded a reluctant consent to her
rival's return, her jealousy still smoldered. She took offense at
the phrase "I count the days until Friday week" in Chapman's letter to Miss Evans. But Marian knew better how to
act now; she resumed her place in the household September
29, 1851, and lived there continuously for two years. No evidence survives of further disagreements among the three ladies who shared so queerly in Chapman's heart. There may
have been some recorded in the Diary, since a number of
leaves containing the entries for October 11–17 and November 15–21 have been cut out. On the latter date Marian wrote
the Brays that "there are four or five boarders in the house,
so Mrs. Chapman is rather hurried, Miss Tilley being ab-
sent."[22] Though her absence may have been temporary, Elisabeth's star was in its decline; by the time the Chapmans
moved from the Strand to Blandford Square in May 1854 it
had probably set.

21. Diary, 21 September 1851.   22. 21 November 1851.

CHAPTER IV

"A Wretched Helpmate"

A WEEK after Miss Evans returned to the Strand, Chapman completed the purchase of the *Westminster Review* by the payment of £300. Preparations began in earnest for their first number—January 1852. The Editors were in daily conference now and took long walks together in the regular course of business. They called on the importers, Williams and Norgate, Nutt, Dulau, and William Jeffs, who agreed to give them French and German books for review in the Contemporary Literature section. In Jeffs's shop they met an ugly little man whom Chapman introduced to her as Mr. Lewes— "a sort of miniature Mirabeau in appearance," she wrote Mr. Bray.

A few days later they went to Chelsea, and while Marian wandered alone up and down Cheyne Walk, Chapman called on Carlyle and tried to persuade him to write the article that Mr. Lombe had requested on the Peerage.[1] Carlyle was not to be persuaded; but after Chapman had gone he sat down and wrote to his friend Robert Browning:

A certain *John*[2] Chapman, Publisher of Liberalisms, "Extinct Socinianisms," and notable ware of that kind, in the Strand, has just been here: really a meritorious, productive kind of man, did he well know his road in these times. It appears he has just effected a purchase of the *Westminster Review* (Friend Lombe's) and has taken Lombe along with him, and other men of cash; his intense purpose now is, To bring out a Review, Liberal in all senses, that shall charm the world. He has capital "for four years' trial," he says; an able Editor (name can't be given), and such an array of "talent" as was seldom gathered before. Poor soul, I really wished him well in his enterprise, and regretted I could not help him myself, being clear for silence at present. Since his departure, I have

1. GE to Charles Bray, Wednesday [8 October 1851].
2. Carlyle's emphasis is probably to distinguish John Chapman from Frederic Chapman (1823–95) of Chapman and Hall, publishers at 186 Strand until January 1851, when they moved to 193 Piccadilly.

bethought me of you! There you are in Paris, there you were in Florence, with fiery interest in all manner of things, with whole Libraries to write and say on this and the other thing! The man means to pay handsomely; is indeed an *honest* kind of man, with a real enthusiasm (tho' a soft and slobbery) in him, which can be predicated of very few. Think of it, whether there are not many things you could send him from Paris, and so get rid of them? If you gave me the signal, I would at once set Chapman on applying to you;—only I fear you won't![3]

There was no need to give the signal. Carlyle's younger brother John had already suggested that Browning, who knew Lombe in Florence, might be interested in the *Review*. At Chapman's invitation he called in the Strand August 26; they had a pleasant interview, during which, Browning wrote Carlyle, "he told me all about it;—how he had got in some measure rid of his *Lombago,* under which he must have been stiffened past even writhing. I conceive your kindness in pointing out a way to him, had I wanted it."[4]

Life in the Strand was exciting enough in those days. The Great Exhibition brought many celebrities to town, some of whom stayed at Chapman's. Frederika Bremer, the Swedish novelist, fresh from her American triumphs, impressed Miss Evans at first as "a repulsive person, equally unprepossessing to eye and ear"; but the judgment mellowed on better acquaintance, when Miss Bremer told her amusing stories at breakfast, "all the prettier for her broken English," or showed her sketchbooks with original portraits of Jenny Lind and Emerson, until at the end of a month she was sorry to see her go.[5] London was swarming with exiles driven from their homes by the revolutions of 1848—men like Mazzini, Louis Blanc, or that "dreamy genius" Pierre Leroux, to whom George Sand had dedicated some of her novels. These men were always welcome. There were a good many American boarders, too, who pleased Miss Evans less. "The house is

3. Alexander Carlyle, ed., *Letters of Thomas Carlyle to Mill, Sterling, and Browning,* London [1923], pp. 288–289. By permission of T. Fisher Unwin, Ltd.

4. T. L. Hood, ed., *Letters of Robert Browning,* New Haven, 1933, p. 36.

5. GE to Charles Bray, Wednesday [8 October 1851]; GE to Sara Hennell, 9 October [1851] and 2 November 1851.

brimful of Americans with varying degrees of disagreeable-
ness," she wrote the Brays, "but one is glad to think they pay
well for their lodging."[6]

On Friday evenings the drawing room was filled with interesting people: Robert W. Mackay; William Rathbone
Greg; Sir David Brewster, the physicist; George Combe, the
phrenologist, with his wife, a daughter of the great Mrs. Siddons; William Ballantyne Hodgson; James Anthony Froude;
Harriet Martineau; Professor Richard Owen, the Conserva-
tor of the Hunterian Museum; Robert Owen, the New La-
nark Socialist, now an ardent believer in spiritualism; William
Ellis, founder of the Birkbeck Schools, and his wife, who were
particularly cordial to the new assistant editor, "inviting me
to visit them without ceremony." A decade later when it became known that George Eliot was really Marian Evans, many
of them recalled the strange charm of the sallow-faced woman
with the lovely low voice, whose conversation had so astonished them at these parties.

The articles for the first number of the *Westminster* under
its new Editors were gradually assembled. Chapman had temporarily accepted Miss Evans's opinion that he ought not to
write for it. He laid aside the article he had begun on suffrage. After failing to get Spencer to do one on the subject,
he went to the veteran William J. Fox, who had written the
first article for the *Westminster* in 1824. Fox agreed to write
if Chapman would furnish the facts, and his article called
"Representative Reform" was placed first in the initial number of the new series. Dr. Samuel Brown of Edinburgh contributed a popular and satisfactory essay on shellfish. Greg
discussed "The Relations between Employers and Employed"; Froude wrote what he termed a "light article" on
Mary Stuart. "The Latest Continental Theory of Legislation"
—the proposal of Rittinghausen and Considérant for direct
legislation by popular vote—was discussed and refuted by
Francis William Newman, brother of the future cardinal. In
"The Ethics of Christendom," James Martineau attacked the
perversion of "the accidental and transient form of the primi-

6. Wednesday [2 June 1852].

tive Christianity into essential and permanent doctrine," defending free will and the "ideal type of a perfect soul, to which all others rise as they approach."

Lewes, whom Miss Evans had seen a number of times since their meeting in Jeffs's shop, had agreed to do the article on the modern novelists that Chapman once proposed for Miss Brontë and later planned to ask Miss Evans herself to write. Chapman suggested

that he should give the characteristics of each of the leading novelists, describe their relative and intrinsic merits, erect a standard of criticism whereby to judge them, with a view of elevating the productions of the novelists as works of art and as refining and moral influences. If more were claimed from the novelist, the best of them would accord more. But Lewes is a "bread scholar" and lacks that enthusiasm of thought and earnest purpose which I must alone seek for in contributors to the Westminster.

Lewes may have felt the difficulty of writing an article that would answer these requirements. For some reason he substituted one on Julia von Krüdener, the adventuress and religious fanatic who played such an important part in forming the Holy Alliance.

There followed an article on French political parties, published as an "Independent Contribution." A note explained that the Editors dissented from the opinion in the concluding paragraph "that the possession of power by the French Socialists would, in the present stage of things, be an immediate national benefit." When they were drawing up the Prospectus, Chapman and Miss Evans thought the Independent Section an admirable device for admitting the most advanced opinions. They were soon to realize, however, that such isolation implied a needless approval of all the other articles, and after the second number the Section was abandoned. Contributors like James Martineau, who looked on the *Review* as an organ for advancing a definite program, did not want it to be open to differing opinions. Others like Spencer objected to all limitations imposed by the Prospectus: "A journal of progress should have no such formula, but content itself with declaring a determination to follow truth wherever she may

lead, and whoever and whatever she may pass by."[7] Nevertheless, Spencer's review in the *Economist* entitled "The New
and the Old" contrasted the *Westminster* with the *Quarterly*
to the decided advantage of the former.

Miss Evans was pleased with her first number. It is "superior . . . to either the *Edinburgh* or the *Quarterly*," she
wrote Mr. Bray.[8] She had good reason to be proud; the contributors were a distinguished group, every one of whom
made his mark in the world of letters and was duly admitted
to *The Dictionary of National Biography*. A modern editor
must wince to think that with all of these "great names" the
articles appeared anonymously.

While the more conservative journals gave the new *Westminster* little notice, dubious perhaps of its trend, those that
welcomed "advanced" ideas found it rather too timid.

Those persons who have been looking out for this number will
note that the two perils besetting Mr. Chapman's path, or confidently supposed to beset it—viz., heaviness and exclusiveness—
have been skilfully avoided. But we miss the boldness such a Review ought to adopt. We miss the positive convictions of which it
should be the organ. That Mr. Chapman will not allow it to fall
into vague routinary orthodoxy his position in the publishing
world assures us: it will be fatal if he *do*, for the orthodox *have*
their organs already.

This was the warning of the *Leader*,[9] a radical weekly run by
Lewes and Thornton Hunt, who disliked nothing so much as
orthodoxy.

Mild as it seems today, standing on the library shelf in
dusty, crumbling binding, the *Westminster* was read with
consternation in 1852. The clergy in particular feared its effect on their flocks. Its exclusion from the Edinburgh Select
Subscription Library on grounds of heresy promptly brought
defenders. When the *Westminster* was in other hands, the
Leader said,

7. *Economist*, 17 January 1852, p. 71.
8. [23 January 1852.]   9. 10 January 1852, p. 37.

its "heresies" were avowed without scruple; yet the Institution quietly gave them shelter, because its members had a laudable desire to see the *Review*. No sooner does Mr. JOHN CHAPMAN take it into his hands than the *nasum theologicum* (quicker at detecting stinks than perfumes) at once scents out "heresy"; although, in point of fact, the reproach which we "heretics" all bring against the *Review* is, that it is too orthodox![10]

Fear of the *Westminster* was not confined to Presbyterian Scotland. In Sheffield the Mechanics' Library banned it. In Nottingham, a city of 100,000 inhabitants, it was not to be had at any public library. At Warwick a clergyman wrote on the back of the October number, "The article on the Restoration of Belief [it was by James Martineau] is full of awful blasphemy," and straightway exerted himself to see the library rid of such a periodical.[11]

One feature in which the new *Westminster* surpassed every rival was its review of contemporary literature. The brief miscellaneous notices of the old series were supplanted by four long articles on the literature of England, America, Germany, and France, which discussed all the most important works in those countries. It was Miss Evans's task to see that the reviews by various hands were woven together into these comprehensive accounts. The thoroughness with which she revised the work of others makes identification of her own reviews difficult. During her editorship she wrote parts of the English and American sections from time to time and the French and German sections regularly. Joseph Neuberg, who was helping Carlyle with *Frederick the Great* and boarding for long periods at Chapman's, supplied some information for the German article and suggested books to be noticed. Mr. Syme also contributed reviews.[12]

Spencer's suggestion that the reviews would be more usefully classified by subject than geographically was adopted in January 1854 with sections for theology, science, classics, history, belles lettres, and art. Aside from this change of classifi-

10. *Leader,* 24 January 1852, p. 86.   11. *Leader,* 20 November 1852, p. 1116.
12. The American article for January and the English articles for July and October 1852.

cation and the abandonment of the Independent Section after April 1852, the general pattern set in the first number was followed in all those edited by Miss Evans.

The most significant article in the April number[13] was "A Theory of Population" by Herbert Spencer, the first of a number of essays in the *Westminster* that enunciated the various hypotheses he later combined in his *System of Synthetic Philosophy*. Chapman was the instigator of this article. In his Diary, January 4, 1851, he notes that Spencer

was astonished to find me propounding a theory regarding population which he conceived to be peculiarly original with him; *viz.*, that the power of reproduction is in an inverse ratio with the perfection of the individuals constituting the race; and several important applications of the doctrine, it seems, have been equally worked out by both of us. He told me the ideas had been familiar to him these two years. I told him I worked them out for myself in Paris, eight years ago, and that I was glad there was a chance they would now get utterance.[14]

Chapman proposed an article on this subject for his first number of the *Westminster,* which Spencer twice refused to write. His change of mind is perhaps attributable to Miss Evans, to whom he was introduced in October at the first evening party after her return to the Strand. The story of their relations is a strange one, which I hope to discuss in detail in another volume, though the general outline may be indicated here.

In any list of the remarkable intellects of the nineteenth century Spencer and George Eliot would certainly stand very

13. The authors of the articles in April 1852 are as follows:
"The Government of India," John Chapman (1801–54).
"Physical Puritanism," Dr. Samuel Brown.
"Europe: Its Condition and Prospects," Giuseppe Mazzini.
"A Theory of Population," Herbert Spencer.
"Shelley and the Letters of Poets," George Henry Lewes.
"The Commerce of Literature," John Chapman (1821–94).
"Lord Palmerston and His Policy," Thomas Colley Grattan.
14. In *An Autobiography*, 2 vols., London, 1904, I, 388, Spencer, writing long after, sets his conception of the theory a year or two earlier, "1847 at the latest, when I remember propounding it to a friend."

near the top. There were curious similarities between them. Both were born in the Midlands, only five months apart, and had come to London to earn their living as writers. Both were engaged as assistant editors of liberal periodicals and lived with their employers, exactly opposite each other in the Strand. On such subjects as dogmatic theology they were in complete accord. Spencer shared also her love for music; having frequent press tickets to the opera and theaters, he began soon after their meeting to invite her to go with him. 142 Strand abutted at the back on Somerset House, and Chapman, either by favor of the authorities or by some clause in his lease, had a key to the terrace. Here Spencer and Miss Evans on pleasant days would walk up and down, looking out over the Thames and Waterloo Bridge, discussing all things in heaven and earth. They took long walks in the country, too, at Richmond or Kew, during which Spencer would expound his theories of plants—"*proof*-hunting" expeditions, she called them, for "if the flowers didn't correspond to the theories, we said '*tant pis pour les fleurs.*' "[15]

In *Social Statics, or the Conditions Essential to Human Happiness Specified, and the First of Them Developed,* 1851, he had expressed his conception of the place of woman in the modern world as an independent being who ought to be treated in every respect as the equal of man. Although living specimens were hard to find in a day when woman was "the lesser man, . . . as moonlight unto sunlight" in comparison with her lord and master, in the assistant editor of the *Westminster* Spencer seemed to have discovered a fit companion even for a philosopher. In writing his friend Lott, April 23, 1852, he spoke of

Miss Evans whom you have heard me mention as the translatress of Strauss and as the most admirable woman, mentally, I ever met. We have been for some time past on very intimate terms. I am very frequently at Chapman's and the greatness of her intellect conjoined with her womanly qualities and manner, generally keep me by her side most of the evening.[16]

15. GE to Sara Hennell, Tuesday Morning [29 June 1852].
16. Herbert Spencer, *An Autobiography,* 2 vols., London, 1904, I, 394–395. By permission of the D. Appleton-Century Company.

The admiration was mutual; there was no one in whose company Miss Evans would rather be. Their friends watched the increasing intimacy with approval, and perhaps fostered the match as they could. When the Brays invited them both to Coventry, Marian replied:

We certainly could not go together, for all the world is setting us down as engaged—a most disagreeable thing if one chose to make oneself uncomfortable. "Tell it not in Gath" however—that is to say, please to avoid mentioning our names together, and pray burn this note, that it may not lie on the chimney piece for general inspection.[17]

The rumor was disagreeable to Miss Evans because, for some weeks, it had been perfectly clear to her that they never would be engaged. The specifier of the conditions essential to human happiness, who was to die a bachelor at eighty-four, had no intention of marrying. "I think it is too much trouble," he told a friend in 1850; ". . . and as I see no probability of being able to marry without being a drudge, why I have pretty well given up the idea. After all it does not much matter."[18] Confronted now with an emancipated and intellectual woman who, far from making him a drudge, would have contributed in every respect to his welfare, Spencer was compelled once more to go "proof-hunting." A reason was not far to seek in this case: Miss Evans, he decided, however brilliant her mind and affectionate her nature, did not measure up to his standards of beauty. Perhaps with her in mind he wrote in his *Autobiography:* "Physical beauty is a *sine quâ non* with me; as was once unhappily proved where the intellectual traits and the emotional traits were of the highest."[19]

They faced the problem in the calm, rational manner that befits philosophers. "We have agreed that we are not in love with each other, and that there is no reason why we should not have as much of each other's society as we like," she wrote the Brays.[20] But on her part there must have been a larger admixture of emotion than Spencer betrays. Hers was a passion-

17. GE to the Brays, Monday [14 June 1852].
18. Herbert Spencer, *An Autobiography*, 2 vols., London, 1904, I, 369.
19. *Ibid.*, II, 445.   20. Tuesday [27 April 1852].

ate nature, ill-concealed by her lack of beauty; "she was not fitted to stand alone." In Spencer she seemed close to the ideal she had once imagined in Dr. Brabant and later in Chapman, the same ideal that Dorothea was to imagine in Casaubon—a man whom she could dedicate her life to helping with a great work, whether a *Key to All Mythologies,* a *Westminster Review,* or a *System of Synthetic Philosophy* and its Universal Postulate.

It is interesting to speculate on what the consequences of their union might have been. One imagines Marian, like Dorothea, turning her whole intellect to the service of Spencer's work, perhaps taking the place of the amanuensis he was shortly to hire. It is unlikely that she would have influenced him much more than she did. But of one thing we may be reasonably sure: there would have been no George Eliot. Living with Spencer, the critical and speculative tendencies of her mind would surely have predominated over a creative talent never strong enough to stand without encouragement.

To Mr. Chapman's domestic difficulties some serious worries had been added by his bookselling business. Since the beginning of the century the price of books had been fixed by a small group of London publishers who controlled an organization known as the Booksellers' Association. To members they granted discounts of 30 to 45 per cent on condition that the books should not be retailed at a discount of more than 10 per cent. Each bookseller who signed the Regulations was given a ticket permitting him to purchase on these terms; but if he were found underselling—and the Association maintained spies to detect violations—his ticket was forfeited, and the publishers would furnish no books to fill his orders.

Chapman had signed the Regulations under protest and adhered to them faithfully in his English trade. But he maintained that the London publishers had no jurisdiction over American books; in January 1852 he announced that henceforth he would sell imported books at cost plus a small commission. To his surprise he was summoned before the committee of the Booksellers' Association and "threatened with excommunication if he did not suppress the obnoxious advertisement." Upon his refusing to do so, his ticket was canceled and the fact placarded in all the London shops, so that the majority of publishers refused to sell him their books.

Although many booksellers had been ruined by attempts to defy the Association, Chapman was not the man to yield without a struggle. He set out to stir up rebellion, conscious that the right was on his side. Advertising his own publications at "a large discount," he offered to supply "miscellaneous English books on the same terms," though he could obtain them only by subterfuge. He wrote to Cabinet Ministers and members of Parliament. He called on influential authors, who assured him of support. Most important of all, he wrote for the April number of the *Westminster Review* an article entitled "The Commerce of Literature," which exposed the shabby racket in effective but moderate terms and precipitated a public discussion.

Most of the London papers, which counted the publishers among their largest advertisers, spoke loudly in defense of the Association. Two notable exceptions, the *Athenæum* and the *Times*, sided with the "Free Traders," as Chapman's party was soon labeled. Two influential members of the Association, John W. Parker and Richard Bentley, publisher-in-ordinary to the Queen, deserted to join the rebels. Soon the criticism of the monopoly had grown so strong that the Association was compelled to act. At a meeting April 8, 1852, they agreed to submit their case to a committee consisting of Lord Campbell, Chief Justice of the Queen's Bench, Dr. Milman, Dean of St. Paul's, and Mr. George Grote the historian. The opinion of these gentlemen was to be accepted without appeal; if it were adverse the Booksellers' Association agreed to "convene the trade and resign their functions."

The hearing was held at Strathenden House, Lord Campbell's residence in Kensington, April 14. None of the "undersellers" was represented, though Chapman sent a letter complaining that longer notice had not been given him. Two of the great publishers, William Longman and John Murray, stated the case for the Association, which relied in lieu of stronger argument on the weight of authority: Dr. Johnson, they observed, had defended the system of price fixing in

1776! When Lord Campbell declined to give a judgment until he had heard representatives of the "undersellers," a second hearing was set for May 17.

In the meantime Chapman planned a meeting of the rebels to be held on May 4 at his house in the Strand. Spencer went about with him to solicit help. Authors, who suffered the most from the restriction of trade, were unanimously in favor of ending the monopoly and gladly promised to attend. When the meeting was called to order by Charles Dickens as chairman, the distinguished group present included Wilkie Collins, R. H. Horne, F. W. Newman, Lewes, Spencer, Dr. Roget of the *Thesaurus,* Tom Taylor of *Punch,* Henry Crabb Robinson, George Cruikshank, and Richard Owen. Of those who could not attend Carlyle, Cobden, J. S. Mill, Gladstone, W. J. Fox, George Combe, Robert Chambers, and several others sent letters, which Dickens read aloud with enthusiasm. Next he called upon Chapman, who read a long and able statement of the Free Traders' position, in the composition of which he had been aided by Miss Evans and Spencer. Five resolutions on the baneful effects of the monopoly were then passed with little opposition and ordered sent to Lord Campbell with a letter from Dickens stating the reasons why the Free Traders declined to send representatives to him, "as they could not consent to defer to his arbitration or abandon the position they had assumed."[21] By midnight, when "the last magnate—except Herbert Spencer—" was out of the house, Marian saluted Mr. Chapman with "See, the Conquering Hero Comes" on the piano. She wrote the Brays next day that he

read his statement very well and looked distinguished and refined even in that assemblage of intellectuals. . . . So now I hope poor Mr. Chapman will have a little time to attend to his business, which is needing him awfully—in fact, his private affairs are wearing a melancholy aspect. However, he has worked well and in a good spirit at this great question and has shown a degree of talent and power of mastering a subject which have won him general admiration.[22]

21. *Leader,* 8 May 1852, pp. 433–434.
22. GE to the Brays, Wednesday, 5 May [1852].

Chapman printed an account of the meeting with the letters that were read; Carlyle's, a very long and characteristic one, had already appeared in the papers. Gladstone took the occasion of a debate on the paper duty to castigate the Booksellers' Association in Parliament. By May 19, when Lord Campbell gave the committee's decision, public opinion was solidly behind the "undersellers." The judgment, a long and carefully considered document, was unanimous in their favor. The *Leader* printed it in full, paying tribute in an editorial to the energy and skill of Mr. John Chapman, "who brings into the trade the feeling of a literary man, the far sight of a philosopher, and the public spirit of a leading reformer."[23]

May 28, 1852, the Booksellers' Association met for the last time. When his case was referred to, Chapman, generous in victory, rose to bear testimony to the character of the committee and praise the conscientiousness of their conduct, but his words "could not be reported on account of the constant interruption to which the speaker was subjected." In a final speech Mr. Longman formally announced the result of their appeal to Lord Campbell, adding that, though he regretted the destruction of the old system, he felt it his duty to state that it had involved practices repugnant to his feelings. He then resigned his functions, and after a brief discussion the Booksellers' Association voted to dissolve.[24]

For Chapman it was a Pyrrhic victory. He could freely advertise "the liberal terms on which he is now enabled, by the destruction of the Booksellers' Association, to supply books of all kinds" at a discount of twopence in the shilling, and his own publications to anyone, "whether bookseller or private individual," at discounts up to 40 per cent. But as all the other booksellers were now at liberty to do the same, his trade never regained its former volume. "You talk of poor Mr. Chapman's laurels," Miss Evans wrote Mrs. Bray, "—alas,

23. *Leader,* 22 May 1852, p. 493.
24. Sympathy with Chapman's opinion of price fixing prompted R. H. Macy & Co., Inc., to publish an account of his struggle with the Booksellers' Association in *The Author's Wallet,* compiled by Paul Hollister, New York, 1934. The statement Chapman read at the meeting is reprinted on pp. 46–64.

alas, he is suffering the most torturing anxiety, advertising for a partner in half-despair of getting another kind of aid. . . . He sits in the shop the greater part of the day now, and is about to part with Mr. Beveridge, as a step in retrenchment."[25] Though the Association was dissolved, its members still found ways to injure his business. An advertisement on the inside wrapper of the *Westminster Review* for July 1852 shows how sharply they made their power felt:

During the last six months, in the course of which MR. CHAPMAN has acted as the leading opponent of the Booksellers' Association, he has experienced a marked diminution in the sale of his publications. . . . He has received, from various parts of England, letters complaining of the difficulty of obtaining them; and hence he can only ascribe the above result to a disposition on the part of the Booksellers to impede the sale of the works published by him. Under these circumstances he will feel obliged to all those who meet with any obstacles in the way of procuring works either published or imported by him, if they will apply for them direct to him, when he will immediately forward them through the post-office, or otherwise as instructed.

The melancholy aspect of his affairs arose also from the financial plight of the *Review*. Like most ventures of the sort it was sustained by loans from well-disposed friends, willing to risk their money in the good cause, and by outright gifts of rich philanthropists, whose views it was expected to forward.

Mr. Edward Lombe had been for years an outstanding donor to the *Westminster Review*. He was a rather eccentric gentleman of Melton Hall, Wymondham, who had not been in England for twenty-five years. He lived in Florence, presumably on account of his health, bestowing by letter his benefactions in support of free thought and the secular control of education. He outraged the Norfolk gentry by allowing his sixty-eight tenants to shoot game on their farms and to vote for members of Parliament according to their own opinions, without consulting him on the merits of the candidates as other landlords required. He established institutions

25. 27 May [1852].

for popular education in Sheffield and Norwich, and contributed largely to the agitation for a national educational system independent of religion.[26] His offer to pay Chapman for reprinting certain liberal theological works has already been mentioned; without his help the *Westminster* would probably never have come into Chapman's hands. One of Lombe's hobbies was a fundamental reform called "organic change"; even though no one knew just what it meant, the phrase appeared in the Prospectus of the new *Review*, well guarded with *ifs* and *yets*. Chapman tried at the outset to make it clear that he must have a free hand, but the stiffness of his patron's opinions, which Browning had alluded to as "Lombago," was not easily overcome.

In July 1851 Harriet Martineau had proposed an abridged translation of Auguste Comte's *Cours de philosophie positive* to Chapman, who sent her letter on to Lombe, inquiring if he would assist in the publication of such a work. In reply he received the following notes, which he copied into his Diary:

Florence, August one, 1851.

My dear Sir,
 Yours of the 24th ult. was received this day. Annexed is my answer to the enclosure it contained. On other matters another time.

Yours very sincerely,
EDWARD LOMBE.

John Chapman.

The second, addressed to Messrs. Barclay, Bevan, Tritton and Company, the London bankers, read as follows:

Gentlemen,
 On receipt of this letter I request you will do me the very great honour of transferring Five Hundred Pounds, say £500, to the credit of Miss Harriet Martineau in support of a great literary work.

Your very obliged servant,
EDWARD LOMBE.

26. See Charles Gibbon, *The Life of George Combe*, 2 vols., London, 1878, II, 293–294.

Since the sum was much larger than necessary to secure a good translation, Chapman rather unwisely wrote back, proposing that the amount should be divided between the Comte and reprints of other books like Theodore Parker's *Discourse on Religion*. This only irritated Lombe, who insisted upon his notions rather tyrannically, but paid handsomely for the privilege. On August 28 Chapman was obliged to tell Miss Martineau the good news and give her the check. It was plain to her that, even though the amount was excessive, Lombe had intended her to have the money in recompense for the work. However, Chapman was persuasive in spite of her ear trumpet, and she finally agreed to take £150 for herself and allow the rest to be used to defray the cost of publishing the translation.

On March 1, 1852, before the second number of the *Westminster* was ready for the printer, Mr. Lombe died. When the news reached England Miss Martineau, who had his £500 already safely invested in the Three per Cents, added a codicil to her will appointing Miss Evans and Henry G. Atkinson joint trustees in case she died before the translation was completed,[27] a needless precaution, as it turned out. Miss Martineau was constantly making such provisions and informing the public of the imminence of her demise, which came as a distinct anticlimax in 1876, twenty-three years after the abridged translation of Comte had appeared.

To Chapman, Lombe's death was a more serious matter, for the *Review* depended greatly on him. A few weeks later Dr. Brabant, who had lent Chapman £800, called with the unwelcome news that the money must be paid back within two years. Under such circumstances it would have been tempting to economize a little in payments to authors of the *Westminster* articles, which came to £250 a number, an enormous sum for a quarterly that printed only 650 copies.[28] The Editors did not yield. The July number, though it had no

27. GE to Mrs. Bray, Tuesday [30 March 1852]. Miss Martineau does not mention her name in this connection. See M. W. Chapman, ed., *Harriet Martineau's Autobiography*, 2 vols., Boston, II, 67.

28. *Christian Union*, 26 January 1881, p. 80.

controversial article to cause a stir, maintained the excellent standard set by the preceding issues.[29] So closely did the Editors guard the anonymity of their contributors that James Martineau, who was not on speaking terms with his sister Harriet, expressed great admiration for her article on Niebuhr under the delusion that it was by Newman.

As soon as the July number was out, Miss Evans was escorted by Mr. Chapman—or rather (she adds in her letter to Mr. Bray[30]), by Mr. *and Mrs.* Chapman—to Broadstairs on the Kentish coast. She settled down in two little rooms for which she paid a guinea a week, wondering if it would not be well to retire from the world and live there always.[31] Of this summer Spencer remarks with the careful vagueness he injected into his *Autobiography:* "Two of my weekly vacations were spent at the sea side; and, later on in the season, I had a few pleasant days with Miss Evans's friends, the Brays, at Coventry."[32] This was the visit that had been postponed until Miss Evans could be there; from the close association in his thought it seems not unlikely that the weekly vacations at the seaside were spent in the neighborhood of Broadstairs. He and Marian now knew, as Dorothea and Sir James Chettam were to know, "the delight there is in frank kindness and companionship between a man and a woman who have no passion to hide or confess."[33]

Marian could not shake off the cares of the Strand by mere flight to the coast. Her heart was involved there. Her interest in the *Review* sprang as much from personal feeling for Chapman as from the need for bread-and-butter. "I feel that I am a wretched helpmate to you," she wrote him, "almost out of the world and incog. so far as I am in it. When you can

29. "Secular Education," George Combe.
"England's Forgotten Worthies," J. A. Froude.
"The Future of Geology," Edward Forbes.
"The Tendencies of England," F. W. Newman?
"The Lady Novelists," G. H. Lewes.
"Political Life and Sentiments of Niebuhr," Harriet Martineau.
"The Restoration of Belief," James Martineau.
"Sir Robert Peel and His Policy," W. R. Greg.
30. 23 June [1852].   31. GE to Mrs. Bray [4 July 1852].
32. I, 407.   33. *Middlemarch* (Cabinet ed.), I, 106.

afford to pay an Editor, if that time will ever come, you must get one." She then went on to sketch an ideal editor for the *Westminster* and what he should believe. The letter contains such an important statement of her philosophical position at this time and so vivid a picture of her editorial work that it must be read in its entirety:

> Broadstairs,
> Saturday Evening,
> [24/25 July 1852].

Dear Friend,

I laid Mr. Gilpin's[34] note with the accompanying pamphlet on my desk the morning I left London, meaning to commend them to your care. I dare say you will find them in my room. If not, I believe the purport of Mr. Gilpin's note was that the writer of said pamphlet wished to know if an article on "Free Schools in Worcestershire" (the subject of the pamphlet) would be accepted for the Westminster. I am not sure whether it was requested that the pamphlet should be noticed by us.

I return Froude's letter and Martineau's. Of course you will let Froude have his twenty-six pages. As to Martineau, there is no doubt that he will write; "Self-interest well understood" will secure that. Pray, how came you to tell him that J. S. Mill was going to write? I have told you all along that he would flatly contradict Martineau and that there was nothing for it but to announce contradiction on our title-page. I think M. is right as to the "idea" of a quarterly, but it is plain that the Westminster can't realize that "idea." However, if I were its proprietor and could afford to make it what I liked, it should certainly not represent the Martineau "School of thought." Not that I mean to decry him, or to speak superciliously of one so immeasurably superior to myself. I simply mean that I can't see things through spectacles of his colour.

What do you think of sending the note which I enclose to Miss Bronty? The thrice announced parcel has just arrived. As to my disgraceful mistake about the stamps, I can only say—peccavi, peccavi. The only excuse I have to make is that I just glanced at the envelope in which you forwarded the same M.S. to me, and saw only two stamps on it. I need not say that I did not pause to use my reasoning faculty in the matter.

34. Charles Gilpin, London publisher and bookseller.

Don't suggest "Fashion" as a subject to any one else. I should like to keep it.

Sunday—This morning came (with the Athenæum and Leader, for which thanks) a letter from Geo. Combe announcing Dr. S. Brown's refusal to write said article for October. I enclose the letters of both. Please return Geo. Combe's with *the one of his which I sent you some time ago.** I am sorry for Dr. B's defection, as I am very favourably impressed with the character of his mind. I wish Mr. Bastard35 would wait until January and still get Dr. B. to write. I shall say so to Geo. Combe. If yes, what do you say to Lewes on Lamarck?

I have noticed the advertisement of the British Quarterly this morning. Its list of subjects is excellent. I wish you could contrive to let me see the number when it comes out. They have one subject of which I am jealous—"Pre-Raphaelism in Painting and Literature." We have no good writer on such subjects on our staff. Ought we not, too, to try and enlist David Masson, who is one of the British Quarterly set? He wrote that article in the Leader36 on the Patagonian Missionaries, which I thought very beautiful. Seeing "Margaret Fuller" among their subjects makes me rather regret having missed the first moment for writing an article on her life myself, but I think she still may come in as one of a triad or quaternion.

I feel that I am a wretched helpmate to you, almost out of the world and incog. so far as I am in it. When you can afford to pay an Editor, if that time will ever come, you must get one. If you believe in Free Will, in the Theism that looks on manhood as a type of the godhead and on Jesus as the Ideal Man, get one belonging to the Martineau "School of thought," and he will drill you a regiment of writers who will produce a Prospective on a larger scale, and so the Westminster may come to have "dignity" in the eyes of Liverpool.

If not—if you believe, as I do, that the thought which is to mould the Future has for its root a belief in necessity, that a nobler presentation of humanity has yet to be given in resignation to individual nothingness than could ever be shewn of a being who believes in the phantasmagoria of hope unsustained by reason, why then get a man of another calibre and let him write a

* See last page of my letter.

35. Thomas Horlock Bastard of Charlton Marshall, Dorset, a philanthropist, interested like Combe in educational reforms.
36. 8 May 1852, pp. 442-443.

fresh Prospectus, and if Liverpool theology and ethics are to be admitted, let them be put in the "dangerous ward," *alias*, the Independent Section.[37]

The only third course is the present one, that of Editorial compromise. Martineau writes much that we can agree with and admire, Newman ditto, J. S. Mill still more, Froude a little less, and so on. These men can write more openly in the Westminster than anywhere else. They are amongst the world's vanguard, though not all in the foremost line; it is good for the world, therefore, that they should have every facility for speaking out. Ergo, since each can't have a periodical to himself, it is good that there should be one which is common to them, id est, the Westminster. The grand mistake with respect to this plan is the paragraph in the Prospectus which announces the Independent Section and which thus makes the Editors responsible for everything outside that railing—Ah me! how wise we all are *après coup*.

If we don't have Lewes's article on Lamarck, I think you had better sound him when he comes back and see what hope there is

37. Although George Eliot's metaphysics cannot be adequately discussed here, this extraordinary statement of her belief during the most critical period of her life must not be passed without comment. Brought up in the orthodox Anglicanism pictured so kindly in *Scenes of Clerical Life* and *Adam Bede,* she was early touched by a stern and ascetic form of Evangelicalism held by her teachers. Her keen appetite for reading was further directed toward theology by a Chart of Ecclesiastical History that she began to compile in 1840; and such books as Isaac Taylor's *Ancient Christianity,* which in defense of the simple teaching of the Bible attacked superstition and clerical fraud, unconsciously laid the foundation for her later scepticism.

At Coventry in 1841 she found in the circle of the Brays and Hennells the speculative freedom needed to develop this latent trait. C. C. Hennell's *Inquiry Concerning the Origin of Christianity,* 1838, was the precipitating factor that brought her to the conclusion she was never to discard: that Christianity was not a divine revelation, but only the purest form yet existing of natural religion. She had already begun to study German; by 1844 when the opportunity came to translate Strauss's *Das Leben Jesu,* she had so far anticipated his destructive criticism as to be little influenced by it.

Charles Bray's *Philosophy of Necessity; or the Law of Consequences,* 1841, must be considered more important than Strauss in her development, for it first brought her the idea that "a man could in no case have acted differently from the manner in which he did act," because mind is subject to fixed laws just as matter is. This conception was shortly reinforced if not absorbed by Spinoza; she got hold of Dr. Brabant's copy at Rosehill in January 1843, and began a translation, which was continued at intervals, notably in 1849–50 and in 1854–55, but, so far as I know, never published. Her debt to Spinoza is a profound one, and deserves a detailed study. The best to date is Paul Bourl'honne, *George Eliot: Essai de biographie intellectuelle et morale, 1819–1854,* Paris, 1933.

in him for October. Defective as his articles are, they are the best we can get *of the kind*.

An article on Chalmers would not be "light." It is important that this Hereditary Transmission business should be settled as soon as possible, and so I shall tell Combe, that we may know whether we want one article or two. Apropos of Combe, I think you are too sore on the subject of the "Copyright"; you did not tell him the terms when you agreed that he should write. Besides for your purposes his article is a bone picked quite clean; let him use it up in his Papin's digester if he will.

It is amusing to see J. Martineau so confidently setting down the Niebuhr article as Newman's and so deluding himself into praising it. It is to me the most entirely satisfactory article in the number. I thought Lewes's criticism in the Leader very poor and undiscriminating.

The publishing world seems utterly stagnant—nothing coming out which would do as a peg for an article. I am running on, scribbling to no purpose and you will hardly thank me. Miss Hennell writes the following opinion of the English article: "I have just read Syme's English article. Most of it is very good; whenever he is in earnest he is good. But in the theological it is mostly slash and scoff, without giving us any confidence that he has any opinions of his own, and in other parts his style is quite too coarse, especially Nell Gwyn. One feels that he does not write as a gentleman." I congratulate you on your ability to be cheerful *malgré tout*.

Yours etc.,

MARIAN EVANS.[38]

A less sanguine person than Chapman would have succumbed long since to the "agonies of anxiety about money matters" that he suffered. No one had been found to replace Mr. Lombe's lavish support of the *Review* and of Chapman's publishing business as well. His friends did what they could. George Combe "is indefatigable in writing and thinking for us," Miss Evans wrote; he persuaded his friend Bastard to give £60 for articles, but that did not go far. Bray also concerned himself with Chapman's affairs, though his own business was in an alarming condition; he talked of supporting the *Westminster* for Marian's sake too, a gesture that she re-

38. This letter is in the collection of Mr. Morris L. Parrish.

fused to countenance. He did persuade his friend Edward Flower, the Stratford brewer, to lend Chapman money. Their efforts led to some embarrassment. Either through ignorance or deliberate misrepresentation Chapman seemed habitually unable to give a true account of his financial state; he went to Coventry July 7 to "explain" to Bray, and on the thirteenth went again to "explain his explanation." Miss Evans warned Bray of the impending visit.

I trust your benevolence and fellow-feeling, or rather your sense of the importance, on other grounds than personal ones, that his position should be maintained, will enable you to bear these visitations with patience. Of course, I am in great anxiety about him, and what is worse, I can do nothing. I have had a letter from Geo. Combe today containing the same hopeless opinion as the one you forwarded to me. I am surprised that you and he think so ill of Mr. C's affairs. My impression was that the business was in a thoroughly promising condition apart from the need of temporary assistance in capital.[39]

Two weeks later Chapman went again to Coventry for the week-end, and on Tuesday, August 3, he accompanied the Brays to Broadstairs, where they made their visit to Marian, postponed from the month before. There was further discussion of ways and means. Cobden, proposed as a possible rescuer, proved to be a Churchman, quite out of sympathy with the liberal religious views of the *Westminster*.

Chapman was always more appealing in person than in correspondence; his letters, when they had not been revised by his assistant editor, were likely to prove unfortunate. Miss Evans characterized a passage Mrs. Bray quoted to her as

a good specimen of Mr. Chapman's skill in "the art of sinking," not in poetry, but in letter-writing. But it is nothing worse than bungling. He feels better than he writes, just as some other acquaintances of ours write better than they feel. I am sure I ought to have sympathy enough with people who mean well and do ill, for the grand occupation of my life has been contributing to hell-paving.[40]

39. Wednesday [14 July 1852].   40. Thursday [12 August 1852].

Somehow, with the help of his friends Chapman got together enough money to go on.

The October number appeared more brilliant than ever.[41] Froude filled the twenty-six pages he had asked for with a temperate but trenchant criticism of Oxford, which his own experience as a fellow enabled him to make with excellent effect. John Stuart Mill, who had been propitiated by George Grote after a year of coldness, contributed a scathing article on Whewell's *Moral Philosophy*. Lewes wrote on Goethe as a Man of Science. Although Spencer assured Miss Evans that his article on the Philosophy of Style would have a "light appearance" by reason of its quotations, which break the page, she wrote Miss Hennell, in the bantering tone that now begins to characterize her references to him, "I suspect it will be like those stone sweetmeats which cheat the children."[42] It was an excellent number, and Lewes did not exaggerate when he wrote in the *Leader*[43] at the beginning of a three-column review:

It is a matter of general remark, that the *Westminster Review,* since it passed into Mr. CHAPMAN's hands, has recovered the former importance it acquired when under the editorship of JOHN STUART MILL. It is now a Review that people talk about, ask for at the clubs, and read with respect. The variety and general excellence of its articles are not surpassed by any Review.

Subscriptions were beginning to come in steadily. With careful management the *Westminster* might soon have been almost self-sustaining. Unfortunately, its funds were so hopelessly mixed with those of the unprofitable publishing business that only a miracle could float it through the sea of debt still threatening. Mr. Flower had refused to lend any more

41. "The Oxford Commission," J. A. Froude.
"Whewell's Moral Philosophy," J. S. Mill.
"Plants and Botanists," Edward Forbes.
"Our Colonial Empire," John Chapman (1801–54).
"The Philosophy of Style," Herbert Spencer.
"Goethe as a Man of Science," G. H. Lewes.
"The Duke of Wellington," W. R. Greg.
42. 2 September [1852].   43. 2 October 1852, p. 949.

money. George Combe, whom Miss Evans was visiting for two weeks in Edinburgh, took a grave view of the future. Bray, too, saw the hopelessness of trying to help Chapman. "I do not think you need trouble yourself to write that long letter you talk of to Mr. Bray," Miss Evans wrote from Coventry on her way home. "He seems to know very well how matters stand."[44]

Back in the Strand, she found Beatrice ill from scarlet fever. Chapman listened most amiably to Marian's report of the fault people found with him. There was still no money in sight. His affairs are "just like the fog," she wrote the Brays. "Instead of a *thousand,* he wants £1200 now! The Lord have mercy on him!"[45] Micawber was not more optimistic; at times she could not help laughing at him.

He was talking of the hopefulness of certain "aspects" of his business, such as that several publications have been recently offered him etc. "Then," he said, in rather an affected, 'proper' drawl, looking pious, "there are these 'Letters from Ireland' which I hope will be something rather better than a *poke in the eye.*" "Let your moderation be known unto all men," I said. That is better than the Swedish woman cooking the rail that the bird had sat on.[46]

That same day, when the "affairs of Chapmandom" never looked more dismal, the miracle occurred. Mr. Samuel Courtauld, a wealthy manufacturer and philanthropist, *volunteered* to interest himself in Chapman's business. The eldest son of George Courtauld, founder of the silk business at Braintree, Samuel had set up for himself and made a great fortune in mourning crape. He was a liberal in politics and a Unitarian in religion; for fifteen years he had been fighting for the abolition of compulsory Church Rates. His benefactions were as unexpected as they were munificent. Without previous warning he presented William J. Fox with an annuity of £400. He contributed £500 to the founding of

44. GE to Chapman, Wednesday [27 October 1852]. This letter is in the collection of Mr. Morris L. Parrish.

45. Saturday [13 November 1852].

46. GE to the Brays, Saturday Morning [4 December 1852]. *Letters from Ireland* by Harriet Martineau, reprinted from the *Daily News.*

Bedford College. And now, when the exchequer of the *Westminster* was all but exhausted and no one knew how the authors of the January number were to be paid, he offered to lend Chapman £600.

CHAPTER V

The Paths Diverge

ALTHOUGH Susanna showed some coolness after Miss Evans returned to live with them, her resentment soon thawed, for she had of necessity developed a great capacity for forgiveness. Marian, as she came to appreciate the difficulties Mrs. Chapman labored under, began to respect her patience and fortitude. Still she was not happy; her first number of the *Westminster* was hardly out before she wrote Mr. Bray: "I have declared my resolution to leave at the end of this quarter—*but say nothing about it.* Mrs. Chapman is increasingly polite and attentive, and I have many comforts here that I could hardly expect elsewhere, but——."[1]

When the end of the quarter arrived, she was so absorbed in her new friendship with Herbert Spencer that she did not want to move away from him. Nothing more is heard of her leaving until September. Then Chapman pled with her to stay, and the separation was postponed. "He makes a great point of my remaining here till Christmas, at all events, and I cannot under present 'cums' say no." Yet ever since her return from Broadstairs she had felt oppressed by "something like the madness which imagines that the four walls are contracting and going to crush one."[2] In the dark November days she was ready to vow not to live in the Strand again after Christmas. "If I were not choked by the fog, the time would trot pleasantly withal, but of what use are brains and friends when one lives in a light such as might be got in the chimney?"[3]

Once more she yielded. In February 1853 she wrote Mr. Bray:

At last I have determined to leave this house and get another home for myself. Many reasons, besides my health, concur to

1. [23 January 1852].
2. GE to Sara Hennell, 2 September [1852].
3. GE to the Brays, Saturday [13 November 1852].

make me desire this change. I suppose I must stay here, however, until the April number is out of our hands.

You once said that you would help me in such a case, and if you do not repent of that word I shall be most grateful for the kindness. I hope you will arrange to spend a quiet hour with me when you come to town.

A month later, as the April number was going to press, she wrote:

Instead of changing my street, I have changed my room only, and am now installed in Mr. Chapman's. It is very light and pleasant, and I suppose I must be content for a few months longer. Indeed, I think I shall never have the energy to move—it seems to be of so little consequence where I am or what I do.

Miss Evans's unhappiness did not go unnoticed by the other members of the household. One American visitor, Professor Noah Porter, later president of Yale, who boarded for a time in the Strand, was deeply impressed by what he interpreted as "her fervid yet unaffected sensibility."

She was free and affable with the family and guests, but unmistakably wore the air of a person preoccupied with many engagements, and living apart in her own works [world?] of elevated thoughts and intense feeling. The writer remembers once being greatly moved at seeing her, after having come late to the breakfast table and being left almost alone, give way to a mood of abstraction during which the tears flowed in streams over her strong yet gentle face.[4]

Miss Evans's tears sprang, not from fervid sensibility, but from other quite adequate causes. Her most oppressive grief at this time was the plight of her sister Chrissey, whose husband Edward Clarke had died just before Christmas 1852, leaving her with six children and almost nothing to support them. Her brother Isaac allowed them to live in an "ugly small house" he owned in Attleborough, near Nuneaton—a

---

4. "George Eliot. Personal Recollections with Comments," *Christian Union*, 26 January 1881, p. 80. I am indebted to Professor Wilbur L. Cross for this reference.

house that was once Chrissey's—but treated her with a meager generosity that George Eliot was to recall in her picture of Mr. Tulliver and his sister Gritty Moss in *The Mill on the Floss*. With her own future so uncertain Miss Evans dared not take the responsibility of bringing Chrissey and her brood to live with her; and, she wrote Mrs. Bray, "To live with her in that hideous neighbourhood amongst ignorant bigots is impossible to me. It would be moral asphyxia, and I had better take the other kind—charcoal myself and leave my money, perhaps more acceptable than my labour and affection."[5] Emigration to Australia was the current panacea for poverty; Marian proposed to send the whole family thither, and even offered to accompany them and see them settled, but Chrissey refused to consider the plan. This was one explanation for Miss Evans's tears at the breakfast table in April 1853.

There was also another problem that had begun to vex her: her relations with Mr. Lewes. The subject has been admirably studied in Anna T. Kitchel's *George Lewes and George Eliot* [1933], but so much misinformation is still current about this extraordinary Victorian romance that a brief summary of the facts may not be out of place here.

With a face like a monkey's, thick lips, excessively narrow jaw, hollow cheeks, and deep-set eyes, Lewes was said to be the ugliest man in London. He was certainly one of the most versatile. He had studied medicine; he had been an actor; he had written plays and novels and a *Biographical History of Philosophy* that went through numerous editions; for years he had earned his living as a journalist, writing with ease and surprising penetration on every sort of subject—political, literary, philosophical, or scientific. In 1850 he joined his friend Thornton Hunt and others in establishing the *Leader*, a liberal or radical weekly. The Hunts and Leweses lived together, sharing everything in common according to coöperative socialistic principles. They held the freest views on marriage, too. But when Mrs. Lewes, after bearing her husband three sons, proceeded to have two more children by his friend Hunt, Lewes felt that his home was hopelessly broken up.

5. Saturday Morning [16 April 1853].

Life seemed dreary and wasted; he gave up "all ambition whatever, lived from hand to mouth, and thought the evil of each day sufficient."[6] It was at this period that his acquaintance with Marian Evans began.

At first she was rather repelled by his appearance and manner. Before long, however, his genuine charm and the essentially serious character of his mind were revealed to her. When Spencer came to the Strand to make his usual afternoon calls on Marian, he often brought Lewes with him. On one of these occasions as Spencer rose to go, Lewes signified that he would stay. This marked the beginning of their intimacy.[7] Lewes's work as dramatic critic of the *Leader* required him to attend the theater regularly; now she often accompanied him. Once he took her behind the scenes between the acts and into the greenroom when Rachel was acting at the St. James's with her French company. "People are very good to me," she wrote Mrs. Bray April 16, 1853.

Mr. Lewes especially is kind and attentive, and has quite won my regard, after having had a good deal of my vituperation. Like a few other people in the world, he is much better than he seems. A man of heart and conscience wearing a mask of flippancy.

The assistant editor's earlier dissatisfaction with his articles for the *Westminster* now disappeared, and she became a staunch defender of everything he did. She is annoyed that Harriet Martineau in a letter (to Atkinson) jeers at Lewes for introducing psychology as a science in his Comte papers in the *Leader*.[8] She assures Sara Hennell that "poor Lewes" was not responsible for a certain article in the *Westminster,* which "is as remote from his style both of thinking and writing as anything can be."[9] She is particularly anxious that Mr. Bray should not think him the author of a wretched play called *The Hope of the Family,* perhaps because the plot revolves about an unfortunate gentleman who has what Mrs. Slipslop

6. Lewes's Journal, 28 January 1859, quoted in J. W. Cross, *George Eliot's Life,* 3 vols. Edinburgh and London, II, 76.

7. Herbert Spencer to J. W. Cross, 13 January 1884. In the collection of Professor Chauncey Brewster Tinker.

8. GE to Sara Hennell, 2 September [1852].

9. GE to Sara Hennell, Monday Morning [10 January 1853].

calls a "fondling" palmed upon him as his own son.[10] When Huxley pointed out serious errors in the biology of Lewes's book on Comte, Miss Evans wrote Chapman, begging him not to send the manuscript to the printer until she had seen him again.

I think you will wish for the sake of the Review as well as from your own sense of justice that such a purely contemptuous notice should not be admitted unless it be well-warranted. The case is the more delicate as the criticism of Mr. Lewes comes after the unmitigated praise of Miss Martineau. I hope to see you tomorrow afternoon. How came you to mention to Miss Martineau that you saw the proof of Mr. Lewes's book "in Miss Evans's room"? I think you must admit that your mention of my name was quite gratuitous. So far you were naughty—but never mind.[11]

Though all the objectionable criticisms remained in the review,[12] Miss Evans's effort to suppress it betrays the deep solicitude she had come to feel for Lewes. He was gay and amusing and made her life pleasanter than it had ever been. Her own pleasure always meant less to Marian than the opportunity to devote herself to helping someone else; but Lewes provided this too. He suffered from most painful headaches, which lasted sometimes for weeks and made it impossible for him to work. During these periods Marian corrected proof for him and wrote articles for the *Leader* at his dictation.[13] Possibly the difficulty of seeing him as freely as she desired was a deciding factor in her removal from the Strand

10. Lewes's review in the *Leader*, 10 December 1853, p. 1195, is full of veiled allusions to a similar situation in his own family: "One is always the son of somebody; but, happily, one is not always the father of somebody. I congratulate myself in ranging under that category every time I see my friends revelling in the 'blessings of boys' . . . . But then, as I always say, if men will have sons, why their blood be on their own heads!"

11. From B. C. Williams, *George Eliot*, New York, 1936, p. 99. By permission of the Macmillan Company. Lewes's book was published early in October by Henry G. Bohn; Miss Martineau's was published by Chapman about 18 November 1853.

12. *Westminster Review*, 61 (January 1854), 254–257. Lewes replied in a long signed article in the *Leader*, 14 January 1854, p. 40, demonstrating very convincingly that his "errors" were based on the most recent French and German research, with which Huxley was apparently unacquainted.

13. GE to Sara Hennell [3 April 1854].

early in October 1853 to lodgings at 21 Cambridge Street, Edgware Road. Here Lewes was in and out almost daily; he poured out to her all the unhappy story of his marriage, which could not fail to move her impressionable heart to pity. According to one biographer,[14] at this time their union commenced.

Pity was reinforced in a curious way by the chief work that was occupying her during these months, a translation of Ludwig Feuerbach's *Das Wesen des Christentums*. Her correspondence sheds no light on how she happened to engage in this project. Her reviews of contemporary German books in the *Westminster,* though they never mention Feuerbach, may have brought his philosophy to her attention. Perhaps Lewes interested her in the book. At any rate she had begun it late in the spring of 1853 and by the end of the year was well on with her work.

In June 1853 Chapman launched a new publishing scheme —the Quarterly Series—to consist of works "by learned and profound thinkers, embracing the subjects of theology, philosophy, Biblical criticism, and the history of opinion," issued quarterly, at an annual subscription of £1. The first two numbers were Theodore Parker's *Atheism* and F. W. Newman's *A History of the Hebrew Monarchy.* The original advertisement[15] also announced two books by "The Translator of 'Strauss's Life of Jesus,' "—one, the English version of Feuerbach, the other, an original work entitled *The Idea of a Future Life.* Subscriptions for the Quarterly Series proved a failure; even the inclusion of Miss Martineau's translation of Comte, subsidized by the late Mr. Lombe, did not save it. To sell such books at an average price of five shillings a volume required a larger trade than Chapman commanded. His zeal outweighed his prudence in this as in many other cases where, if they seemed important, he published works no other publisher would undertake. Though he had agreed to pay Miss Evans only two shillings a page for the translation, he seemed likely even at that rate to lose by the bargain.

14. Oscar Browning, *Life of George Eliot,* London, 1890, p. 37.
15. *Leader,* 18 June 1853, p. 600.

There was a good deal of visiting back and forth between the Strand and Miss Evans's new lodgings in Cambridge Street. Mr. and Mrs. Chapman called together, bringing a package Mr. Bray had left for her. A few days later Chapman came in alone, fagged to death from having chased along the Strand a thief who had managed to get into his house and out of it with £8 worth of plate. Marian went often to the Chapmans, too; but when she put her head into 142, she wrote Bray, "I feel that I have gained, or rather escaped, a great deal physically by my change."[16] November 24, 1853, Chapman called on her to intimate that under the circumstances perhaps it would be better not to publish Feuerbach in the tottering Quarterly Series, since the reviewers would certainly treat it harshly.

Miss Evans was no longer the shy and susceptible young woman who had come to the Strand two years before; she talked to him now as a shrewd businesswoman, determined to sell her work for what it was worth. It seemed a propitious moment to tell him that she intended to give up all connection with the editorship of the *Westminster*. Describing the conversation to Sara Hennell, she added:

He wishes me to continue the present state of things until April, but admits that he is so straitened for money and for *assistance* in the mechanical part of his business that he feels unable to afford an expense on the less tangible services which I render. I shall be much more satisfied on many accounts to have done with that affair, but I shall find the question of supplies rather a difficult one this year, as I am not likely to get any money either for Feuerbach, which, after all, Mr. Chapman I think will be afraid of publishing in his Series, or for "The Idea of a Future Life," for which I am to have "half profits" $=\frac{0}{0}$![17]

Chapman invariably appealed to her compassion when he was with her so that she could never be severe. Sympathy with his personal troubles had interfered too long with her own work; she could not make her living by gratuitous editing of

16. [5 November 1853].
17. GE to Sara Hennell, Friday Morning [25 November 1853].

the *Westminster Review*. By translating German theological books for the Quarterly Series at two shillings a page she might continue the career begun with Strauss; but Marian realized that she could achieve literary distinction only with an original work like *The Idea of a Future Life*. In their conversation Chapman had not even mentioned that. Taking advice, perhaps of Lewes, a veteran in dealing with publishers, she wrote the following letter to make her position quite clear:

21 Cambridge Street,
Friday Morning,
[25 November 1853].

Dear Friend,

Have the goodness to confine the perusal of this letter to yourself, and not to leave it about for the amusement of your amateurs of *lettres inédites*.

There is one subject which I omitted to mention to you yesterday, but which will perhaps be better committed to paper, as it will then be understood to be a matter of business. Friendship is not to be depended on, but business has rather more guarantees.

You seem to be oblivious just now of the fact that you have pledged yourself as well as me to the publication of another work besides Feuerbach in your Series. For the completion of the historical part of that work, *books* are indispensable to me. If I could do as I pleased I would much rather become myself a subscriber to the London Library and save both myself and you the trouble of speaking to you on the subject. But as this said work will occupy nearly the whole of next year and as I am to have no money for it—since the "half profits" are not likely to have any other than a conceptional existence, a "gedachtsein"—I don't see how I can possibly go to any expense in the matter.

I bitterly regret that I allowed myself to be associated with your Series, but since I have done so, I am very anxious to fulfil my engagements both to you and the public. It is in this sense that I wish you to publish Feuerbach, and I beg you to understand that I would much rather that you should publish the work and *not* pay me than pay me and not publish it. I don't think you are sufficiently alive to the ignominy of advertising things, especially as part of a subscription series, which never appear. The two requests then which I have to make are first, that you will let me know whether you can, *as a matter of business*, undertake to supply me with the necessary books, and secondly, that you will consider the question of Feuerbach as one which concerns our *honour* first and our pockets after.

I have been making a desk of my knee so I fear some of my words may be illegible, which will be a pity because of course you can't substitute any half as good.

Yours faithfully,

MARIAN EVANS[18]

Chapman's reluctance in this affair was augmented by financial difficulties, which, temporarily relieved by Mr. Courtauld's loan, were now once more drawing toward a crisis. Susanna had done what she could to be a good helpmate to him. In 1852 when his business was nearly at a standstill on account of his fight with the Booksellers' Association, she had advertised for boarders:

MRS. JOHN CHAPMAN begs to announce that, as the House occupied by Mr. CHAPMAN is larger than requisite for the purposes of his Business, arrangements have been made, enabling her to offer to Persons who may be VISITING LONDON for a short or long time, the Advantages of an Hotel with the Quiet and Economy of a Private Residence.[19]

Even with boarders the house was too large for them; rent and taxes alone amounted to £500 a year. By the spring of 1854 it was plain that they must find a smaller one. In Dorset Street there was one they liked very much, still a little larger than necessary, but feasible if they could count on a regular boarder. They urged Miss Evans to return to the family. After considering the proposal, she finally decided against it on the ground that

I could not feel at liberty to leave them after causing them to make arrangements on my account, and it is quite possible that I may wish to go to the continent or twenty other things. At all events, I like to feel free. Apart from the comfort of being with people who call out some affection there would be no advantage in my living with the C's—at least none that *I* take into account.[20]

18. This letter is in the Henry E. Huntington Library.
19. *Leader*, 31 July 1852, p. 740.
20. GE to Charles Bray, Saturday [13 May 1854].

The Chapmans rented a house at 43 Blandford Square, into which they moved the first week in June. Later they took as their boarder Miss Julia Smith, an aunt of Miss Evans's friend Barbara Leigh Smith, who lived near by at number 5.

William Chambers of Edinburgh was horrified at the way the London publishers conducted their business, trading beyond their means and

substituting sanguine expectations, along with borrowed money, for capital. . . . The whole transactions subside into a system of bills—bills to wholesale stationers, bills to printers, bills to artists, bills to writers, bills to everybody. In the same wild way, bills that are received are hurried off for discount. There is great seeming prosperity, but so is there too frequently a great bill-book—dismal record of difficulties and heart-aches.[21]

There could hardly be a better description of Chapman's methods. He borrowed from everyone, confident that prosperity could not fail to come his way. Neither the *Westminster Review* nor his publishing business flourished. His encounter with the booksellers had left him few friends in the trade. The popular impression of his publications as "atheistic" scared off timid and conventional readers and prevented the volume of his sales from rising to the point where books could be profitably sold at a discount of two pence in the shilling. The *Review* printed only 650 copies at this time, and as he told Noah Porter with some bitterness, was not "taken in" at any reputable reading room in the United Kingdom.[22] Still he kept afloat somehow, borrowing right and left, and never failing to look brighter when (as George Combe remarked) he had added a new letter to his alphabet, getting a G or an H to satisfy the claims of E and F.[23]

Harriet Martineau, the H of the moment, lent Chapman £500, taking the *Westminster Review* as security. She insists in her *Autobiography* that

Mr. Chapman never, in all our intercourse, asked me to lend him money. . . . It was entirely my own doing; and I am anxious, for

21. William Chambers, *Memoir of Robert Chambers with Autobiographic Reminiscences of William Chambers*, New York, 1872, pp. 279–280.
22. *Christian Union*, 26 January 1881, p. 80.
23. GE to Mrs. Bray, Wednesday [28 June 1854].

Mr. Chapman's sake, that this should be understood. The truth of the case is that I had long felt, as many others had professed to do, that the cause of free-thought and free-speech was under great obligations to Mr. Chapman; and it naturally occurred to me that it was therefore a duty incumbent on the advocates of free-thought and speech to support and aid one by whom they had been enabled to address society. Thinking, in the preceding winter, that I saw that Mr. Chapman was hampered by certain liabilities that the review was under, I offered to assume the mortgage,—knowing the uncertain nature of that kind of investment, but regarding the danger of loss as my contribution to the cause.[24]

By such loans the day of reckoning was long postponed.

In July 1854 Chapman was finally compelled to admit that he was insolvent. A meeting of the creditors was called for August 4, at 11 A.M. Most of them, including Miss Martineau, were content to leave the *Review* in Chapman's hands; but her brother James Martineau and W. B. Hodgson, who were minor creditors living away from London, did not attend the meeting and refused to accept the decision. Under the editorship of Chapman and Miss Evans the *Westminster* had grown more and more uncongenial to the philosophical and religious convictions of Martineau and his friends, who resented the appearance of their articles sandwiched between others of quite an opposite tendency. The *Prospective Review,* which Martineau had under his direction, was too liberal for most Unitarians and too Unitarian for anyone else; in Chapman's failure he saw an opportunity to amalgamate it with the *Westminster* to the benefit of both.

All the other creditors accepted the definite composition promised them if the *Westminster* were left in Chapman's control. Martineau, however, refused to receive his share unless a second meeting were called at which a vote should be taken with the *Review* listed among the assets. Harriet Martineau was already on bad terms with her brother; she had not spoken to him since 1851, when he wrote a most scathing

24. M. W. Chapman, ed., *Harriet Martineau's Autobiography,* 2 vols., Boston, 1877, II, 97.

review of her *Letters on the Laws of Man's Nature and Development*. His action seemed to her a plot to upset the mortgage and throw the *Review* into the market at the most disadvantageous season, when London was empty because of the cholera. Zeal and animosity joining forces, she sent Chapman a check for the full amount of his debt to James Martineau, instructing him to get it deposited in her brother's bank account without his knowledge, since he declined to accept the composition. Rather perplexed by this unusual commission, Chapman wróte to ask the advice of Mr. Courtauld, who with Octavius Smith and George Grote, the principal creditors, had guaranteed the settlement. Courtauld replied.

November 9th, 1854.
My dear Sir,

I really don't know what to say; it is purely a matter for yourself and Miss Martineau, and I scarcely feel *free* to take the reference of it, which I should do if in reply to your note I offered the advice which you say beforehand you would take.

Miss Martineau's offer and the sympathy with you in the unfair position in which J. M. places you, are very generous, and you will hardly know how to refuse taking the course she so warmly urges when she says "that my peace of mind really requires it." At the same time my own opinion is not favorable to that course in itself, nor do I see any *material* difference between your sending the money as now proposed and the making legal tender of it as previously suggested. In my own case I should not *like* to run about to discover if J. M. had a Banker in order to get the money entered to the credit of his account without his knowledge, and so far to outgeneral him. If I chose to send him the money, I would do so in the ordinary way of remitting your cheque to himself by letter; he may then keep it, or return it, as it may please him; but that is only what he may and will do all the same, if you attempt to steal a march upon him by paying it, unknown to him, to his Banker.

Now if you send the cheque (your own I mean) in a letter, or pay it at his Banker's, he must of course either return, or keep it.

If he returns it, you are rebuked for attempting to force upon him a payment he had told you he would not receive; if he keeps it, he falsifies himself, and makes a most vulgarly impotent conclusion of the whole matter, reminding one of the lower class of Higglers in our markets, who staunchly refuse a price, but at actual *sight* of the gold, and sound of its fascinating clink, are forthwith overcome and subdued; this is a degradation Martineau will not exhibit, but if there were any danger of his doing so, I should be sorry to be any way accessory to it.

I hold Martineau's position to be radically a false and wrong one. The state of the Law may enable him to keep you his debtor, so long as he does not demand payment, but morally he has no right to prevent your discharging your liability to him. We have already represented this to him; we may do so again and more fully if we please; and if we should make the attempt and succeed, he will take the composition, but not the full amount of the debt, and give you a release; but he won't do either; he has taken his position and his pride will maintain it.

I don't know why I enter again so much into consideration of the intrinsic merits of this question, since Miss Martineau's appeal is somewhat upon other grounds, and I must finish as I began, by saying it is your affair and not mine, and I would not wish to make it mine by response to your inquiry "what shall I do." Had Miss M. sent me the money, with request that I should change her cheque for my own and send it to J. M., I should, after my last note to her, have considered myself under engagement to act as her agent in the matter, irrespective of my exact approval of the particular course adopted by her.

Yours, my dear Sir,
Very truly,
SAM COURTAULD.

John Chapman, Esq.

Whether Martineau accepted the money thus offered does not appear. In spite of his obstructions the *Review* never came into the market. It "was saved from the hammer," he wrote,

but only to be delivered into the hands of a Comtist coterie, and to suffer the defection of a whole group of its most reliable contributors. So next, having both staff and funds in readiness, and in the opinion of experienced publishers, an open field of unrepresented feeling and opinion between the heavy Whiggism and decorous Church-latitude of the Edinburgh on the one hand, and the atheistic tendency and Refugee-politics of the "Westminster" on the other,—we proposed to start "The National Review,"[25]

which superseded the *Prospective* in July 1855. The settlement of Chapman's business was deferred indefinitely. According to Martineau: "Some years after, when the insolvent pressed for my signature to his discharge, I qualified myself for duly giving it, by receiving in exchange his surrender of the copyright of articles which I had contributed to the 'Review' during his proprietorship."[26] Thus the long association between Martineau and Chapman, whose entrance into the publishing business in 1843 had resulted indirectly from his reading the former's *Endeavours after the Christian Life,* ended as so many of his friendships did, in bitterness.

The Feuerbach translation was all in type early in June 1854. Preliminary notices of it in the newspapers read "By the Translator of 'Strauss's Life of Jesus.'" At the last moment, however, Miss Evans changed her mind; and when the book was published in July the title page, for the first and only time, bore her real name, "By Marian Evans, Translator of 'Strauss's Life of Jesus.'" Miss Hennell reviewed it in the Coventry *Herald* with some pleasant personal references that vexed Marian, who wrote to protest. "I shall soon send you a good bye," she added, "for I am preparing to go to 'Labassecour.'"[27] On Wednesday evening July 19 she wrote the often-quoted letter of farewell to the Brays,[28] and the next day set sail with Lewes for Antwerp on their way to Weimar.

Her decision to take this step was not an impulsive one. It was reached only after many months of most searching consideration. Lewes's need for help was probably the factor that turned the balance. All during the spring of 1854 he was suf-

25. James Martineau to Charles Wicksteed, 18 February 1855, in James Drummond, *Life and Letters of James Martineau,* 2 vols., New York, 1902, I, 269. By permission of Dodd, Mead and Company, Inc.

26. *Ibid.,* I, 265.

27. Monday [10 July 1854]. Cross prints this: "I am preparing to go abroad (?)." *Labassecour* is Charlotte Brontë's name for Brussels in *Villette,* a book which greatly impressed Miss Evans in 1853.

28. J. W. Cross, *George Eliot's Life,* 3 vols., Edinburgh and London, 1885, I, 325.

fering intensely from pain in his head. Ordered to rest for a month, he went off to visit his friend Arthur Helps, while Miss Evans supplied articles each week to make up his quota for the *Leader*. He came back in May and worked again for a few days, but was soon compelled to stop and return to the country. At length, in July, when his head was "still unwell," Marian resolved to flout convention in order to give him the care he needed so badly. No doubt her own yearnings for affection confirmed her in the sacrifice. In Lewes she had at last found someone to lean upon. He understood the various and contradictory elements in her character, and could share her most serious philosophical speculations at one moment and raise her spirits with gay nonsense the next. He satisfied both the intellectual and sensual sides of her nature.

The sensual side seems to have developed to a marked degree while she was translating *The Essence of Christianity*. The powerful influence this book had upon her sprang, not from its humanism—*Homo homini Deus est*—for she was already perfectly familiar with that idea, but from Feuerbach's conception of love. "Love is God himself, and apart from it there is no God, . . . not a visionary, imaginary love—no! a real love, a love which has flesh and blood, which vibrates as an almighty force through all living."[29] Feuerbach distinguishes between a "self-interested love" and "the true human love," which "impels the sacrifice of self to another."[30] Such love is, and must always be, particular and limited, finding its expression in the sexual relation, the frankest recognition of the divine in Nature. Marriage, according to Feuerbach, is therefore almost essential to the full development of human personality; but it must be "the free bond of love,"

for a marriage the bond of which is merely an external restriction, not the voluntary, contented self-restriction of love, in short, a marriage which is not spontaneously concluded, spontaneously willed, self-sufficing, is not a true marriage, and therefore not a truly moral marriage.[31]

29. Ludwig Feuerbach, *The Essence of Christianity*, translated from the second German edition by Marian Evans, London, 1854, p. 47.
30. *Ibid.*, p. 52.   31. *Ibid.*, p. 268.

That Miss Evans was in complete accord with this doctrine her subsequent behavior would show, even if there were no direct evidence to that effect. While translating the sections in which most of these passages occur, she sent the manuscript to Sara Hennell, begging her

to read as quickly as you can the portion of the Appendix which I send you by today's post, and to tell me how far it will be necessary to modify it for the English public. I have written it very rapidly and have translated it quite literally so you have the *raw* Feuerbach, not any of my cooking. I am so far removed from the popular feeling on the subject of which it treats that I cannot trust my own judgment. With the ideas of Feuerbach I everywhere agree, but of course I should, of myself, alter the phraseology considerably. Before I do this however, I want you to tell me what I *must* leave out. Mind, I want to keep in as much as possible.[32]

When the moment came to take the fateful step "so far removed from the popular feeling," she was quite prepared for it. She was convinced that Lewes's marriage had become immoral, and that her unconventional union was sanctioned by a law higher than any made by man. "I am quite prepared to accept the consequences of a step which I have deliberately taken and to accept them without irritation or bitterness," she told Mr. Bray in a letter of extraordinary interest:

> 62a Kaufgasse,
> Weimar,
> [23 October 1854].
>
> Dear Friend,
> I yesterday wrote to my brother to request that he would pay my income to you on the 1st of December. I also requested that, in future, he would pay my half yearly income into the Coventry and Warwickshire Bank, that I might order it to be sent to me wherever I wanted it, as he has sometimes sent me a cheque which I could not get cashed in London. Is there anything to be done—any notice given to the Bank in order to make this plan feasible?
> It is possible that you have already heard a report prevalent in London that Mr. Lewes has "run away" from his wife and family.

32. GE to Sara Hennell, Saturday [29 April 1854].

I wish you to be in possession of the facts which will enable you to contradict this report whenever it reaches you. Since we left England he has been in constant correspondence with his wife; she has had all the money due to him in London; and his children are his principal thought and anxiety. Circumstances with which I am not concerned, and which have arisen since he left England, have led him to determine on a separation from Mrs. Lewes, but he has never contemplated that separation as a total release from responsibility towards her. On the contrary he has been anxiously waiting restoration to health that he may once more work hard, not only to provide for his children, but to supply his wife's wants so far as that is not done by another. I have seen all the correspondence between them, and it has assured me that his conduct as a husband has been not only irreproachable, but generous and self-sacrificing to a degree far beyond any standard fixed by the world. This is the simple truth and no flattering picture drawn by my partiality.

I have been long enough with Mr. Lewes to judge of his character on adequate grounds, and there is therefore no absurdity in offering my opinion as evidence that he is worthy of high respect. He has written to Carlyle and Robert Chambers stating as much of the truth as he can without very severely inculpating the other persons concerned; Arthur Helps, who has been here since we came, already knew the whole truth, and I trust that these three <rational> friends will be able in time to free his character from the false imputations which malice and gossip have cast upon it.

Of course many silly myths are already afloat about me, in addition to the truth, which of itself would be thought matter for scandal. I am quite unconcerned about them except as they may cause pain to my real friends. If you can hear of anything that I have said, done, or written in relation to Mr. Lewes, beyond the simple fact that I am attached to him and that I am living with him, do me the justice to believe that it is false. Mr. and Mrs. Chapman are the only persons to whom I have ever spoken of his private position and of my relation to him, and the only influence I should ever dream of exerting over him as to his conduct towards his wife and children is that of stimulating his conscientious care for them, if it needed any stimulus.

Pray pardon this long letter on a painful subject. I felt it a duty to write it.

I am ignorant how far Cara and Sara may be acquainted with

the state of things, and how they may feel towards me. I am quite prepared to accept the consequences of a step which I have deliberately taken and to accept them without irritation or bitterness. The most painful consequences will, I know, be the loss of friends. If I do not write, therefore, understand that it is because I desire not to obtrude myself.

Write to me soon and let me know how things are with you. I am full of affection towards you all, and whatever you may think of me, shall always be

Your true and grateful friend,

MARIAN EVANS.[33]

After George Eliot's death many of her friends recollected that she had confided in them her intention of going abroad with Lewes. Spencer had "a faint impression" that he had been told at Kew shortly before they left; Madame Belloc was quite positive that Miss Evans told her in Park Lane in May. Against such *ex post facto* reminiscences one must place Miss Evans's very precise statement to Mr. Bray that, besides himself, Mr. and Mrs. Chapman were the only persons to whom she had ever spoken of Lewes's private position and her relation to him. Not one of them ever betrayed her confidence.

Chapman wished the rebels all happiness. Though the critical condition of his business forbade more substantial assistance, he proposed that she write an article on Victor Cousin's *Madame de Sablé* for the October *Westminster*. She accepted gladly, and a month later sent off her article under the title "Woman in France." It opened with the admission that, though science has no sex, "we think it an immense mistake to maintain that there is no sex in literature." The reason that woman's influence on the development of literature has been felt in France alone Miss Evans attributes to "the laxity of opinion and practice with regard to the marriage-tie," the discussion of which sheds considerable light on her state of mind during the early months of her liaison with Lewes.

Heaven forbid that we should enter on a defence of French morals, most of all in relation to marriage! But it is undeniable, that

---

33. This letter is in the collection of Mr. Morris L. Parrish.

unions formed in the maturity of thought and feeling, and grounded only on inherent fitness and mutual attraction, tended to bring women into more intelligent sympathy with men, and to heighten and complicate their share in the political drama. The quiescence and security of the conjugal relation, are doubtless favourable to the manifestation of the highest qualities by persons who have already obtained a high standard of culture, but rarely foster a passion sufficient to rouse all the faculties to aid in winning or retaining its beloved object—to convert indolence into activity, indifference into ardent partisanship, dulness into perspicuity. Gallantry and intrigue are sorry enough things in themselves, but they certainly serve better to arouse the dormant faculties of woman than embroidery and domestic drudgery. . . . The dreamy and fantastic girl was awakened to reality by the experience of wifehood and maternity, and became capable of loving, not a mere phantom of her own imagination, but a living man, struggling with the hatreds and rivalries of the political arena; she espoused his quarrels, she made herself, her fortune, and her influence, the stepping stones of his ambition; and the languid beauty, who had formerly seemed ready to "die of a rose," was seen to become the heroine of an insurrection.[34]

Madame de Sablé was not a genius, not a heroine, "but a woman whom men could more than love—whom they could make their friend, confidante, and counsellor; the sharer, not of their joys and sorrows only, but of their ideas and aims."[35] Written about a Frenchwoman of the seventeenth century, these words sum up vividly Miss Evans's own attitude toward marriage.

The article is bright and readable. Lewes and Sara Hennell thought highly of it. But its author

feared that Mr. Chapman did not approve it, as he has said no word of satisfaction about it, and though he had been urgent on me to write for the Review before, he has made no proposition to that effect since. I have not seen the Westminster, but Mr. Lewes *has* seen it at the Library here. He told me about the notice of Feuerbach, which appears to be rather stultifying to Mr. Chapman as publisher of the *Series*. I am very sorry for Mr. Chapman.

34. *Westminster Review*, 62 (October 1854), 451–452.
35. *Ibid.*, p. 472.

Whatever may have been his mistakes I think he must have been
hardly used by Dr. Hodgson and J. Martineau.[36]

The trouble with Martineau may account for Chapman's
extreme tardiness in paying her. Instead of on the date of
publication, her check arrived November 30 and was for £15,
just a trifle less than usual for an article of this length. She
records Chapman's reply to her letter of acknowledgment as
"a chef d'œuvre of bad taste."[37] She had other work in hand
and also helped Lewes by occasionally scribbling off an article
for the *Leader* to appear over his signature, "Vivian." But as
none paid so well as the *Westminster,* solvent or otherwise,
Miss Evans was grateful when Chapman wrote her in January, proposing an article on Vehse's *Court of Austria* for the
April number.[38]

Lewes and Marian (henceforth styling herself Mrs. Lewes)
landed March 13, 1855, at Dover, where she took lodgings
while he went up to London to reconnoiter. She wrote Chapman announcing her return. In reply came a note asking her
to undertake the Belles Lettres Section of the Contemporary
Literature reviews at £12. 12 a number, a welcome proposal
that she accepted at once. Beginning with the July number
she continued to write this section until January 1857, when
the success of "The Sad Fortunes of the Reverend Amos Barton" put her beyond need of Chapman's help. During the five
years since she came to London he had been the principal
source of her earned income; in the eighteen months after

36. GE to Sara Hennell [22 November 1854]. The "stultifying" review in
the *Westminster,* 62 (October 1854), 559–560, was quite harsh: "It is a sign of
'progress,' we presume, that the lady-translator who maintained the anony-
mous in introducing Strauss, puts her name in the title-page of Feuerbach.
She has executed her task even better than before: we are only surprised that,
if she wished to exhibit the new Hegelian Atheism to English readers, she
should select a work of the year 1840, and of quite secondary philosophical
repute in its own country. . . ."

37. Journal, 7 December 1854.

38. Journal, 20 January 1855. At the same time he asked Spencer for an
article on the Maine Law and the Sunday Beer-Bill, a subject Spencer declined in favor of "Progress: Its Law and Cause," which marks the inception
of his general doctrine of evolution. Herbert Spencer, *An Autobiography,* 2
vols., London, 1904, I, 461–462; *Westminster Review,* 67 (April 1857), 445–485.

her return from Germany her payments from the *West-minster* alone amounted to more than £200.[39]

Chapman was also the first friend her Journal mentions as visiting them at East Sheen, where they settled after two weeks in London. He came to dinner on June 24, bringing for her criticism the manuscript of an article he had written on "The Position of Woman in Barbarism and among the Ancients," which was already in type for the *Westminster*. The tone of Marian's comments upon it discouraged him. With editorial blue pencil she went through the manuscript, pointing out that to "emerge from a catalepsy" was questionable and that "stepping stones" could not be "forged into fetters."[40] At the same time she indicated more fundamental defects of structure with such clarity that Chapman withdrew the article from the July number. When he wrote plaintively to ask if she thought it worth publishing at all, she reassured him:

There is no reason for you to be despondent about your writing. You have made immense progress during the last few years, and you have so much force of mind and sincerity of purpose that you may work your way to a style which is free from vices, though you perhaps will never attain felicity—indeed, that is a free gift of na-

---

39. The following is a complete list drawn from George Eliot's Journal of her contributions to the *Westminster Review* in 1855–56:

	£ s d
"Memoirs of the Court of Austria," 63 (April 1855), 303–335,	20– 0–0
"Belles Lettres," 64 (July 1855), 288–307,	12–12–0
"Evangelical Teaching: Dr. Cumming," 64 (October 1855), 436–462,	15– 0–0
"Belles Lettres," *ibid.*, 596–615,	12–12–0
"German Wit: Heinrich Heine," 65 (January 1856), 1–33,	20– 0–0
"Belles Lettres," *ibid.*, 290–312,	12–12–0
"Art and Belles Lettres," 65 (April 1856), 625–650,	12–12–0
"The Natural History of German Life: Riehl," 66 (July 1856), 51–79,	17–10–0
"Belles Lettres and Art," *ibid.*, 257–278,	12–12–0
"Silly Novels by Lady Novelists," 66 (October 1856), 442–461,	12–10–0
"Belles Lettres," *ibid.*, 566–582,	12–12–0
"Worldliness and Other-Worldliness: The Poet Young," 67 (January 1857), 1–42,	25– 0–0
"History" and "Belles Lettres," *ibid.*, 288–326,	22– 1–0
	————
	207–13–0

40. B. C. Williams, *George Eliot*, New York, 1936, pp. 112–113. By permission of the Macmillan Company.

ture rather than a reward of labour. You have plenty of *thoughts*, and what you have to aim at is the simple, clear expression of those thoughts, dismissing from your mind all efforts after any other qualities than precision and force—any other result than *complete presentation* of your idea. It would be the best possible symptom in you if your sentences became rather rugged. It would prove that you no longer introduced words for the sake of being *flowing*.[41]

Throughout the summer Chapman worked at revising the article. Marian's incisive criticism, though valuable, was scarcely calculated to soothe his ego. He could not turn to Susanna for sympathy with an article on "The Position of Woman"; Elisabeth seems to have departed from the household when the Chapmans moved from the Strand. "A well-to-do brother of Miss Tilley's is come from Australia," Miss Evans wrote Sara Hennell, "and will do something for her, I hope."[42]

Elisabeth had already been supplanted in Chapman's affections by his neighbor in Blandford Square, Miss Barbara Leigh Smith, later Madame Bodichon. She was a granddaughter of William Smith (1756–1835), the great abolitionist and emancipator, who defended Joseph Priestley after his flight to London. His descendants were numerous and distinguished. The eldest son, Benjamin Smith (1783–1860), succeeded his father in Parliament, where he carried on the liberal traditions of the family by supporting the repeal of the Corn Laws. Because of illegitimacy the Benjamin Smiths were known as "the *tabooed* family,"[43] and their more respectable cousins, who among others included Florence Nightingale, looked on them somewhat askance. Mrs. Gaskell thought that Barbara became such an ardent rebel against established opinion in consequence of her birth;[44] it undoubtedly exaggerated in her a penchant for reform that had occupied the family for three generations. Her brother Benjamin Leigh Smith, later known

---

41. *Ibid.*, pp. 113–114. 42. Saturday Morning [3 June 1854].
43. GE to Sara Hennell, 16 July [1852].
44. Jane Whitehill, ed., *Letters of Mrs. Gaskell and Charles Eliot Norton, 1855–1865*, London, 1932, p. 52.

as an Arctic explorer, led the fight against the exclusion of Dissenters from degrees at the Universities and in 1857 was the first Nonconformist to receive his A.B. from Cambridge.

Barbara turned her attention to improving the lot of women in England. Contributing generously to early efforts to provide them with education, she was one of the founders of Girton College, to which she gave the first £1,000. Her own education was of the sort, less common then, that ignored such elementary studies as penmanship and spelling to concentrate upon the arts. Having a talent for painting, Barbara received the best instruction available under William Henry Hunt, Corot, and others. She knew Rossetti and did what she could in 1854 to benefit Miss Siddal's health by inviting her to Clive Vale Farm, her country place near Hastings—the same farm where Holman Hunt painted his sheep.[45] With her friend Bessie Parkes, later Madame Belloc, Barbara occasionally came to the evening parties at Chapman's. Here in June 1852 she first met Marian Evans. They liked each other at once; and Barbara's unconventional opinions made it possible for her to remain one of George Eliot's few close friends during the years of social ostracism.

Barbara's intimacy with Chapman began in the summer of 1854, about the time he moved to Blandford Square, and reached its astonishing climax a year later. A series of letters he wrote her between August 8 and September 22, 1855,[46] reveal their deliberate plan to form an extramarital union, ostensibly for the benefit of Barbara's health. Although he had not yet become a doctor, Chapman did not hesitate to prescribe for her. His letters are a most singular mélange of love-making, petty economies, and quite unprintable clinical

45. Margaret Howitt, ed., *Mary Howitt, An Autobiography*, 2 vols., Boston and New York, 1889, II, 111.

46. I have been unable to find the originals of these letters; the quotations are taken from a typewritten transcript made for Clement Shorter about 1915, which is now in the Yale University Library. Shorter seems to have contemplated writing a life of Chapman, for the volume containing the letters has also a partial transcript of the Diaries for 1851 and 1860 and a number of newspaper clippings relating to them.

details. On one occasion he even wrote to a certain physician in Susanna's name, describing Barbara's symptoms and asking an opinion.[47]

Hitherto the affair had been conducted in complete secrecy. In August 1855 at Chapman's request her friends Bessie Parkes and Anna Mary Howitt were taken into her confidence. Chapman wanted to go even further: he wanted Barbara to announce openly to her family that she intended to live with him. "You would then maintain your right and equal relation towards them, and would be able without fear and undue anxiety and without the knowledge of the world to be really united with me and to look forward with joyous anticipation to becoming a Mother."[48] He intended to take a separate house in his own name for the children and Susanna, to whom he had already broached the plan. Of course, he wrote Barbara, Susanna "feels unsettled, . . . and in justice and kindness to her I desire to speak with as much certainty as I can." Susanna's reproaches and bitterness seemed to him nonetheless unreasonable.

She does not object so much to my attachment to you as to its becoming known. In short, love of approbation is her strongest feeling. But I am much concerned about the utter absence of discipline with respect to Beatrice. Her temper is being utterly ruined. Oh she does love me so intensely! Ernest too is very fond of me.[49]

Barbara hesitated. An earnest and serious person with nothing of the flirt about her, she was not altogether sure that she loved him enough to take such a step. She was determined not to marry in the regular way because of a deeply ingrained sense of the injustice of English law toward married women, who could not own property or even make a will. The previous year in an effort to ameliorate their lot she had drawn up and published *A Brief Summary, in Plain Language, of the Most Important Laws Concerning Women*, which attracted much attention. Through her exertions in circulating petitions some relief had been obtained, though the law was

47. Chapman to Barbara Leigh Smith, 27 August 1855.
48. *Ibid.*, 29 August 1855.   49. *Ibid.*, 4 and 7 September 1855.

not properly amended until 1882.[50] Barbara had an adequate income of her own. One of her father's liberal notions was that daughters should have an equal provision with sons; when she came of age in 1848 he gave her an allowance of £300 a year to spend as she saw fit,[51] and planned to divide his fortune equally among his three sons and three daughters.

Her objection to the law giving a husband control over his wife's property was certainly not based upon love of money, for she was of a most generous disposition, looking on wealth as a mere responsibility, "a power to do good."[52] On Chapman's part one cannot feel quite sure that her fortune was not at least a stimulus to his affection. He made careful inquiries about her income and prospects. Either Lady Stephen is wrong or Barbara, suspecting his motives, deliberately misstated the amounts. He replied September 4, 1855:

You have at present *less* money and expect finally to have *more* than I had been led to suppose. I thought you had now £250 and would ultimately have £500 a year. I am sorry for your sake that I am mistaken. Never fear however, but that if we have health we shall get sufficient for our needs.

Although Chapman's income, after Susanna's allowance was provided for, would be only about £100, he counted on the *Westminster Review,* which was growing more popular all the time, to make him independent in about three years more.

Chapman seems to have believed that Mr. Smith would approve of his unconventional proposal and perhaps even assist it. "*I* wish Pater knew," he kept telling Barbara. One day when in talking with her father she adverted in a general way to her belief in free love, her enthusiasm had been dampened by his telling her that she ought to go to America to practise it. Chapman pointed out her mistake at this point:

50. Barbara Stephen, *Emily Davies and Girton College,* London, 1927, pp. 40–42. This book contains the best account of Madame Bodichon.
51. *Ibid.,* p. 34.
52. See her pamphlet, *Woman and Work,* 1857.

When he advised you to go to America and practise your principles, you had a splendid opportunity of getting from him a formal acknowledgement of their truth; had you obtained that, he would be constrained either to sanction your practice of them in England, or to confess that his not doing so is simply from regard to Mrs. Grundy. That confession he will never make. . . . Oh that your father could see and understand all as I do! He would then welcome me as your lover and devoted help-mate for life.[53]

The fatuous man actually began to compose a letter that she could show Mr. Smith to make the whole matter clear. A few days later he wrote that he found the task more difficult than he expected: "I scarcely knew what to say." But optimism never deserted him. "Try to be hopeful and peaceful," he added; "rely upon it we shall be happy yet. Lewes and M.E. seemed to be perfectly so."[54]

Spurred on perhaps by Marian's conspicuous example, Barbara finally found courage to tell her father that she intended to live with Chapman without benefit of church or state. Mr. Smith's strenuous objections are easily inferred from the next letter: "It is out of your father's deep love and the bitterness of his disappointment that his present unkindness comes," Chapman assured her. "He will and must change. . . . He will not see his child pine away. *Now* he knows not what he does."[55] Chapman's advice that she continue to discuss the subject frequently seems not to have mollified Mr. Smith's opposition, since this letter, signed "Yours until death, J.C.," concludes the remarkable correspondence. The only further allusion to the affair is found in the 1860 Diary, where Chapman describes going to an evening party with Barbara's successor. "Sir George and Lady Grey and *Ben.* Smith (!) were there. Of course I never spoke with the latter."[56]

One may surmise from this that her brother Ben had a hand in terminating the relationship between Barbara and her curious suitor. Soon after it ended, he took all three of his sisters off to Algiers, where Barbara forgot her disappoint-

53. Chapman to Barbara Leigh Smith, 14 September 1855.
54. *Ibid.*, 17 September 1855.   55. *Ibid.*, 22 September 1855.
56. Diary, 5 March 1860.

ment in sketching the interesting landscape and making pleasant new acquaintances. One of the latter was Dr. Eugène Bodichon, a Breton about forty-five years old, who had lived in Africa since 1836. A friend of Louis Blanc and other French revolutionaries, his broad social sympathies had prompted him to practise medicine among the natives and lead a successful campaign for the abolition of slavery in the colony. He was an attractive and romantic figure, tall, dark, and dignified. In spite of the difference in their ages he quickly dispelled the image of John Chapman from Barbara's thoughts. This time her family did not oppose the match. In 1857 Dr. Bodichon came to England and married her July 2 at the Unitarian Chapel in Little Portland Street.[57]

57. Barbara Stephen, *Emily Davies and Girton College*, London, 1927, pp. 43-44.

CHAPTER VI

Dr. John Chapman

IN her reply to one of Chapman's letters of prescription Barbara remarked that he would make a good doctor. If she was unaware of his youthful experience as "surgeon," he did not enlighten her.

> And so you really think I should make a good Doctor! I have always felt that I should, and I wish I were one. It would be a great relief to me, when I am no longer in business, to have a medical degree to fall back upon. Page 1 of the enclosed paper will show you the lectures I should have to attend and the total cost, were I to resolve on becoming a Doctor in May 1857. If I never practised, the status of Doctor of Medicine would be a great advantage to me.[1]

Now, when his hopes of another career had been dashed by Mr. Smith's unforeseen behavior, Chapman felt more strongly the desire to begin his studies.

His lack of any formal education seems an almost insuperable obstacle until one realizes the state of the medical profession at the time. While Oxford and Cambridge conferred very few M.D. degrees, and those chiefly honorary, the Scotch universities vied with one another in soliciting candidates for the sake of the fees. In the eighteenth century a degree at St. Andrews could be procured *in absentia* for £10;[2] the story is told of a servant who bought one at Edinburgh when he accompanied his master there for the same purpose. In 1857 the abuse still flourished, in spite of Parliamentary committees and pamphlets by earnest physicians, genuinely distressed by quackery. The fee had risen to about £25, and the revenue, divided between the examiners and the university, formed no negligible portion of their income.

1. Chapman to Barbara Leigh Smith, 15 September 1855.
2. John D. Comrie, *History of Scottish Medicine*, 2d ed., 2 vols., London, 1932, I, 575.

St. Andrews was probably the worst offender. With no hospital or laboratory, with only one professor of medicine and almost no medical students, "the University of St. Andrews conferred a larger number of medical degrees than any other University in Scotland or England."[3] The lone professor had to call in two outsiders to help with the formality of examining the candidates, the great majority of whom came from England. Eighty-four degrees were granted in 1860; the following year the number rose to 107; by 1862 it had reached the scandalous total of 605.[4]

But the M.D. degree gave no one the right to practise in London. This privilege was held by three societies, the Royal College of Physicians, the Royal College of Surgeons, and the Royal Society of Apothecaries. Of these the first was the most exacting both in its examination and in its fee for the diploma, which amounted to £56.17. In addition to a university degree the candidate was required to present certificates of attendance during a period of three years on the lectures and medical practice of a hospital containing at least one hundred beds. He was then examined in physiology, pathology, and therapeutics before the president and censors of the College. He was asked to translate Galen from the Greek, though he might decline this test in favor of translating parts of Celsus or some other Latin author. These examinations were passed in most cases with the help of "grinders," who crammed the students in a brief period with the answers to the usual questions, while the requirement of hospital practice was a mere formality of quite literally "walking the hospital."[5] It was charged, very justly at this time, that the fee was the principal requirement for the license. Under such a system there is little wonder that England was called the "Paradise of Quacks."[6]

Regarding the profession of medicine as something "to fall

3. James Donaldson, *Addresses Delivered in the University of St. Andrews from 1886–1910,* 1911, p. 432.

4. *Ibid.* Thereafter it was limited by ordinance to ten; now no special medical degrees are given.

5. Edwin Lee, *The Medical Profession in Great Britain and Ireland,* London, 1857, Part I, pp. 120, 141.

6. *Ibid.,* p. 93.

back upon," Chapman naturally chose the easiest course. Perhaps he managed to secure credit for his work in Paris or for his experience as a "surgeon" before his marriage. By hook or crook he managed to compress the whole of his medical education into nineteen months. Though his name never appeared on the matriculation rolls, he heard some lectures at University College and others at King's College, hard by his house in the Strand. His hospital attendance was at St. George's, where his friend Dr. Edwin Lankester lectured on *materia medica*. He also owed much to the "grinders," whose methods of teaching he warmly defends.[7]

Chapman's publishing business could ill afford the time these studies required. His debts were enormous. Mr. Courtauld's £600 had been followed by further loans; and a new patron, Barbara's uncle Octavius H. Smith, had added his support, probably at Spencer's suggestion. Many smaller subscribers like Rufa Hennell were already demanding a settlement which Chapman was in no position to make. If the creditors insisted on liquidating the business at once, he would be unable to continue his medical work. He wrote Mr. Courtauld, pleading for delay. The honest old man's reply casts a dubious shadow over Chapman's business ethics.

Carey Lane,
November 29, 1855.

Sir,

Since receiving your letter of the 13th Inst. I have been endeavoring in vain to obtain some communication from Mr. Octavius Smith upon the subject of it, by which I might be guided in my reply to you.

As you seem to entertain some expectation of finding some one to take the business if it were not pressed to conclusion at the coming Christmas, which you say is the most unfavorable season for dealing with it in *any way,* and as also you tell me that in the event of winding up the business, failing all endeavours to dispose of it, some further delay in doing so to let the dead Christmas Season pass over would be advantageous to all interests, I am

7. John Chapman, *Medical Institutions of the United Kingdom*, London, 1870, p. 94.

willing to suspend that winding up for two months after Christmas.

I should see no reason for more protracted delay in disengaging myself, as I best may, from affairs with which I feel the most extreme repugnance to be any longer connected in any way whatever. Because you will have time to make up your balance sheet for the current year; because all reasonable time will have been had for seeking a Party to take the business, if any such might be found; and because the early Spring will be as good a time as any other for realizing the Stock. And to these specific considerations I might add my general impression, that the longer a settlement is delayed, the worse its result will be.

Certainly your new pursuit of the study of medicine is not calculated to invigorate the management of a business that hitherto has not been successfully conducted; and you must, I think, be aware how little confidence can be felt in the *general representations* of one with whose philosophy it consists to obtain a desired concurrence of trusting friends by the suppression of whatever truth would be adverse to it.

And here let me say in reply to one part of your letter that in determining not to avail myself of Mr. Brewitt's guarantee for my *last* advance, my object was not the pecuniary advantage of Mrs. Chapman under her marriage settlement, but it was simply to maintain the *integrity* of my own action towards her Trustee.

In respect of the several inquiries you make as to my course of proceeding in winding up the business, I could not reply by anticipation—circumstances as they occur ought to guide that course; but I may at least say that I should not under any circumstances take any one step without previously conferring with all parties who might be affected by it.

> I am, Sir,
>> Your obedient Servant,
>>> SAM COURTAULD.

John Chapman, Esq.

Having won this respite (which he managed to prolong until 1860), Chapman leased his house in Blandford Square for a year and sent Susanna and the children into lodgings at Redhill, Surrey. Ernest had developed a tendency to scrofula that made country life advisable.[8] Chapman himself was thin

---

8. GE to Sara Hennell, 19 February [1856].

and ill, struggling to attend to his studies and keep the publishing business and the *Westminster Review* going at the same time. For the April 1856 number he wrote an article entitled "Medical Despotism," opposing a Parliamentary bill for reform of the profession on the grounds of "legislative interference" and "flagrant encroachment on the fundamental rights of English citizens."[9]

Marian Evans continued to contribute articles and reviews until January 1857, when "Worldliness and Other-Worldliness: The Poet Young" appeared in the *Westminster* at the same time that "The Sad Fortunes of the Reverend Amos Barton" was published in *Blackwood's*. Though she had told no one but Lewes and Spencer the secret of her new occupation, Chapman may have sensed a new importance in his former editor that prompted him to keep in her good graces. He had paid her £20 for the article on Young, at the usual rate of £10 for a sheet of sixteen pages; now he sent a check for £5 more with the following letter:

8 King William Street, W.C.,
January 15, 1857.

Dear Friend,

Of course it is impossible to adopt any scale of remuneration whereby I could graduate the payments to contributors to the W.R. so that each writer may be rewarded according to his (*or her*) merit. Still there are cases where a departure from the rule usually acted on would be so obviously just that I can have no hesitation as to the propriety of treating them as exceptional.

Your articles are so uniformly excellent that I desire to express my appreciation of their merit by paying for what you may hereafter contribute at the rate of £12.12.0 per sheet.

While paying you for the article on Young, as per agreement, both as to terms and length, I felt that you were inadequately remunerated; but knowing that the number, being a sheet and a half too long, would be a costly one, I acted according to *rule*; now, however, that I have read your article again with greatly increased delight, I shall not feel satisfied without sending you the enclosed, which, though when added to the £20 already sent on account of the article, will not represent its value, but which you

9. *Westminster Review*, 65 (April 1856), 538.

will perhaps regard as an assurance of my high estimation of it, and of my hope that you will let the "Westminster" be the medium of publication of whatever quarterly review articles you may be able to write.

Yours faithfully,

JOHN CHAPMAN.

Blackwood was clamoring for more manuscript of *Scenes of Clerical Life* and enclosing checks in his letters that before the end of 1857 amounted to nearly £500. It was impossible for George Eliot to explain to Chapman why she could not afford to write for the *Westminster,* even at twelve guineas per sheet. Still she wished him well. When Sara Hennell was proposing to have Chapman publish her *Christianity and Infidelity,* Marian advised against it, perhaps as much in his interest as in hers. Yet she did not want Sara to misunderstand her feelings toward Chapman:

I should not like you to be under the mistake of supposing, that I would not *go out of my way* to do him any real service; for example, I would write an article for his review rather than for any other, though that other might give me a few more guineas. But self-defeating actions do no one any good. And for you to publish with him would in my opinion be an action of that kind.[10]

On May 6, 1857, Chapman took his M.D. degree at St. Andrews, and later in the same year passed the examinations before the Royal College of Physicians and became a Licentiate. Susanna and the children now returned from the country. March 2, 1858, they moved into a house at 1 Albion Street, Hyde Park West, where, with the inevitable complement of boarders, they were to live for the next five years. Under the usual difficulties Susanna did her part, trying to make ends meet.[11] The new dignity vested in her husband added nothing

10. GE to Sara Hennell, 19 August [1857].
11. The Morgan Library has an undated letter in GE's hand that I believe she wrote to Mrs. Chapman about this time:

"My dear Susanna,
    With my usual imperfection in such matters, I forgot the pocket of the dress. Eccola! Treat my work just as it suits you with regard to time.

Yours affectiona[te]ly,

MARIAN."

to his income; and though the *Westminster* was holding its own against the menacing competition of Martineau's *National Review,* it produced no surplus for amortizing old debts.

Chapman could not understand why Miss Evans, whose kindly feelings toward him seemed as strong as ever, refused to contribute. For April 1858 she had promised an article on Francis W. Newman's books, of which Chapman had just published a new one entitled *Theism.* When he inquired as to her progress, she replied in a most unsatisfactory way:

Alas! I have not done a stroke towards the article on Newman, and before your letter came I was intending to send you the books and letters with a confession of my hopelessness; for since I cannot do the article, it would perhaps be well for someone else to write on the appearance of Newman's new book. I have been quite unhappy about the article and disgusted with myself that I undertook it even in a problematic way, for I can't bear to be shilly-shally about things. . . . It is almost needless to say that I don't neglect the opportunity of working for the W.R. in order to do work for any other review, and that I have no grounds for my negation except inability.[12]

Despite her perplexing behavior they remained good friends. When she made her will, Chapman and his clerk Mr. Birt were called upon to witness it.[13] Chapman continued to bring for criticism articles that he wrote.[14] Though she was usually severe with his faults, her editorial strictures were sometimes tempered by pity for his troubles. She wrote Sara Hennell October 11 [1858]:

Dr. Chapman came yesterday, in spite of the weather, and in spite of a bad headache, poor man! . . . I felt deep compassion for him. His health seems to be threatening again, and the load of anxieties he has to carry about his neck, while he is making efforts so strenuous and in many respects so disagreeable that few men would have the courage for them! That hideous Martineau-

---

12. 12 January 1858; in B. C. Williams, *George Eliot,* New York, 1936, pp. 143–144. By permission of the Macmillan Company.
13. Journal, 7 March 1858.
14. e.g., the article on "Medical Reform," 69 (April 1858), 478–530. See GE to Sara Hennell, 10 May 1858.

correspondence gave me almost a sick-headache only to think of. He seems to have enjoyed his visit to Coventry, and gives me a pleasant idea of you all.

But the friendship between Chapman and his "helpmate," which had survived so many shocks, was now suddenly and irreparably shattered. Since the beginning of 1858 all London had been agog over the great new Unknown, George Eliot, who had risen at one step to the topmost rank of English writers. All sorts of rumors and suspicions circulated. Only three persons actually knew George Eliot's secret—her "husband" Mr. Lewes, her publisher Mr. Blackwood, and her excellent friend Herbert Spencer. On November 5, when Spencer came to dine with her, he "brought the unpleasant news that Dr. Chapman had asked him point blank if I wrote the Clerical Scenes."[15] Marian immediately sent a letter "to check further gossip on the subject." Its tone must have been unfortunate, for Chapman, who cannot be called thin-skinned, was hurt and did not answer. Three weeks later, after recording an offer of £30 from Tauchnitz for a continental reprint of *Scenes of Clerical Life,* she added in her Journal:

I may also note, by way of dating the conclusion of an acquaintance extending over eight years, that I have received no answer from Dr. Chapman to my letter of the 5th, and have learned from Mr. Spencer that the circumstances attending this silence are not more excusable than I had imagined them to be. I shall not correspond with him or willingly see him again.[16]

A month later Chapman finally replied. Her acknowledgment must have made it painfully clear that the woman who once begged him in tears for some intimation of the state of his feelings was no longer even "an acquaintance":

Richmond,
January 1, 1859.

Dear Friend,
    I have received your letter of the 30th, in which you state the reasons that, in your opinion, justified you in leaving unanswered my letter written two months ago.

15. Journal, 5 November 1858.   16. Journal, 30 November 1858.

If that letter of mine implied any misconception or contained any word not strictly just, I beg so far to apologize for it.

Several of your observations and statements I have read with much surprise, but I forbear commenting on them, since it does not seem likely that further letter-writing would advance our mutual understanding.

I remain,
Yours very sincerely,
MARIAN LEWES.

John Chapman, Esq. M.D.

Adam Bede was published February 1. Having now a very good idea why she had been too busy to contribute to the *Westminster,* Chapman once more attacked Spencer, certain that, if anyone knew the secret, he did.

"By the way, Mrs. Dunn told me the other night that Miss Evans is the author of *Adam Bede:* is it true?"
"Mrs. Dunn!" I replied; "who told Mrs. Dunn any such thing?"
"Oh, that she didn't say."
"I do not see how Mrs. Dunn should know anything about it; she can have no means of learning."
Thus I fenced as well as I could, but all to no purpose. Chapman soon returned to the question—"Is it true?" To this question I made no answer; and of course my silence amounted to an admission.[17]

When Spencer called on the Leweses, now in their new house at Wandsworth, to tell them what had occurred, he was blamed for not having given a denial, "the case of Scott being named as justifying such a course." Spencer felt that, quite apart from the ethical question, denial would have been futile; a coolness arose between him and his friends that lasted for many months.

Lewes now took the problem in hand. On February 12 his Diary records an unpleasant correspondence with Dr. Chapman,

who had annoyed us with his indelicate conduct about the authorship of *Adam Bede,* which in very emphatic and distinct terms I

17. Herbert Spencer, *An Autobiography,* 2 vols., London, 1904, II, 38. By permission of the D. Appleton-Century Company.

have denied on Marian's behalf. She was reluctant that I should do so, but the very existence and possibility of anonymity would be at an end if every impertinent fellow could force us either by confession or implication to admit the truth of his questions. . . . If the thing is to be denied at all, I am for distinct effective denial rather than equivocation.[18]

His letter was certainly not equivocal:

> Holly Lodge,
> Wimbledon Park, Wandsworth,
> Saturday [12 February 1859].
>
> My dear Chapman,
> Not to notice your transparent allusion in your last, would be improperly to admit its truth. After the previous correspondence, your continuing to impute those works to Mrs. Lewes may be *meant* as a compliment, but *is* an offence against delicacy and friendship. As you seem so very slow in appreciating her feelings on this point, she authorizes me to state, as distinctly as language can do so, that she is not the author of "Adam Bede."
>
> Yours faithfully,
> G. H. Lewes.[19]

It was too late, even by such questionable means, to stay the tide of public curiosity. During the summer George Eliot's identity became generally known. Though Spencer was soon forgiven, the break with Chapman was final. When he wrote her January 17, 1860, asking consent to republish her articles from the *Westminster* on the old basis of "half-profits," she merely turned the letter over to Lewes, who records the "cool request" in his Diary with the laconic comment: "Squashed that idea."[20]

Chapman had contrived to postpone for nearly two years Mr. Courtauld's announced intention of winding up the business. In November 1858 when pressure again became severe, he discovered another patron, who advanced £600 to pay Courtauld's initial loan and keep the water-logged vessel float-

---

18. A. T. Kitchel, *George Lewes and George Eliot*, New York [1933], pp. 185–186.
19. This letter is in the collection of Mr. Morris L. Parrish.
20. A. T. Kitchel, *George Lewes and George Eliot*, p. 196.

ing a while longer. The new contributor was Lord Stanley, later fifteenth Earl of Derby. When he came to Chapman's rescue at the eleventh hour, he was the Colonial Secretary in his father's Cabinet, and his interest was undoubtedly quickened by the attention the *Westminster* had given to the Indian question—a lively one since the recent Mutiny. He could hardly have expected to be repaid. At Chapman's request in 1860 he made the loan a free gift.[21]

Chapman's other large creditor, Octavius H. Smith, though liberal in his religious views, was reactionary in opposition to the growing trades-union movement or anything which tended to hinder his business. As owner of the largest distillery in England he viewed with alarm what he characterized as "overlegislation" and government interference with free enterprise. In this matter his views coincided exactly with those Herbert Spencer had enunciated in *Social Statics*. He and Spencer became fast friends, and their joint influence is apparent in drawing the *Review* away from its advanced social and political principles toward a more conservative policy.

The *Westminster's* gallant campaign for general education now gives way to warnings that the education of laborers "threatens greatly to augment their power of working political evil," since "the artisans from whose mistaken ideas the most danger is to be feared, are the best informed of the working classes." One also reads much about how to "prevent mischievous meddling with the relations between labour and capital."[22] At the beginning of 1859 Smith proposed that Spencer should take over Chapman's publishing business, confident that after he had got it in order, he would find ample time to complete his *System of Synthetic Philosophy*. But Spencer recognized that he could not succeed without devoting all his time to the business and was not wholly sorry when the matter "dropped through." The business was carried on for the following year by Chapman's former assistants, Birt and Fergusson.[23]

21. Diary, 14 January 1860.
22. From Spencer's article, "Reform: The Dangers, and the Safeguards," *Westminster Review*, 73 (April 1860), p. 500.
23. Herbert Spencer, *An Autobiography*, London, 1904, II, 33–34.

The growing conservatism of the *Westminster* was naturally accompanied by an increased circulation. In 1853 only 650 copies were printed, not all of which were sold; in 1860 Chapman notes with satisfaction that only 10 copies are left from a printing of 1,620.[24] If he could only free himself from the debts of his publishing business, he felt sure that he could manage to live very well on his income from the *Review*.

He therefore proposed to form the Westminster Publishing Company, in which the claims of all creditors should be commuted into stock, leaving him unincumbered to devote himself to the *Review*. Lord Stanley and George Grote agreed to the plan at once, while W. B. Carpenter and other scientific men seemed willing to join. On the other hand Spencer felt that the scheme was unnecessary and certain to fail. He convinced O. H. Smith, Huxley, and a number of other creditors that if it were formed the Company ought to control the *Westminster Review*. That was exactly what Chapman wished to avoid.

Finally, after prolonged negotiations which occupy much of the 1860 Diary, a young man named George Manwaring, who had already invested £180 in Chapman's publishing business, was persuaded to buy it for the sum of £900, Chapman and Smith becoming his creditors. The provisional agreement was signed March 29, 1860, just in time to be announced in the April number of the *Review,* where Chapman took advantage of the opportunity to point out his distinctive character as a bookseller and publisher:

In commencing and continuing his Publishing Business, Mr. Chapman designedly offered in his establishment a platform from which opinions and doctrines, however diverse or opposed to each other, might be placed before the public, and during the last sixteen years he has issued numerous Theological and Philosophical works which have exerted a great and growing influence over English thought. Engrossing occupations, apart from the business, have for a considerable time past made Mr. Chapman wish to withdraw from it, but he was unwilling to do so before finding a successor prepared to continue it on the broad catholic principle

24. Diary, 31 January 1860.

by which it has hitherto been distinguished. He has reason to believe that Mr. Manwaring will fulfil this condition. . . .

He concluded by asking support for the new proprietor as
publisher and bookseller.

The transfer was decidedly to Chapman's advantage, leaving him in complete control of the *Westminster*, but saddling
Manwaring with the debts the publishing business had ac-
cumulated during the past decade. The young man had been
reluctant to undertake the responsibility and was clearly ill-
qualified to carry it. From the first there were disagreements.
A few days after the change was announced Chapman wrote
in his Diary:

Extremely annoyed today to learn that Mr. Manwaring thinks I
have altered a part of the draft deeds of agreement in my own
favour concerning the renewal of certain bills! After a considerable talk he at length withdrew the odious imputation.[25]

Payments were never made on time. When Manwaring went
away for two weeks without warning, Chapman was afraid
that he had absconded:

No letter has come yet from Manwaring. His conduct is as extraordinary as it is indefensible. Fears have crossed me that he
designs starting for America with the money which I know he has
at present in the bank. He owes me, including his acceptances,
£240, besides the amount of the purchase money of the business,
which is £900. I am liable for an acceptance of his for £35, and
for the rent of the business premises due at Midsummer; probably
also for various accounts contracted before last April and which
he may not have paid, as he is bound to do. The worst of it is I
cannot take summary measures to make him pay by proceeding
to remove the Review from him without lessening my prospect of
getting a release from O. H. Smith, which he has now twice promised me. He called upon me on Wednesday, and then promised he
would return my acceptances forthwith; but he has not done so.
He also promised to send me a release from all claims as soon as
I send him a letter from Manwaring acknowledging that he holds
Mr. Smith's stock on certain agreed upon conditions.

25. Diary, 3 April 1860.

Since Mrs. C's return home this time we have persistently avoided all reference to painful topics, and by being cold, distant, but respectful, I have secured more peace during the last few days than I have experienced in the same length of time with her in previous years.[26]

The most painful topic between Dr. and Mrs. Chapman at this time was a young lady named Johanna von Heyligenstaedt. She had boarded with them in Albion Street since the end of 1858, when she came from Germany to study for the operatic stage. It was not long before she held the same central position in Chapman's affections that Elisabeth Tilley and Barbara Leigh Smith had occupied at earlier periods. He felt a

restless unhappiness unless basking in the smiles of Johanna, who though in respect to beauty of form and voice and certain mental qualities is a glorious and fascinating creature, is nevertheless very capricious and often both ungenerous and unjust.[27]

Susanna was quite properly outraged by her husband's infatuation with the temperamental soprano, whose primadonna mannerisms had developed long before her voice was trained. Having endured the humiliation well over a year, Mrs. Chapman determined to leave him. After one especially violent quarrel, she actually went to stay at a friend's house. But she was back next day, aggrieved and querulous, and (according to Chapman's Diary) telling Ernest "to remember that whenever anything goes wrong in the house I always scold Mama!"[28] Ten days later there was another tempest:

The Fräulein passed the morning in crying with vexation at the insult which she has just discovered herself to have received in the fact of the disappearance from her room of the key which locks the door between her room and mine. She says that she knows it to have been in the door some days ago, and missed it this morning.

26. Diary, 24 August 1860.   27. Diary, 6 January 1860.
28. Diary, 9 February 1860.

In the afternoon

Susanna confessed to having taken it out of the door on Saturday. I requested her to return it, which she has done. After I went to bed last night Johanna began a discussion with her on the subject, when words ran high. This I am very sorry for, and consider Johanna greatly to blame after I had undertaken to speak in order to save her from needless excitement—so injurious to her voice. Thus have passed two days of useless and uncalled for misery.[29]

The contemptible wretch apparently believed that he was treating his wife with unusual consideration.

I have thought a great deal about Susanna with much compassion lately: precisely because her temper is so incontrollable, her domestic management such hopeless inefficiency and confusion, and her incapacity of being cheerful or of allowing others near her to be so. I feel extremely sorry for her, try to be friendly and kind to her, and frequently reprove Johanna for her least want of considerateness toward her. But alas! it is all in vain. She *determined* to have a scene with me this morning.[30]

At this point Johanna's mother and sister Idalie arrived from Berlin. Pondering over the causes of her daughter's depression and impaired health, Frau von Heyligenstaedt "asked Idalie whether it were possible that Johanna liebt den Doctor?" If she could not see that Johanna *did*, Frau von Heyligenstaedt was the only one in the house who failed to. Ernest and Beatrice, now fourteen and fifteen, were both aware of their father's intimacy with "the Fräulein"; according to Chapman, "the painfulness of my whole position has been greatly and needlessly increased by Mrs. C's unjustifiable discussion of all matters with them."[31]

He had been acting as Johanna's banker. In August when Frau von Heyligenstaedt was leaving with her daughter for the Isle of Wight, Chapman rendered his account showing a balance of £80 due him.

29. Diary, 19, 20 February 1860.   30. Diary, 6 April 1860.
31. Diary, 24 July 1860.

She was taken by surprise. Much more money has been spent than she counted on. She therefore got into a towering passion which she vented on Johanna, who resented it very ill temperedly, and at last burst out crying. In fact, the last night of their stay in the house was made wretched by this occurrence.[32]

Chapman spent most of a day and a night analyzing the accounts. He sent the cashbook showing that between January 1, 1859, and April 7, 1860, when her mother arrived, Johanna's expenditure had amounted to £296, nearly a third of it for lessons. Johanna's letter of acknowledgment was not very agreeable in tone.

The instability of her position as Chapman's mistress worried her. She wrote from Paris where she had gone to continue her studies, urging him to divorce Susanna; otherwise, she suggested, in view of the difficulties it might be better if they forgot each other. That possibility Chapman could not face; he promised "at no very distant time" to learn "all that can be known and done for the accomplishment of my freedom."[33] Meanwhile he assured her that if

another influence should prove more attractive to you in the future, the bond which now binds you to me will spontaneously dissolve and you will be wholly free to follow the guidance of your instincts. Why then refuse to accept joyously the affection which is tendered you today?[34]

They met briefly and at infrequent intervals now in Brussels, Trouville, St. Valery, or, more often, Paris, where Chapman's landlady in the Rue du Bac knew her as his niece.[35] Letters passed between London and Paris every few days with all the familiar romantic concealments. The Yale University Library has seventeen of them in Chapman's hand, dated between June 21, 1859, and May 1, 1863, which constitute the principal source of information about his activities during these years. His passionate eloquence has grown more mechanical but it never falters, though the juxtaposition of lofty

32. Diary, 11 August 1860.
33. Chapman to Johanna von Heyligenstaedt, 18 October 1860.
34. *Ibid.*, 17 November 1860.   35. *Ibid.*, 4 July 1862.

sentiment and trivial economy is often unintentionally comic:

Oh my angel! if I may but be assured of winning thee at last, impose upon me any tasks, any trials, any number of years' waiting. I love thee with every drop of my heart's blood, with every fibre of my being,—"with all my heart and soul and strength."
Have the kindness to keep yesterday's and today's Times (November 15th and 16th) for me.[36]

After a year in Paris, Johanna was advised to go to Italy for her debut. In February 1862 when she wrote from Florence that she expected soon to appear in *Macbeth*, Chapman set the staff of the British Museum to work to discover what sort of costume the historical Lady Macbeth might have worn; he also consulted Charles Kean the tragedian, an authority on such matters. The results of both attempts were nugatory, and he could offer only vague advice.

A month later her opportunity came when, through the illness of the regular prima donna, Johanna was called upon to sing the part. Chapman wrote immediately to congratulate her on the "long-expected and complete triumph," expressing the hope that she would soon "have another performance of Macbeth with all the music properly adapted to your beautiful high notes so as to show the Florentines what you can do."[37] He was really more concerned with the hope of her singing in London "this very season"—it need scarcely be said, a vain hope. The newspaper clippings she sent, Chapman took to his friend Justin McCarthy, who wrote for the *Morning Star* a little paragraph on the "New Italian Prima Donna":

The Florentine journals are filled with enthusiastic accounts of the "debut," made under singular circumstances, of a new "prima donna," in the Theatre della Pergola of Florence. The new soprano is Signora Giovannina Stella, a lady of twenty-one years of age, and endowed, according to the journals of Florence, with singular attractions of face and figure. The opera of "Macbeth" was to be performed, when the illness of the regular "prima donna" left the part of Lady Macbeth a blank. The Signora

36. *Ibid.*, 16 November 1861.   37. *Ibid.*, 24 March 1862.

Stella, at the request of the management, undertook the part, and actually accomplished it without any previous rehearsal. The "debut," which would, it appears, have been a complete triumph in any case, was of course rendered a far more brilliant success by the peculiar difficulties it surmounted. The audience were rapturous in their enthusiasm, and the journals are unanimous in predicting a splendid career for the young singer. Signora Stella is described by one of the journals as having an exquisite voice of the true soprano quality, of a tone at once peculiarly sweet and powerful, a style perfectly trained in the best schools, and a dramatic power which bespeaks the genuine article.[38]

After her "triumph" the correspondence dwindles. In a letter numbered 50 Chapman writes July 4, 1862, in great perturbation because his last three letters have gone unanswered. He plans to join her in Paris within a week, whether she writes or not. As if in reply to inquiries on the subject, he informs her that his income in 1859 was £619.10.8, in 1860, £871.13.8, and in 1861, £837.11.0. In 1862 he hopes for still more, and expects by "early next year" to be wholly free of debt. Here again he was oversanguine. In the next letter, May 1, 1863, which concludes the series, he is forced to announce that a subsidy had suddenly been discontinued, while the "ordinary sale" of the *Westminster* had decreased in 1862 by £70, so that he is able to send only half of the £20 that was to be paid Johanna "as before" at Oporto. No more is heard of her.

By the end of 1861, when it became obvious that Manwaring could not meet his obligations, Chapman and Smith were forced to take back the business. At a creditors' meeting attended by Chapman, Octavius H. Smith, Spencer, Fergusson, and a lawyer representing F. W. Newman, it was decided to declare Manwaring bankrupt at once. When the trustees to whom he had assigned his estate pointed out that they hoped to get from four to five shillings in the pound if this were not done, it was agreed to await a settlement. Chapman refers to

38. *Morning Star and Dial,* 5 April 1862, p. 5. The authorship of this notice is given in Chapman's letter to Johanna von Heyligenstaedt, 8 April 1862.

Manwaring as "a hardened rogue," who had shammed illness to avoid questioning; for two years he had drawn £80 a year more than he should have, and there was still a deficit of £675 that he could not account for. By a curious coincidence Chapman's own income for the period of Manwaring's management averaged £230 per year more than in 1859.[39]

Chapman had come to believe with his chief creditor Mr. Smith "in the necessity of gradually stripping government of all functions except those of defending the nation from foreign enemies, and of administering justice—enforcing contracts."[40] In opposing the various humanitarian reforms the lower classes were demanding, the *Westminster Review* was a valuable and influential ally that Mr. Smith did not intend to relinquish. He agreed to join with other like-minded men in establishing a fund to support it, Chapman retaining the editorship as before. Accordingly, an arrangement was made with Trübner and Company to take over all the publications, including the *Westminster Review*. A notice in the number for April 1862 announcing the change asked to have subscriptions henceforth paid to the new publisher; those who had paid Manwaring before his failure were to be given the *Westminster* "at the Proprietor's expense."

Chapman's optimism was not at all diminished by these changes. In the first year of the American Civil War he was anticipating a large additional market for the *Review* if the seceding States should adopt Free Trade. He also hoped for an increased circulation in India. In the latter case, at least, his wish came true for a time. In 1862 Theodor Goldstücker, Professor of Sanskrit at University College, London, introduced him to a wealthy Hindu, a freethinker among his people as Chapman was in England, who wanted to subscribe for 500 copies of the *Westminster* each quarter, with the understanding, of course, that the editorial policy toward India should be such as he could approve. Before concluding the agreement Chapman insisted on commercial guarantees, which the Hindu promptly furnished. Thus without additional editorial expense, the *Review* found itself £400 richer

39. Chapman to Johanna von Heyligenstaedt, 11 March and 4 July 1862.
40. *Ibid.*, 6 March 1862.

at the end of a year, when the subsidy was abruptly discontinued.[41]

Ever since taking his medical degree Chapman had been debating how to divide his time between editorial and professional work. In his Diary July 24, 1860, he wrote:

I am greatly embarrassed to decide which of the following courses I shall adopt: 1st. To go on editing the Review, living in the same house and waiting for practice as now and endeavouring to secure what subsidies for the Review I can; 2nd. To try to get a government situation, continuing on as in No. 1 meanwhile; 3rd. To continue on as in No. 1. but to endeavour to cultivate a practice among insane patients; or 4th. While still editing the Review to avoid writing and to qualify myself for medical practice generally so as to be able to take a country practice hereafter.

If he were to go to the country as a general practitioner, Chapman would have to know surgery as well as medicine. So in the autumn of 1860, after Johanna had left England, he put himself in the hands of Mr. Hind, the "grinder" in Newman Street, who promised to get him through the examinations of the Royal College of Surgeons after two months of study.[42] Hind was as good as his word; in 1861 Chapman's name appears on the lists as a member of the College.

While in many respects country practice would be pleasanter and more profitable for a man of Chapman's limited skill, it had disadvantages that he had not considered until his friend Andrew Johnson pointed them out to him. Since 1832 Johnson had been employed by the Bank of England as a clerk in the Bullion Office, of which he rose to be Principal in 1866.[43] Paradoxically enough, his sympathies lay with the revolutionists. He befriended Freiligrath and Karl Marx in London; Engels sent his more important letters to Marx in care of Johnson at the Bullion Office. Whatever his real opinions were, Johnson conformed outwardly to the prejudices of his neighbors and lived a calm and happy life; but he knew

41. *Ibid.*, 20 February, 11 March 1862, and 1 May 1863.
42. *Ibid.*, 18 October 1860.
43. Information supplied by the Librarian of the Bank of England.

that Chapman could never follow this course. Chapman reported their conversation in a letter to Johanna March 6, 1862:

His opinion is strongly against my going into the country with a view to practise my profession. As he says, if I do that I must be prepared to live what is called "respectably," to conform to present ideas in respect to my social life, as he does, and to forego all expression of my real convictions: to go to church and seemingly to acquiesce in all the superstitions of the stupidest old ladies with whom I may come in contact. A nice life that would be—would it not? I hope thou wouldst hate me if I so degraded myself as to live it. Wouldst thou not? I should certainly hate myself.—No! Wherever I go I will strive above all things to be and seem myself. . . .

Only if I cannot live here in modest comfort should I be justified, as it seems to me, either on public grounds or by expediency, in leaving this country. Of course, I claim the right to order my own private and domestic life as shall seem to me best, and if as a condition of obtaining an adequate income English Society insists that I shall live in the same house with a person who is repulsive to me, then I shall feel it my duty to live in such place and in such manner as will best insure my individual freedom.

They ordered this matter better in France, Chapman believed. He would gladly have flown to Johanna, had circumstances not compelled him to compromise in accordance with his friend's prudent counsel. Whether he continued to live in the same house with Susanna does not appear. On January 22, 1863, he moved to 25 Somerset Street, Portman Square, but the house in Albion Street was kept as his office and for the accommodation of boarding patients, principally insane.[44]

Chapman's career as a physician is open to strong suspicion of quackery. Never excessively modest about trumpeting his achievements, he had unusual temptation to self-advertisement in his easy access to the public press. He had hardly received his diploma from the Royal College of Physicians before he issued a seven-page pamphlet on *Chloroform and Other Anæsthetics; How They Act, How They Kill, and How*

---

44. Note in Clement Shorter's Transcript.

They May Be Safely Used.[45] Except as it told the public that the author was now "John Chapman, M.D., Licentiate of the Royal College of Physicians," this work was of no importance. At least, it brought him no patients, and Chapman was always candid in declaring that profit was his first consideration in the medical profession. To obtain reputation by arduous study and long practice was never his aim; he meant to startle the world with some marvelous nostrum that would make his fortune.

He soon fixed upon a method of treating certain functional diseases of women by means of heat and cold applied along the spine. He had recommended a similar treatment to Barbara Leigh Smith as early as 1855; now he refined and complicated it by insisting on the use of a spinal ice bag of his own devising placed on very limited portions of the back according to the symptoms of each case. By this method he claimed to cure not only functional maladies, but diarrhœa, epilepsy, paralysis, and diabetes. His pamphlet on the subject describes a patient, one of whose breasts was quite undeveloped while the other was swollen; by the application of an ice bag to one side of the spine and a hot-water bag to the other they were brought in a few weeks "so nearly equal, that the difference between them is scarcely distinguishable."[46]

My discovery is a blessed reality [he wrote Johanna[47]], and when it is matured and published I am confident I shall soon have many *paying* patients. Last Tuesday morning at 9:30 I began to treat a girl who had on an average *6 fits an hour* (!) every day; from that, she has ceased to have fits, except when she has neglected my orders.

For seasickness and hysteria Chapman's method was probably as effective as any other and certainly involved no public danger. But when he began to describe the "cure" of cholera by spinal ice bags during the great epidemic of 1866, his colleagues grew justly suspicious. He insisted that cholera was "neither infectious nor contagious," but "a disease of the

45. Reprinted from the *Medical Times and Gazette,* 23 and 30 October 1858.
46. John Chapman, *Functional Diseases of Women,* London, 1863, pp. 41–42.
47. 1 May 1863.

nervous system."[48] Even after 1883, when Koch demonstrated the vibrio that causes it, Chapman rejected the scientific evidence and continued ascribing cholera to such factors as high temperature, disturbances of atmospheric electricity, absence of ozone, "nocturnal influences," fear, and insanity.[49]

He used every means at his command to advertise his "discovery." In a letter to the editor of the *Athenæum* he protests that, though his book had been out more than a year, it had not yet been reviewed.

I am so far a believer in myself as to venture the assertion that the time will come when the medical doctrine and method I am preaching will be so generally known and practised that spine-bags will become articles of domestic furniture as indispensable as tea-kettles! If there is just ground for a tenth part of my faith, the subject assuredly deserves the attention of the *Athenæum*—especially as it notices medical books. . . . I confess, however, that for the sake of profiting a little from my own ideas while I am still in the flesh, I am most anxious for the public to know of my success in the treatment of Epilepsy, Paralysis, and Neuralgia.[50]

His friend Dr. Lankester, Chapman adds, is willing to contribute an article on the book if the *Athenæum* will print it. The offer seems to have been declined, since in the notice the *Athenæum* finally published nearly six months later, Chapman's belief in the effect of external heat or cold on the sympathetic nervous system is declared highly improbable, and the whole theory of its use in the treatment of cholera "too good to be true."[51]

In London Chapman was on the staff of the Metropolitan Free Hospital and the Farringdon Dispensary, of which Dr.

48. John Chapman, *Cases of Diarrhœa and Cholera*, London, 1871, p. 2.

49. "The Non-Contagiousness, Causation, and Scientific Treatment of Cholera," *Westminster Review*, 122 (October 1884), 472–533. Koch's *Cholera and Its Bacillus* is among the books reviewed in this article. It is interesting to note that Chapman revived the "Independent Section" for his contribution.

50. Chapman to William Hepworth Dixon, 10 March 1868. Further efforts to puff his own work appear in a letter written to Chapman by Thornton Hunt, 8 March 1865, explaining that J. M. Levy, the chief editor [of the *Daily Telegraph*], had declined to enter into any physiological question.

51. *Athenæum*, 15 August 1868, pp. 214–215.

Lankester was chief physician. These positions he resigned in 1874, when he moved to Paris to practise among the English colony there. His departure marked also the end of all pretense of living with Susanna. She remained in England until her death in March 1892.[52] I have been unable to ascertain whether Chapman secured a French divorce or merely forewent the ceremony of marriage; it appears, however, that in 1879 he took as his second wife a widow named Hannah, twelve years his junior. The Yale University Library has four of his letters to her[53] which give a momentary glimpse of their domestic life in 1880.

Chapman always calls her "Pres"; he addresses her as "my darling wife" or "my own darling child" and implores her to "love your Doc, for he wants a great deal of love from you." Pres has gone to London to see about the renting of their house there, but is having some difficulty, as it is only half furnished and Peter Robinson refuses to supply any more merchandise until Chapman's bill is paid. Another Oxford Street furnisher, W. S. Burton, is willing to supply £200 worth of furniture, including bedding, if paid cash for half the amount. Since certain prior claims make a second mortgage impossible, Chapman advises Pres to try to let such of the rooms as are furnished until they can decide what to do.

In Paris, meanwhile, life is not going too smoothly. Their house at 212 Rue de Rivoli, if not a hotel, seems, at least, like every house Chapman lived in, to have been adapted for boarders. There is a possibility that a certain Mr. Senders and his wife—the latter a patient of Chapman's—may take a suite of rooms in the house, which will involve repapering the "chambre de bonne No. 30" for their maid. However, he writes, "four guineas a week will be so much gained." Like most doctors he had trouble collecting his bills: the sum of debts, good and bad, due him was over £500; £200 was owed by one person. But Chapman was still unfailingly hopeful. In a letter he wrote February 10, 1880, to greet Pres "on the

---

52. *Note and Queries,* 11th Series, 12 (14 August 1915), 125, says: "In 1842 he married Susannah Brewitt of Nottingham, who predeceased him in March, 1892."

53. 26 and 29 January, 5 and 10 February, 1880.

DR. JOHN CHAPMAN, M.R.C.P., M.R.C.S.

morning of the anniversary of our betrothal-day," he says, "though at present our outward circumstances are surrounded by dark clouds, I rejoice in feeling assured that our souls are more thoroughly one and indivisible than they ever were. . . ."

In 1888 they were living at 46 Avenue Kléber. Chapman had his office at 224 Rue de Rivoli, above Galignani's, looking across the Tuileries Gardens. He was frequently consulted by foreign guests at the hotels in the neighborhood, who found his name prominently listed among the recommended physicians in English editions of Baedeker. His drawing room was frequented by French, English, and American radicals and literary people. Hely Bowes, Edward King, Theodore Stanton, Campbell Clarke, Theodore Child, and Richard Whiteing were among them,[54] but the circle never approached in brilliance the group that used to gather in the Strand.

A passage copied for Clement Shorter, apparently from a Diary of this period, gives one more curious glimpse of Chapman's domestic life:

October 21, 1888. At 3.15 p.m. I went in a cab, intending that we should go to 224 Rue de Rivoli. Before starting, we met Mme. McKaye: I suppose that I was in a half-dreamy state, for I imagined her to be la Baronne de Salvador! While she was talking with Pres, I noticed with surprise that her hair was white. While we were passing along the Champs Elysées in the cab, I remarked to Pres that the Baronne's hair had become white. Pres, evidently, did not understand me; and when it dawned upon her that I was referring to Mme. McKaye, she delivered me from my extraordinary delusion and reviled me violently for my stupidity: she told me that rather than see a man commit such a folly as that she would prefer to see his head cut off! I, unfortunately, replied— "I am much obliged to you." She became much more excited, reviled me more vehemently, and, when I attempted to defend myself by remarking that if I were to use like language to her she would not tolerate it for a moment, or words to that effect, she became still more excited, stopped the cab, got out, and commanded the driver to take me to the Rue de Rivoli; and he did

54. *Critic* (New York), 35 (1899), 782.

so. If I had not been a fool or had not lost half my senses, I should have got out of the cab too.

Chapman's removal to France did not affect the *Westminster Review*, which he continued to edit from Paris until his death, November 25, 1894. According to one account he died as a result of being run over by a cab;[55] but the obituary notice in the *Westminster*,[56] announcing the first change in its editorship in forty-three years, speaks of "an intermittent illness of some months." He was buried December 1 at Highgate Cemetery in London, "close to the grave of George Eliot, his revered co-worker."

As we bid farewell to him in his resting-place [the notice continues], it seems that no more fitting epitaph for that silent tomb could be placed thereon than George Eliot's own verse. No more eloquent tribute can be paid to the memory of Dr. John Chapman than to think of him as one of the

> "Choir invisible
> Of those immortal dead who live again
> In minds made better by their presence: live
> In pulses stirred to generosity,
> In deeds of daring rectitude, in scorn
> For miserable aims that end in self,
> In thoughts sublime that pierce the night like stars,
> And with their mild persistence urge man's search
> To vaster issues."

Circumstances must excuse the exaggeration in the *Westminster's* four-page eulogy, which was directed as much toward Chapman's widow as toward the public. During his latter years Mrs. Chapman had helped increasingly with the *Review;* after his death she continued as editor, at first from Paris and then (until 1907) in London.[57] The author of the obituary looked to her

55. *The Dictionary of National Biography*, First Supplement, 1901, I, 414.
56. *Westminster Review*, 143 (January 1895), [1]–4.
57. *Notes and Queries*, 162 (23 January 1932), 64. "His second wife still survives him at the age of 82, and at the present time is being cared for by Mrs. Cobden Sanderson, as readers of a recent notice in the Press will be aware." (*Nottingham Guardian*, 4 May 1915.)

for the Life of her husband, and to no living person could such a work be more safely confided than to the one so closely and so unswervingly associated with Dr. Chapman's labours, the inseparable companion of his intellectual, as of his social life.

Unfortunately, the expectation was never gratified, whether because she knew too little about him or too much the reader of this volume may decide.

"If ever Chapman's history is written fully and accurately," said Sir W. Robertson Nicoll, "it would form a romance of the most extraordinary kind."[58] No character of fiction presents a more baffling paradox. Vanity and humility, shrewdness and generosity, quackery and zeal for reform mingle unpredictably in him. Using money secured by dubious means to bring out important books that no one else would publish, he exerted a stimulating influence upon English thought. A man of sudden and shifting enthusiasms, he edited the *Westminster Review* continuously for forty-three years. Throughout a life of deliberate sensuality his Diaries show him striving, apparently quite sincerely, for moral improvement. Though he refused to publish a novel containing an objectionable love scene, he maintained in the heart of mid-Victorian London a household no novelist would then have dared to describe. It seems never to have occurred to him that his contemptible treatment of his wife was anything but magnanimous.

In the years of George Eliot's fame he must sometimes have recalled their remarkable friendship. The secrets that she entrusted to him before she found someone else to lean upon he never betrayed. During the fourteen years he survived her, when the slightest acquaintance prompted writers to gratify an eager public with reminiscences, Chapman held his peace. In one not given to reticence such persistent silence should not pass uncommended.

58. *A Bookman's Letters*, New York, 1913, p. 372.

JOHN CHAPMAN'S DIARIES

𝕷𝖊𝖙𝖙𝖘'𝖘 𝕯𝖎𝖆𝖗𝖞,

OR

BILLS DUE BOOK,

AND

AN ALMANACK,

FOR

1851,

BEING THE FOURTEENTH OF THE REIGN OF HER PRESENT MAJESTY,

QUEEN VICTORIA

(Accession 20th June, 1837.)

PUBLISHED FOR ISSUE, 1 SEPTEMBER, 1850, BY

LETTS, SON & STEER,

Stationers, Printers, and Map-Sellers.

8, ROYAL EXCHANGE, AND PRINTED AT THEIR OFFICE,
24, QUEEN STREET, LONDON.

May be had of any Bookseller or Stationer in the United Kingdom.

AGENTS IN FOREIGN PARTS.

Adelaide—Farmer & Hodgkiss ; Were, Todd & Co.
Bombay—The Office of "The Gentleman's Gazette."
Ceylon—Clarke, Romer & Co.; Medical Hall, Colombo & Kandy; Brodie,
Bogue & Co., Colombo.
Demerara—J. W. Richardson.
Jamaica, Kingston—Thomas Groom; and George Henderson.
Melbourne—J. B. Were & Co.
Sydney—J. B. & G. Were.

Note.—An *Appendix* will be added in November to correct any alteration that may
have taken place after the above date of publication.

TITLE PAGE OF CHAPMAN'S DIARY
FOR 1851

CHAPMAN'S DIARY FOR 1851

13/11/50[1]
See Pleffel's [Pfeffel's] Summaries at the end of each period of his *"History of Germany"*, recommended by Smyth p. 88 vol I. Coxe's Hist. of Austria.
Hist: of France by Michelet & Lamartine.
Abbe de Mably's Hist. (philosophic) of France.
Montesqueau.

14/11/50
English History:—Compare Hume and Rapin and study Millar on the "Constitution," Hallam, Turner, Mackintosh, Lingard.[2]
A terminational Dictionary of latin substantives by B. Dawson, & William Rushton.[3]
Sir Charles Lyell.[4]

Wednesday 1 January 1851

I open the record of this new year with a sad retrospect of the last one,—sad in regard to the trying difficulties I have gone through pertaining to my business, sad in regard to the wretchedness I have endured through my affections, sad that I have wasted much time and seem to have made no intellectual progress,—and saddest of all that I have made *others* sad, and have not at all profited by this year, in the very vigour of my manhood, to become a better man. The misery I experienced yesterday and the causes of it was a fitting close to such a year.—

1. These notes, dated 13 and 14 November 1850, are written on blank pages at the beginning of the Diary.
2. These names are taken from *A List of Books Recommended and Referred to in the Lectures on Modern History* by William Smyth (1765–1849), Professor of History at Cambridge. The authors referred to are Christian Friederich Pfeffel (1726–1807), William Coxe (1747–1828), Jules Michelet (1798–1874), Alphonse Marie Louis de Lamartine (1790–1869), Gabriel Bonnot de Mably (1709–85), Charles Louis de Secondat Montesquieu (1689–1755), David Hume (1711–76), Paul de Rapin-Thoyras (1661–1725), John Millar (1735–1801), Henry Hallam (1777–1859), Sharon Turner (1768–1847), James Mackintosh (1765–1832), and John Lingard (1771–1851).
3. London, 1850.
4. Two of his books are reviewed [by Edward Forbes] in an article entitled "The Future of Geology," *Westminster Review*, 58 (July 1852), 67–94.

There is ground for hope in the coming year that my business at least will cause me less anxiety, but its claims on my attention are so urgent and incessant that I fear my opportunities for study will grow less and less; and alas, even for moral and spiritual discipline and improvement *time* for meditation is a necessary element, and hence my hope of accomplishing much is small. I feel compelled to postpone day by day the needful attention to the claims of my better nature to a more convenient season.—Elisabeth[5] returned from Johnson's[6] party of last night.

Spent the evening at home with Dr Hodgson[7] who came today. Susanna[8] received an answer from Miss Lynn,[9] very sad. Elisabeth described to me 2 letters she had written to Coventry[10] which occasioned much painful conversation. Susanna went to the Dunn's[11] party.

5. Elisabeth Tilley. See pp. 16–17.

6. Andrew Johnson (1815–80) had been since 1832 a clerk at the Bank of England. His translation of F. W. J. von Schelling's *The Philosophy of Art*, 1845, was published in Chapman's Catholic Series. He was a friend of Freiligrath, the German poet, and of Karl Marx; the latter wrote Engels 28 October 1852: "Wenn Du mir *wichtige* Sachen zu schreiben hast, so tu es unter der Adresse: A. Johnson, Esq., (Bullion Office, Bank of England)." (*Marx-Engels Briefwechsel*, Berlin, 1929, I, 424.)

Johnson was the author of *Some Observations on the Recent Supplies of Gold . . .*, 1852, and *Currency Principles versus Banking Principles . . . .*, 1856. He became Principal of the Bullion Office in 1866, was pensioned because of ill-health 8 February 1872, and died at his home, The Laurels, Haslemere, Surrey, 26 December 1880.

7. William Ballantyne Hodgson (1815–80), educational reformer, had been since 1847 Principal of Chorlton High School in Manchester. He was also a member of the council of University College, London.

8. Susanna Brewitt Chapman. See p. 5.

9. Eliza Lynn Linton (1822–98), novelist, came to London in 1845 to earn her living as a writer. She boarded with the Chapmans for a time before they moved to the Strand. See p. 5, and G. S. Layard, *Mrs. Lynn Linton*, London, 1901, p. 134. Her first novels, *Azeth the Egyptian* (1846) and *Amymone* (1848), were criticized for their remoteness from contemporary life; in her next novel, *Realities* (1851), which Chapman had agreed to publish, she leaned over backwards in depicting sordid aspects of the London theater. Although the book evoked an eighty-line tribute in blank verse from Walter Savage Landor, to whom it was dedicated, most reviewers regarded it as a failure, and commented on its lack of reality. Mrs. Chapman's correspondence with her dealt with objectionable passages in *Realities*.

10. After her return from Geneva in March 1850 Marian Evans made her home with Mr. and Mrs. Charles Bray at Rosehill, Coventry. She had spent the last two weeks of November 1851 at Chapman's; Elisabeth Tilley's letters may therefore have been written to her.

11. Robert Dunn was a surgeon who lived near the Chapmans at 15 Norfolk Street, Strand.

Thursday 2 January 1851

1[12]

Susanna answered Miss Lynn's note at length and kindly, but with an air of moral superiority. Accompanied D[r] Hodgson to a party given by M[r] Wills,[13] the editor of Dicken's[14] "Household Words." A M[r] Ross[15] known to Hodgson went with us who is engaged on the "Chronicle". Met M[r] Orr,[16] M[rs] Loudon,[17] M[r] Spence as the only persons I knew;—rather a dull affair with *some* good music. I passed a good part of the time in discussing on religious topics with a young friend of M[rs] Loudon's,—the most thoughtful and capable looking girl or woman in the room, a Miss Houghton of Dudley, Birmingham.—Reached home at 1.15. and found Elisabeth not returned from the Perrys where she had been spending the evening.

Friday 3 January 1851

3   4

Yesterday I sent a copy of the N[o] of the "Westminster" containing an article by Miss Evans on the "Progress of the Intellect" to her and another to Mackay[18] with a note presuming he would wish for one, and that Miss E. should have one on his account. Today he returned me the number I sent him with a shabby-note saying he did not see why I should send one to Miss E. on his account,—and that he could not "undertake to be paymaster for other people ad infinitum", and intimated other disagreeable

12. These numerals refer to Chapman's relations with Elisabeth Tilley.

13. William Henry Wills (1810–80) became assistant editor of *Household Words* in 1849.

14. Another of Chapman's variant spellings is *Dickins*.

15. Probably William Ross, who lived at 4 Howard Street, Strand. The offices of the *Morning Chronicle* were at 332 Strand.

16. William S. Orr, bookseller and publisher, was London representative of Mrs. Wills's brothers, Robert and William Chambers, the Edinburgh publishers.

17. Margracia Loudon wrote on Coöperation and other radical movements. See her letter in the *Leader*, 11 January 1851, pp. 44–45.

18. Robert William Mackay (1803–82), philosopher and author. Miss Evans's review of *The Progress of the Intellect as Exemplified in the Religious Development of the Greeks and Hebrews*, London, John Chapman, 1850, appeared in the *Westminster Review*, 54 (January 1851), 353–368.

things. Answered him at length letting him know my views clearly. D[r] Hodgson read my note and pronounced it very mild and courteous. We had a very pleasant party this evening. Busily engaged in writing to America *all day*. Sat up after the party with D[r] H. until nearly 2 o'clock. He gave me the history of a M[r] Espinasse,[19] a most contemptable fellow.—

"Asia" for New York[20]

Saturday 4 January 1851

Albion Sale[21] Bill at 12 mo[s] due			22.	15.	0
James Burns " " 4 " "			24.	6.	5
H. G. Bohn " " 3 " "			36.	13.	10
Simpkin & C[o] " " 4 " "			46..	11.	7
Mudie's acceptance due £22. 7. 2.			130.	6.	10
J. S. Smith's " " £69. 18. 3			200		
Ross (promissory notes in hands of Clowes)			213..	6.	8
			343..13.	6

Rose late,—accompanied M[rs] Young and Susanna to see some Pianos, but came to no decision about a purchase, the one I want being higher priced than I like for the present.—Did not reach home until 2. The afternoon passed with D[r] Hodgson succeeded by M[r] Woodfall[22] and afterwards by Herbert Spencer.—[23] In the

19. Probably Francis Espinasse, Carlyle's friend and biographer.

20. Sailing dates, bills due, birthdays, etc., were entered in the Diary in advance.

21. "The great publishers have annual or semi-annual sales, generally held at the Albion Hotel, with the accompaniments of dinners and wine. . . . On these occasions the 'remainders' . . . are offered on reduced terms, or sold by auction, while new works, often even before they are issued, are offered at 10 and 15 per cent. below the trade price, with the advantage of long credit, extending, in cases of large purchases, to sixteen months, and sometimes more." *Westminster Review*, 57 (April 1852), 530–531.

Most of the firms mentioned in this list are publishers, stationers, and booksellers. William Clowes and Son were engravers and printers.

22. George Woodfall, son of the publisher of the Junius letters, was printer of the books Chapman published and of the *Westminster Review*, vols. 57–63 (January 1852–April 1855), to which he subscribed £200. See GE to Sara Hennell, Monday [13 October 1851].

23. Herbert Spencer (1820–1903), philosopher, was at this time subeditor of the *Economist*, at 340 Strand, and had rooms there.

course of conversation the latter was astonished to find me propounding a theory regarding population which he conceived to
be peculiarly original with him;—viz., that the power of reproduction is in an inverse ratio with the perfection of the individuals
constituting the race;—and several important applications of the
doctrine, it seems have been equally worked out by both of us. He
told me the ideas had been familiar to him these 2 years,—I told
him I worked them out for myself in Paris,—8 years ago;—and
that I was glad there was a chance they would now get utterance.—[24] Sat up till 12 with D[r] H. who tried to persuade me to
think of Ireland[25] of Manchester for a partner.

Sunday 5 January 1851

7.

Spent the morning writing business letters,—Elisabeth sat with
me reading the proofs of Miss Martineau's book.—[26] D[r] H. went to
hear Maccall[27] with Susanna. Marrianne[28] arrived, and went with
S. to call on the Howitts[29] where they left Beatrice. E. took Ernest[30] to Islington. I walked with D[r] H. to call on M[rs] Torrens,[31]
not finding her at home I walked with him from Cadogan Place

24. See p. 47.
25. Alexander Ireland (1810–94), a native of Edinburgh, settled in Manchester in 1843, where he published the *Manchester Examiner*, 1846–86.
26. *Letters on the Laws of Man's Nature and Development*, by Henry
George Atkinson and Harriet Martineau, London, John Chapman, 1851.
27. William MacCall (1812–88), a former Unitarian minister, was lecturing
in a hall near Oxford Street. He was noted for virulent reviews; his notice of
a book by Charles Bray began "Fitly art thou called Bray, my worthy friend!"
Carlyle introduced him to Espinasse at one of Chapman's *soirées*. See F. Espinasse, *Literary Recollections and Sketches*, New York, 1893, p. 250, and D. A.
Wilson, *Carlyle at His Zenith*, London, 1927, p. 467. Chapman had published
three of MacCall's books.
28. Marianne Chapman, a schoolmistress, is described as "a little old-
young lady, a cousin of Mr. Chapman's." (GE to Mrs. Bray [8 January 1851].)
Chapman also spells her name *Marianne* and *Marian*.
29. William Howitt (1792–1879) was a chemist at Nottingham, 1823–31; he
wrote his first book, *A Popular History of Priestcraft*, in 1833; Chapman published the seventh edition of it in 1845. From 1844 to 1848 he lived at The
Elms, Clapton, quite near the Chapmans. His wife, Mary Howitt (1799–1888),
collaborated with him on many books.
30. Chapman's elder child, Beatrice, was six years old on 28 December 1850;
Ernest was five, 9 March 1851.
31. Mrs. Torrens was staying with William Torrens M'Cullagh, M.P. for
Dundalk, at 23 Cadogan Place.

across Hyde Park to Sussex Terrace, and then I returned alone and spent the evening with Mrs Torrens.—

Conversed at length in intervals of today with Dr H. concerning a partnership.—I told him I should prefer him to anyone else, and that my [I] fancy the idea of his being a sleeping partner during the time of his travels the next 4 years, and then of his becoming an active partner.—

Monday 6 January 1851

Rose at 7.

Spent the entire day at business, the afternoon not very well, and saddened.—

Went to a party at 8 at Dr Lankester's,[32] met Dr Ramsey,[33] Mr Smith (of the Dictionary),[34] Dr Carpenter[35] & others among whom were Mrs Loudon and Miss Houghton again.—

Mr Smith urged reasons why youths should not learn latin until their reasoning powers are well developed, in which I concur.

Received a proposition to rent my vaults and an office, but I do not see how I can give a proper access that may be mutually convenient.

Tuesday 7 January 1851

Elisabeth removed her writing materials I having given her my Davenport for her use in the Drawing Room.—

Rose at 7. Took Dr Hodgson to call on Mr Crabbe Robinson[36] who was kind enough to accompany us to the Flaxman Gallery consisting I believe of all his works which were carefully pre-

32. Edwin Lankester (1814–74), author of works on physiology and sanitary reform, was at this time Professor of Natural History at New College, London.

33. Andrew Crombie Ramsay (1814–91) became Professor of Geology at University College, London, in 1847.

34. William Smith (1813–93), author of *A Dictionary of Greek and Roman Antiquities* (1842), *A Dictionary of Greek and Roman Biography* (1843–48), etc.

35. William Benjamin Carpenter (1813–85), naturalist, was Professor of Medical Jurisprudence at University College, London, and later Registrar of the University of London.

36. Henry Crabb Robinson (1775–1867), the diarist, was one of the founders of University College, London.

served by Miss Denman[37] and presented to the College. They are of course in clay and are now beautifully arranged in the Dome of the College.—They had a narrow escape of being dispersed. Flaxman's heir, Miss Denman whose life has been devoted to their care offered them to the government, they were declined for want of room, at Mr Robinson's suggestion they were then offered to University College. Before getting there, they were seized by the creditors of her brother in whose house they were and who failed. They were rescued only to be seized again by the landlord from whom they were ransomed at a small cost.—

Called on Miss Lynn who gave me a letter to Susanna to read but not to deliver. A cheerful day, went out with Elisabeth.—

Wednesday 8 January 1851

Rose at 6.40. Saw for the first time Venus and Jupiter through a telescope. The crescent form of Venus was distinctly visible.—

Miss Evans arrived at Euston Square at 3 P.M. where I met her, her manner was friendly but formal and studied.

Miss Lynn called in reference to my corrections of her proofs, only one of which she acquiesced in.

Dr Hodgson spent most of the evening with me, we had a walk on Waterloo bridge,—beautiful starlight. I like him extremely.

I have endured much suffering today.

Thursday 9 January 1851

Had a very busy day, and although the month is so far advanced we have been unable to get any a/cs out yet.

<Had a very painful altercation with Elisabeth the result of her groundless suspicions hence I have been in a state of unhealthy excitement all day.—She gave notice at the dinner table that she intended to leave in the Autumn.—

Miss Evans is very poorly, sat with her a short time and talked about Miss Lynn and her book.>—

Still reading "Vanity Fair".[38]

37. Maria Denman was sister-in-law and adopted daughter of the sculptor John Flaxman (1755–1826). J. M. D. Meiklejohn, ed., *Life and Letters of William Ballantyne Hodgson*, Edinburgh, 1883, pp. 80–82, gives essentially the same account of this visit. See also H. H. Bellot, *University College, London*, London, 1929, pp. 302–303.

38. Thackeray's *Vanity Fair* was published in 1847–48.

Friday 10 January 1851

α

Rose at 5 and lighted my fire dressed at 6, feel dizzy and weak.—
Mr Jarvis[39] left by the Steamer for Havre.—Read Miss Lynn's 5th
proof through.—Felt very poorly all day, entirely owing to mental
excitement which seems to increase rather than diminish with me.

< Miss Evans was very ill all day, but like myself recovered >
towards night being the night for the reception of visitors. I exerted myself and the excitement benifited me.—

My cousin Chapman,[40] Johnson and a Mr Benton were present.—

Saturday 11 January 1851

Day and Son[41] Bill 6 mo^s, due=   41..2. 6
Spent an unprofitable morning, and went out in the afternoon
to choose a Piano with Miss E for her use. Afterwards had a long
walk, and conversed much on *general topics,* and about Miss
Lynn and her social principles.—

Received and read through one of Miss L's "proofs" of a love
scene which is warmly and vividly depicted, with a tone and tendency which I entirely disapprove. Miss Evans concurs with me,
and Elisabeth and Susanna are most anxious I should not publish
the work.—

Miss E. and Susanna had a long talk on the point, when S. became excited and used language in reference to Miss L. unbecom-
ing and unjust. She also said that I, when conversing with Miss L.
in her presence on the subject, had 'lowered myself', but she re-
tracted the expression when I told her she did not believe what
she herself said.

Dr Hodgson woke me up this morning complaining that he had
the most acute pain in the right eyeball,—the result of a general
derangement, he took some medicine, and kept his bed all day.

39. James Jackson Jarves (1818–88), art collector, is described by Marian
Evans in a letter to Mrs. Bray [8 January 1851] as "an American, evidently a
noodle." He made the famous collection of Italian paintings now at Yale University.

40. John Chapman (1801–54). See Diary, 29 April 1851.

41. Lithographers and printers.

+ 10 A.M.[42]

Sunday 12 January 1851

Rose late, sat in Miss E's room while she played one of Mosart's Masses with much expression. The[n] went with her to call on Miss Lynn in the hope of inducing her to cancel some objectionable passages, and succeeded to the extent of a few lines only. I said that such passages were addressed [to] and excited the sensual nature and were therefore injurious;—and that as I am the publisher of works notable for the[ir] intellectual freedom it behoves me to be exceedingly careful of the *moral* tendency of all I issue. I, Susanna and Marianne dined in Sydenham and met Miss Lynn at the House of Mrs Peter Taylor.[43] Had a painful night with S.

Monday 13 January 1851

Harrison's[44] acceptance due for £100.

Rose late, unwell and ate no breakfast. Went at 12 with Dr Hodgson to see the Museum of economic geology which was shown to us by Mr Hunt.[45] Marianne left us to resume her school duties. Went with Miss Hennell[46] to the British Museum and left her at Newman's[47] introductory lecture.—Walked out with Dr Hodgson and was accosted by one woman on account of another (in Bedford Square) whom she declared to be in labor, the Doctor turned away with a rough answer, but I have felt concerned ever

42. An initial [E] before the cross has been erased. These crosses, appearing at regular intervals in the Diary, refer to Elisabeth's physical condition.

43. Clementia Doughty Taylor was the wife of Peter Alfred Taylor (1819–91), a silk mercer in the firm founded by his grandfather, Samuel Courtauld. Of an old Unitarian family, he was a reformer and radical in politics, a friend of Mazzini, and chairman of the Society of Friends of Italy. It was Marianne Chapman who dined with them on this occasion; but Marian Evans met them soon, and Mrs. Taylor became her lifelong friend.

44. William Harrison, bookseller and stationer.

45. Robert Hunt (1807–87), author of many works on mining and minerals, was Keeper of Mining Records at the Museum of Practical Geology in Jermyn Street, which was opened officially by Prince Albert 12 May 1851.

46. Sara Sophia Hennell (1812–99), George Eliot's friend and correspondent for nearly forty years, was a sister of Mrs. Charles Bray. She wrote a number of books on religion and theology.

47. Francis William Newman (1805–97), brother of John Henry Newman, was one of the founders of Bedford College, or the "Ladies' College," where, from 1849 to 1851, he lectured on ancient history, mathematics, philosophy, and political economy.

since. Had a German lesson from Miss Evans,—Elisabeth is very weak and poorly.—

Tuesday 14 January 1851

Burge & Perrin's[48] acceptance due   52. 16. 8

Rose at 6.45. Elisabeth is very sad and ill which causes me the greatest concern and grief;—she treated me with great coldness this morning, and affected indifference,—however I will try to bear it patiently and be only kind to her. Time only can convince her of the strength and intensity of my love. Gave her a short lesson in German. The question has been much agitated today whether she should attend the lectures of the ladies College which I wish her to do. M[r] Birch[49] dined with us. Received an unkind note from Miss Lynn concerning her "proofs". Had a German Lesson.

Wednesday 15 [19] January 1851

Rose at 4.50.
Sunday 19th. I have risen too late to write in my Diary the few preceding days, and I have been very busy.—The most interesting facts of the interval are that we have bought a piano, so that now I shall have some music. D[r] Hodgson left us on Thursday morning from whom I have since received an interesting letter announcing his arrival at Manchester &c &c. Miss Hennell came on a visit for a few days on Friday because Miss Evans is here, and the affair of Miss Lynn's novel has made some decided progress

Thursday 16 [19] January 1851

towards a settlement.—Urged on more strongly by the decided opinions expressed by D[r] Hodgson I wrote to Miss Lynn to say that I could not publish her book unless she consented to suppress the passages to which I objected; and as in spite of the remonstrances of myself Miss Evans, and M[rs] Peter Taylor, who visited her for the purpose on Monday, she would persist in maintaining the work in its original form I had only the alternative of

48. Booksellers at Manchester.
49. In October 1851 Birch subscribed £20 to the *Westminster Review*.

declining its publication altogether. This letter was in answer to
an insulting note from her in reference to my interference in the

(Friday 17 [19] January 1851

9

Westley & Co[50] Bill at 4 mo[s] due   23..13..6)

matter. My letter was answered by Miss Lynn's lawyer and friend
—M[r] Loaden[51]—who asked for [an] interview, in which he expressed a wish that I should make arrangements with some other
publisher to bring out the work,—in order that the thing may be
arranged in a friendly way so as to prevent him from acting "pro-
fessionally". This seemed reasonable. I tried Colburn and Shoberl
who declined, I learnt from Smith & Elder that their reason for
originally declining the work was on account of its intrinsic character,—and at length Churton[52] I found would not object to the

"Canada" for Boston   <M.   P.M.>[53]

Saturday 18 [19] January 1851

Orr & Co[54] Bill 6 mo[s] due   71. 5. 2.

work. Mess[rs] Smith & Elder's Manager, M[r] Williams,[55] called upon
me last night to say they had had a visit from M[r] Loaden & Miss
Lynn requesting them to publish her work on commission which
they declined to do, but urged upon her to submit to the censor-

50. Binders and embossers.
51. William Loaden was the Lynn family solicitor, who had persuaded
Eliza's father to let her come to London to try a literary career; he was a
bachelor, but said his sisters should look after her. See G. S. Layard, *Mrs.
Lynn Linton,* London, 1901, pp. 47–48.
52. Henry Colburn, William Shoberl, and Edward Churton. *Realities* was
eventually published by Saunders and Otley. See the *Leader,* 24 May 1851, p.
500.
53. These deleted letters probably refer to Marian Evans.
54. Publishers and booksellers.
55. Smith Williams had a soft and gentle voice, Mrs. Lynn Linton wrote,
"but his letters were harsh and acrid, and no one could think more cruelly
than he—no one wound more deeply when it came to the pen and ink contradiction of his mild words and half-hinted promises." (*My Literary Life,*
London, 1899, p. 16.) See also W. B. Scott, *Autobiographical Notes,* New York,
1892, I, 134.

ship of Thornton Hunt,[56] which she finally consented to do. In the course of the conversation they told her it would be best for her welfare and reputation to throw the M.S. in the fire.—

This has been a week of much painful experience.—Elisabeth has caused me great suffering and has suffered herself greatly—both mentally and physically,—her headaches seem to have been continual and most oppressive on the coronal region.—My time is dreadfully wasted, and I seem to accomplish nothing.—I would fain rise at 5 every morning but the irregular hours at which I go to bed make it very difficult.

Susanna suffers much from pain in her leg, seemingly from some affection of the nerves, but nothing succeeds in removing it. I hope her expected visit into Cornwall will restore her.—Had a short German lesson.

<M.   A.M.>

Sunday 19 January 1851

10

Rose at 6.45. Saw the crescent of Venus through the telescope.—
Took Elisabeth and Miss Hennell into Hyde Park, and the latter to call on Miss Marshall,[57] E having left us for Islington.—
Finished reading "Vanity Fair". Susanna read aloud Spencer's Rights of Women,[58]—all undeniable and true but very dry and dull.—
Called upon Mrs Torrens to take home her boy where I spent the evening.—Miss Hennell and Susanna played sacred music when I returned.—

Monday 20 January 1851

11.

Heard Newman give his first lecture on Geometry at the Ladies College, and wish much I might hear the course.—Much occupied in business all day. Miss Hennell left us, after w[h]ich I had a

56. Thornton Leigh Hunt (1810–73), son of Leigh Hunt, was editing the *Leader*, which with Lewes and others he had established in 1850.
57. Miss Mary Marshall, at 4 Leonard Place, Kensington.
58. Chapter XVI of Herbert Spencer's *Social Statics*, 1851.

lesson in German from Miss Evans who is not well. She played *well* in the Drawing room tonight.

Elisabeth seems to cherish her unhappiness most sadly.

Thomas Chapman is 35 years old.[59]

Tuesday 21 January 1851

12

William Sallis Bill due =   29..0..0

Rose at 6.20. Read Mackay, and then worked at Arithmetic with Elisabeth until 8.30.—Took E & S. into Hyde Park the sky being most clear and beautiful. Lewes[60] called to effect a reconciliation between me and Miss Lynn, and informed me of her willingness to cancel the objectionable passages, but that her bitterness against me is extreme.—Passed a profitable evening with Miss Evans, having read both Latin and German,—Elisabeth had a lesson from her in German.—

Wednesday 22 January 1851

Rose at 5.40.

Deighton's[61] acceptance due   37. 12. 9

Passed the morning as yesterday, till 8.30. Invited Miss Evans to go out after breakfast, did not get a decisive answer, E. afterwards said if I did go, she should be glad to go,—I then invited Miss Evans again telling her E. would go whereupon she declined rather rudely, Susanna being willing to go out, and neither E. nor S. wishing to walk far I proposed they should go a short distance without me, which E. considered an insult from me and reproached me in no measured terms accordingly, and heaped upon me suspicions and accusations I do not in any way deserve. I was very severe and harsh, said things I was sorry for afterwards, and we became reconciled in the Park.

Miss Evans apologized for her rudeness tonight, which roused

59. Chapman's brother Thomas was a cutler and dressing-case maker at Glasgow. The entry for 23 January 1851 gives that as his birthday. This may have been a reminder to write him in advance.

60. George Henry Lewes (1817–78).   61. Joseph Deighton, bookseller.

all E's jealousy again, and consequent bitterness. S. E. and Miss Evans are gone to spend the evening with M^r and Mrs Holland.—

Thursday 23 January 1851

13   14.

My brother Thomas was born 1816.
Had a sad morning with Elisabeth, and worked with her a little at Arithmetic. Took Susanna and Miss E. a walk into the Park.— The latter suffered from headache in the evening so that I did not get a full German lesson.—The demands of my business have become so imperative and engrossing latterly that I get very little time for any kind of study,—writing seems quite out of the question. A man needs much time for efficient self culture,—even the claims of the spirit for meditation and self scrutiny cannot be neglected with impunity.—

Friday 24 January 1851

5.30 rose   1 A.M. retired

Read Mr J. Willoughby Rope's Pamphlet on the Catholic question entitled "The Duty of England" &c[62] which I admire and concur in. Worked 3 hours at Arithmetic and went to hear Faraday on the magnetism of Oxygen, with Mr Mackay and Miss Evans,—on returning we found Dr Travis[63] whom Susanna engaged to mesmerize Elisabeth the next time she is unwell, the Doctor consented which instantly caused a flush of jealousy to quiver through my frame spite of my reason and my will.—[64]

62. *The Duty of England. A Protestant Layman's Reply to Cardinal Wiseman's "Appeal"* had just been published by Chapman.

63. Henry Travis is described by W. B. Hodgson, *Life and Letters*, Edinburgh, 1883, p. 80, as "an independent gentleman and a staunch spiritualist, . . . a young man with a very fine countenance, beaming with benevolence, and which when once seen it is difficult to forget; but he is obviously an impracticable dreamer, bound in verbal formulas, and rotating darkly in a vortex of insane speculation." Travis contributed articles to the *Leader* on such subjects as a "Reply to Mr. Spencer's Views on Property" (12 April 1851, p. 352) and "The Power of Education" (30 August 1851, pp. 832–833). Cf. Diary, 12 July 1851.

64. The account of this experiment was probably in the entries for 4–7 February, which have been cut from the Diary.

Elisabeth has not spoken kindly to me since Thursday evening, —on account of Miss Evans. Mrs Peter Taylor called when we had a long discussion about Miss Lynn. Susanna was painfully vehement. She had also a long talk with Mr Mackay.—

[Two leaves containing the remaining entries for January have been cut from the Diary.]

Saturday 1 February 1851

Rose at 7. Susanna is not well having been kept awake all night by excitement of the previous evening and annoyance about Mr Nisbet's novel[65] and his sarcastic letters.—I asked Miss Evans to undertake the revision of the work henceforth which she kindly consented to do.

Received a visit from Thornton Hunt and had a long talk with him about Miss Lynn,—he says he wrote her a letter expressing my views in regard to the Chapter in question. I regret extremely that she should have gone down in my estimation by the report of Dr Brabant[66] according to which she told him that I *entreated* her *with tears* to permit me to publish her work! I never thought she would have told a deliberate untruth.

Busily engaged all day in attending to correspondence,—I seem to have no time to read now.—Had a walk with Miss Evans in the Parks, when she did not seem well. Dr Brabant took her to the Theatre.—Susanna is very poorly and overcome, having a sore throat.—

65. James Nisbet, *The Siege of Damascus; A Historical Romance,* 3 vols., London, John Chapman, 1851. Reviewing the book the *Leader* says: "For some time past Mr. John Chapman has shown a disposition to enlarge the province of his publishing, and—without relinquishing that specialty of bold philosophical books for which he has gained a reputation—to include works of more general literature, not excepting even novels. He has here given us a three volume romance . . . such as must arrest attention by its qualities as a work of fiction, and help the good cause of liberty of thought.

"Many novel readers will be scared away by its uncompromising hostility to all dogmatic creeds and the vehemence of its tone with respect to priests of all colours. . . . Nevertheless it cannot be denied that the strong animus of the book gives it great vigour and stirring interest." (29 March 1851, p. 299.)

66. R. H. Brabant (1781?–1866), M.D. Edinburgh 1821, lived at this time in the Marlborough Buildings, Bath. He was the father of Mrs. Charles C. Hennell. See p. 23.

Mr Mudge says that the "Letters" &c of Miss Martineau & Atkinson "mock and deride every principle and sentiment of humanity".—

Sunday 2 February 1851

Rose at 7. Found Susanna had not had a good night but was better.—Did not feel well. Read about half Martineau's Article on the Battle of the Churches,[67] but could not get through, it lacks aim and continuity,—there seems to be no cohesion about it.— Read through the Athenæum and some of Don Quixote. I spent the evening in the Drawing room, Doctor Brabant who remained at home has kindly offered to lend me his telescope. Miss E. gave us a profusion of excellent music.—

Passed a sleepy stupid afternoon. At night Susanna spoke about the chance of E.'s leaving, and said she thought she had some foolish jealousy of Miss Evans, and instanced her bitter remarks.—

Monday 3 February 1851

Rose at 6.30.

Richard Kinder's[68] Bill due   23..6. 10

Elisabeth came after having been to the College, looking and feeling better, but one of the first things she said was that she wished she might never enter the house again. She lunched with us after which I took her to the Omnibus on her return to Shacklewell.—[69]

[One leaf containing the entries for *Tuesday 4 February—Friday 7 February 1851* has been cut from the Diary.]

67. James Martineau in the *Westminster Review*, 54 (January 1851), 441–496.
68. See Diary, 8 August 1851.
69. The next six-and-one-half lines, which concern Johnson, are illegible except for an occasional word.

Saturday 8 February 1851

6.45　　　　　　　　　　　　　　　　　　　　　　　　　10.30.

This very busy week now passed. I begin to feel that I must have more assistance, or what I have must be of a better kind, my business is in constant arrear, and hence I feel constant discomfort.—The business is decidedly increasing and I am confident will soon let me feel comparative comfort in regard to *money,* but I must struggle to prevent it from consuming ALL my time.

<Took M. and> Miss Hennell into St James Park, the day was fine, and the air fresh and exhilerating. <M. talked of returning to Coventry sadly>.—

Henry Crabbe Robinson called and I introduced him to Miss Evans who conversed with him a long time, more especially about the new book of Atkinson & Martineau about which she spoke with great discrimination and beauty of spirit.[70] Had the pleasure of handing Miss H. her £5 prize for the essay on Antichrist.[71]

Johnson came to request my aid in getting a paper into the "Leader" concerning Freiligrath[72] (at his own desire) and the treatment he is receiving from the Prussian government.—Wrote to Hunt about it.

Had a sad struggle with my pets today both having been very naughty, and Beaty much hurt by a blow on the forehead by a stick from Ernest. Beatrice lay in my arms on the sofa tonight which gave me great pleasure.—

70. Robinson recorded their meeting in his diary: "I called at Chapman's and there saw Miss Mary Ann Evans, translator of Strauss—no recommendation to me, certainly, but the contrary, and yet there was something about her which pleased me much both in look and voice. She spoke of Harriet Martineau's and Atkinson's letters as studiously offensive. It seems as if this book is absolutely atheistic!" (E. J. Morley, ed., *H. C. Robinson on Books and Their Writers*, 3 vols., London [1938], II, 707.)

71. The prize was offered 28 September 1850 in the columns of the *Leader* by George Baillie (1802–70), signing himself "A Constant Reader." In the issue of 25 January 1851, p. 80, appeared the following note: "The Prize Essay on I John ii, 18.—The prize has been awarded to the writer of the essay signing S. S. H." In 1857 Miss Hennell won the fifth Baillie Prize for her essay on *Christianity and Infidelity*.

72. Ferdinand Freiligrath (1810–76), German poet and communist, had fled to London after the publication of *ça ira!* in 1846. After the revolution of 1848 he went to Düsseldorf. In May 1851 he returned to London, where he collaborated with Karl Marx. Johnson's article, unsigned, appeared in the *Leader*, 15 February 1851, p. 144.

Sunday 9 February 1851

5.30.   10.45

Looked at Jupiter and Venus through the telescope, the morning being very fine.

Read the various criticisms on "Don Juan" given in Moore's edition of the work.—

Took Susanna a walk, called on Mr Woodfall and went to see the Houses of Parliament.

Wrote to Mr Empson[73] on behalf of Miss Evans of whom I spoke as a man proposing she should write in the "Edinburgh" on Mackay, Martineau & Atkinson's book, on Slavery, or any subject he would name if within her province.—

My dear E. is I fear suffering now.—Susanna has a bad cough.—

Monday 10 February 1851

6.45.—

Elisabeth surprised me agreeably by unexpectedly coming, I escorted her and Mrs Johnson into the City.

Worked late balancing my cash. Johnson with me.—

A Barrister Mr Bailey, Miss Lynn's cousin called on her account to settle our differences, and offered to procure a letter from Miss Lynn releasing me from all claim, conditionally that I would acknowledge she had reason to consider herself aggrieved by my refusal to publish her book, and that I would pay her £5 as a cover for her legal expenses. I consented, as least trouble, and being glad even now to help her.

[Two leaves containing the entries for *Tuesday 11 February—Monday 17 February 1851* have been cut from the Diary.]

Tuesday 18 February 1851

I presume with the view of arriving at a more friendly understanding S. & E. had a long talk this morning which resulted in their comparing notes on the subject of my intimacy with Miss Evans, and their arrival at the conclusion <that we are com-

73. William Empson (1791–1852) succeeded Macvey Napier as editor of the *Edinburgh Review* in 1847. See p. 20.

I presume with the view of arriving
at a more friendly understanding
S. & C. had a long talk this morning
which resulted in their comparing
notes on the subject of my intimacy
with Miss Evans, and their arrival
at the conclusion ~~xxxxxxxxxxxxxxxxx~~
~~xxxxxxxxxxxxxxxxxxxxxxxxxxxxxxxxxxxx~~
~~xxxxxxxxxxxxxxxxxxxxxxxxxxxxxxxxxxxx~~
~~xxxxxxxxxxxxxxxxxxxxxxxxxxxxxxxxxxxx~~
~~xxxxxxxxxxxxxxxxxxxxxxxxxxxxxxxxxxxx~~
~~xxxxxxxxxxxxxxxxxxxxxxxxxxxxxxxxxxxx~~
~~xxxxxxxxxxxxxxxxxxxxxxxxxxxxxxxxxxxx~~
~~xxxxxxxxxxxxxxxxxxxxxxxxxxxxxxxxxxxx~~
~~xxxxxxxxxxxxxxxxxxxxxxxxxxxxxxxxxxxx~~ —

···· **19** WEDNESDAY [50-315] ····

My room upset and the cieling whitened.
Sat in the dining room to write in
the morning where M. joined me, we
talked of course of the excited feelings
of S. & C. I gave her an account of what
had passed and urged her to talk with
S. on the subject to give her an opportunity of dissipating her uncalled for
hatred by expression. — C. made some
bitter remarks on account of our being
in the dining room (i e together), and
I therefore passed the afternoon in S's room
without a fire. — S. had a long talk with M.
before dinner unsatisfactory to S. from the high tone M. took.
Conversation renewed after dinner in my presence
when M. confessed S. had reason to complain,
and a reconciliation was effected. —

A PAGE FROM CHAPMAN'S DIARY

pletely in love with each other.—E. being intensely jealous herself said all she could to cause S. to look from the same point of view, which a little incident (her finding me with my hand in M's[74]) had quite prepared her for. E. betrayed my trust and her own promise. S. said to me that if ever I went to M's room again she will write to Mr Bray, and say that she dislikes her>.—

Wednesday 19 February 1851

My room upset, and the cieling whitewas[h]ed.—
Sat in the dining room to write in the morning where M. joined me, we talked of course of the excited feelings of S. & E. I gave her an account of what had passed and urged her to talk with S. on the subject to give her an opportunity of dissipating her uncalled for hatred by expression.—E. made some bitter remarks on account of our being in the dining room (i e together), and I therefore passed the afternoon in S's room without a fire.— S. had a long talk with M. before dinner unsatisfactory to S. from the high tone M. took. Conversation renewed after dinner in my presence when M. confessed S. had reason to complain, and a reconciliation was effected.—

Thursday 20 February 1851

Crosby & Nichols[75]   87. 0. 2

Susanna made it a condition of our renewed treaties of amity that I should recommence my German lessons, which I grieve to think will pain Elisabeth;—I am sure I have no [other] feeling on the subject than to obtain peace at any cost.—
Last night accompanied S. and the Hardmetts[76] to the Hullah Concert,[77] E. was kind to me before I went and kissed me several times. At parting she kissed me saying "God bless thee thou frail

74. Chapman originally wrote *E's*, then canceled it and wrote *M's* above.
75. Publishers and booksellers at Boston, Massachusetts.
76. Mr. and Mrs. Hardmett came from Ruddington, where Chapman was born. They were in town again at the end of September to see the Exhibition.
77. John Pyke Hullah (1812–84), composer and teacher of "vocal music" at Queen's College and Bedford College. His concerts at St. Martin's Hall, Longacre, were very popular from 1850 to 1860. On this occasion (19 February) Mendelssohn's *Elijah* was sung.

bark!" But alas this morning she is all bitterness and icy coldness, the result I believe of conversation she had last night with M.— who was very severe and unjust to me yesterday.—

Friday 21 February 1851

I

I've often thought I'd better write a book,

But whether prose or rhyme,—'that's $\left\{ \begin{array}{c} \text{the} \\ \text{a} \end{array} \right\}$ question'.

$\left. \begin{array}{l} \text{I have not yet} \\ \text{Not yet to be} \end{array} \right\}$ resolved; for how to hook

A reader on one's line is a suggestion
Vouchsafed by genius only or good luck:
Still being by the author's madness pressed on,
I'll play for reputation by beginning;—
The game's no worse than any other sinning.

Elisabeth makes me very miserable by her continued coldness, she says all love has passed, and that she does not even consider me her friend!—She had a further conversation with M. who came to my room for a Dictionary this afternoon, the result of which was increased bitterness in both their minds. <Had some talk with M. who then accorded me some justice and told me she would help me to be what I wish to be to E. and would sustain me in the right as a "second self" if E   .[78]>

Saturday 22 February 1851

Went with Susanna the children and the Hardmetts to the House of Lords. M. was called for and taken by Miss Martineau[79] to Highbury to stay 2 nights.—

I have just finished the 8th Canto of "Don Juan" which I am glad to read again, as the hatred to war and tyranny and the masterly exposition of their evils makes me respect Byron more than I did before.—

I admire the Stanza of the Poem extremely, and should be

78. The last two words of this deleted passage are illegible.
79. Miss Kate Martineau, daughter of Peter Martineau, lived at 16 Highbury Terrace.

vastly delighted if I found the structure easy. I see Blackwood say[s] Frere wrote it before Byron. I wonder who Frere[80] was.—
I have had a good deal of intercourse with E. today, which has resulted in our becoming friends again, with (I fear) a vain hope of continuing so. Alas it is so much easier in the absence of the offending cause (M), and when she returns and I resume my lessons, I dare say she will feel and express herself as bitterly as ever. —Bless her, I wish she would be a little more charitable and generous. Unhappily she lives so entirely in her affections that if they are disturbed her whole being is in Chaos.

Sunday 23 February 1851

$\overline{\underline{19}}$

Never went out today, though the weather was very beautiful.—
James Orton came with whom I had a long talk about his wretched book he agreed at length to be content to print it without publishing.—[81]
Spent a great part of the day in working at arithmetic with Elisabeth.

Monday 24 February 1851
[No entry.]

[Two leaves containing the entries for *Tuesday 25 February—Monday 3 March 1851* have been cut from the Diary.]

Tuesday 4 March 1851
[No entry.]

Wednesday 5 March 1851
[No entry.]

80. John Hookham Frere (1769–1846), whose *Whistlecraft* (1817–18) was the model for the stanza of *Beppo* and *Don Juan*.
81. *Excelsior; or The Realms of Poesy.* By Alastor. London: Printed for the Author. 1851. This was a volume of miscellaneous "reflections on the Poets," critical essays, and short narratives.

Thursday 6 March 1851

22 B

Friday 7 March 1851

[No entry.]

⧺

Saturday 8 March 1851

⧺

Sunday 9 March 1851

Ernest was 5 years old today.

Monday 10 March 1851

⧺

Tuesday 11 March 1851

[No entry.]

Wednesday 12 March 1851

[No entry.]

Thursday 13 March 1851

Harrison's acceptance for £107. . 13. 8. due.—

Miss Tait took Ernest and Beatrice to Truro today. Beatrice promised me she would return with Mama. I should not like to be without one of them long.—

Went to see the Cyclorama at the Colloseum[82] with Miss Evans.

82. The official spelling was *Colosseum.* The Cyclorama was a sort of annex in Albany Street. At this time it was showing "A Grand Moving Panorama of Lisbon, and the Earthquake in 1775 . . . illustrated by appropriate music on the new Grand Apollonicon." See the *Critic,* 15 February 1851, p. [73]. Cf. Edmund Yates, *Fifty Years of London Life,* New York, 1885, pp. 93–94.

Friday 14 March 1851

[No entry.]

Saturday 15 March 1851

Took Miss M. to the Lyceum to see the first part and Elisabeth the Spectacle.[83]

Sunday 16 March 1851

Posting accounts all day.

Monday 17 March 1851

Paid a visit to M[rs] Torrens, who asked permission to write to me when she is in the Levant.

Tuesday 18 March 1851

Went to the Olympic Theatre with Susanna. The two Pieces were "Charles King & King Charles" and "Sextus the fifth".[84]

Wednesday 19 March 1851

Went to Drury Lane with Miss Evans, Elisabeth being taken by Johnson into the Stalls the same evening. Saw "A morning call"[85] and "Azael or the Prodigal",[86] the views in Memphis were very interesting.

83. Miss Martineau. The Lyceum was almost opposite Chapman's house in the Strand. The first part consisted of *Used Up* and *The Practical Man*; the spectacle was *King Charming, or the Blue Bird of Paradise*, by J. R. Planché, which had been running since Christmas.

84. *Charles King and King Charles* by Holcroft; *Sextus the Fifth, or the Broken Vow*, by Dion Boucicault. See the *Leader*, 22 February 1851, pp. 181–182.

85. One-act comedy by Charles Dance.

86. Freely adapted from Auber's opera, *L'Enfant Prodigue*. See the *Leader*, 22 February 1851, p. 182.

The above was written in mistake here an[d] refers to Thursday night.—Tonight Susanna and Miss Evans went to Hullahs Concert,[87] I and E. staying at home.

Thursday 20 March 1851

See Wednesday

Friday 21 March 1851

Had an interesting evening party, have been very busy all the week.

Saturday 22 March 1851

Took Miss Evans to the Opera which opened tonight, saw Lucia de Lammermoor, and a most absurd ballet.—[88]

Sunday 23 March 1851

Mackay and his Nephew spent the evening with us. M. played.

Monday 24 March 1851

M. departed today, I accompanied her to the railway. She was very sad, and hence made me feel so.—She pressed me for some intimation of the state of my feelings,— <I told her that I felt great affection for her, but that I loved E. and S. also, though each in a different way.> At this avowal she burst into tears. I tried to comfort her, and reminded [her] of the dear friends and pleasant home she was returning to,—but the train whirled her away very very sad.—

Susanna was much excited today and perplexed with her packing, she reproached me, and spoke very bitterly about M.—

87. Among other selections this concert included the first performance in England of the *Credo* from Bach's *Mass in B Minor*.
88. At Her Majesty's Theatre, Donizetti's *Lucia di Lammermoor* and Taglioni's *Ballet, à la Watteau* to music by Nadaud.

Tuesday 25 March 1851

Accompanied Susanna and Miss Bellamy to the train where the old lady was managed extremely well, and went off quite comfortably.

On returning home found the house quite empty and felt a sense of extreme loneliness.—

Wednesday 26 March—Saturday 29 March 1851

[No entry.]

Sunday 30 March 1851

Woodfall came and spent the morning with me.

Visited Mackay in the afternoon—found he was commencing a commentary on the New Testament.

Monday 31 March 1851

[No entry.]

Tuesday 1 April 1851

[No entry.]

Wednesday 2 April 1851

Went with E. to the Lyceum and saw "Cool as a Cucumber."[89]

Thursday 3 April 1851

[No entry.]

89. By William Blanchard Jerrold, played by Charles Mathews.

Friday 4 April 1851

23.

W. Harrison's acceptance due   45.. 17.. 0.
Received from Miss Evans Susanna's letters concerning her
which I sent her to read,[90] the bitter injustice of which caused her
to decline doing the Catalogue,[91]—but she afterwards wrote agreeing to do it conditionally that she should receive for it no remuneration. Received from Susanna a letter which gave me great
pain (about Miss Evans) answered it in tears (and I fear bitterness) and enclosed her Miss Evans' notes.
Had but a small party this evening.

Saturday 5 April 1851

Read Mackay[92] aloud to Elisabeth before breakfast, spent the
morning in looking through old business memoranda, and was
struck with the fact they show me to have manifested much
greater intellectual energy formerly than now.—
Wrote to M. about Susanna's letters and sent her a Catalogue
of such books as I thought might be selected from my publications to constitute the 'Catalogue raisonnée' of liberal philosophical literature. I begged her to be calm and not to let recent circumstances agitate and needlessly pain her. I told her that I feel
even in the midst of the tumult of grief, and in the very moment
of excitement the most intimate essence of my being, or some element of it, <remains> is still no sharer in the enacted scene, but
continues a serene spectator, experiencing only shame and regret
that any part of my nature with which it is allied should be so
moved and agitated by events & affections or the selfish personalities of today and yesterday.
Passed 5 hours of unprofitableness this evening being unable to
do anything after a late dinner.

+

90. This is the packet of letters referred to in Marian Evans's letter to
Chapman 4 April [1851]. See B. C. Williams, *George Eliot*, New York, 1936,
pp. 69–70.
91. *An Analytical Catalogue of Mr. Chapman's Publications,* referred to frequently in the Diary and in letters. It was published the first week in June,
1852; a brief notice of it appears in the *Westminster Review*, 58 (July 1852),
250.
92. R. W. Mackay, *The Progress of the Intellect.*

Sunday 6 April 1851

Elisabeth is suffering considerably but not so much by any means as usual at these times. Read aloud out of Dryden's Fables, and Mackay.

Spent the evening with Mackay who exhibited, despite his philosophy, a little shortness of temper, concerning my proposal to make the coffee in my own way. "Of course," said he, "you consider your own way the best."

He certainly cherishes the idea of writing a Commentary on the New Testament.

As for me I feel and deplore daily how idly and unprofitably I suffer the time to pass.—I fear I shall never use it according to its value.—

Monday 7 April 1851

Mr Bray[93] called, and I accompanied [him] to the "exhibition"[94] where I was admitted as his assistant, he being an exhibitor of Ribbons. It is a wonderful scene, but the foreigners are sadly behindhand.—

Tuesday 8 April 1851

Mr Mackay called and staid some time, to whom I read Miss Evan's letter received this morning concerning the 'Catalogue raisonnée' which I wish to get up. I had thought of prefacing it with an outline sketch of philosophic literature, he suggested instead, some general remarks upon the aspect of religious life in England and an affirmation of the nature of true Protestantism, and then to introduce my books as exponents of it and as indicators of intellectual freedom.—I like his notion much.—Had an interview in Mackay's presence with Mr Hobson[95] a candidate for the situation. He is a Baptist minister and a promising man. <Passed a miserable day with Elisabeth which completely wore me out.—She cannot be happy & I fear never will be.>

93. Charles Bray (1811–84) of Coventry.

94. The Great Exhibition of the Works of Industry of All Nations at the Crystal Palace in Hyde Park was opened officially by Queen Victoria 1 May 1851.

95. Mr. Hobson was the first of a number of men Chapman considered as assistants in his publishing business.

Wednesday 9 April 1851

(O=24)

Wrote to Mr Leighton of the Liverpool Exchange Club, offering him £150 a year if I liked him in other respects. Wrote to Martineau[96] to make some inquiries about Leighton. I feel extremely the need of some such man as he. Rec^d an interesting letter from Miss Martineau about her book.

A Mr Ferrar called this evening about the situation, he seems a promising man, but has never thought on religious topics.—

Bray breakfasted and lunched with me. Elisabeth and, consequently, *I* have been cheerful today.

Thursday 10 April 1851

Wrote to Susanna, and to James Martineau about Leighton. Received yesterday an interesting letter about Charles Knight chiefly, explaining how far it is true that he had advertized to say the publications of Miss M's historical works would cease.[97]

Busy with the advertizing, and ordered £17 worth of Furniture.

Went up to Mackay in the afternoon, who showed me the introduction he has commenced of his Commentary to the New Test. He came and spent the evening with us, and explained some of the features of the distinct Christianities of Paul and Christ.— My throat is more inflamed.

Friday 11 April 1851

Read Mackay in the morning, very busy all day,—received satisfactory letters from Martineau and Hodgson about Leighton, who made his appearance about 5 P.M.—

96. James Martineau (1805–1900), the famous Unitarian, was pastor of the Hope Street chapel in Liverpool. He was also one of the editors of the *Prospective Review*, published by Chapman (1845–55). Mrs. Martineau was a cousin of Mrs. Bray and Sara Hennell.

97. Harriet Martineau's *History of England during the Thirty Years' Peace* was published by Charles Knight, 1846–49. He then commissioned her to write the history of the years 1800–15 in two volumes called *Introduction to the History of the Peace.* But the publication of the Atkinson–Martineau *Letters on the Laws of Man's Nature and Development* in 1851 shocked him, and he sold the whole series to W. S. Orr, a London publisher associated with Chambers of Edinburgh. For her side of the affair see M. W. Chapman, ed., *Harriet Martineau's Autobiography*, Boston, 1877, II, 18–20.

I like him quite as well as I expected. There is much excellency of character clearness and system about him, but perhaps a want of strength. Showed him the a/c books upon which he made some sensible remarks.

Mackay brought me his notes as a preliminary for a Catalogue but would not stay the evening which was a very pleasant one. Mrs Hennell,[98] Miss Skerrett & Thornton Hunt were present.—

Saturday 12 April 1851

Introduced Leighton to the details of the business through Young who explained a good deal to him. He considers it essential to keep the a/cs by double entry for which he gave good reasons. On the whole I think he is as good a man as I can hope to obtain, but wanting in force of character. He mesmerizes his wife's sister with whom he seems to sustain a peculiarly affectionate relation.

Wrote a long letter to M. about the Catalogue (which I copied by machine) giving her as much suggestion and direction as I could.

I feel very anxious for an efficient assistant on many accounts. I am weary and unable to get through the business which now necessarily devolves upon me. I am going on in a painful state of uncertainty as to the actual value and profit of the business, and know not whether I am gaining or losing because I cannot get a balance sheet; and I feel that many very important business details are neglected. My time is all swallowed by business without the reward of feeling that I manage it with complete efficiency; and my own culture, especially the moral side (for which *time* is absolutely requisite) is mournfully neglected. "I am not now that which I have been and the glow which was in [my] spirits is fluttering faint and low."[99]

98. Elizabeth Rebecca (Rufa) Brabant Hennell, daughter of Dr. R. H. Brabant and widow of Charles C. Hennell.

99. Byron, *Childe Harold's Pilgrimage*, Canto IV, Stanza 185:

> The torch shall be extinguish'd which hath lit
> My midnight lamp—and what is writ, is writ;
> Would it were worthier! but I am not now
> That which I have been—and my visions flit
> Less palpably before me—and the glow
> Which in my spirit dwelt is fluttering, faint, and low.

Sunday 13 April 1851

5.45   25

Leighton left me this morning by rail to consult his friends at Chorley, my doubts whether he is strong enough for the place, gather strength. Got up with a headache which continued until refreshed by a long sleep in the afternoon.—

Went with E. to call upon M[rs] Macdanniel[99a] and M[rs] Hennell, the latter seemed concerned at my not looking well.—Read Fowler on Vegetable Diet,[100] which I long to practice.

Prof. Newman came and spent the evening with me. Conversed with him about my catalogue scheme which he approved, but doubted if it could be sold. He told me all about the absurd doings at the Ladies College.—[101]

Monday 14 April 1851

26.

6.0. Wrote to Susanna, and to James Martineau about printing his essays,[102]—the Catalogue &c.—Wrote to Leighton proposing that he should come 2 months on trial, for I do not like making a permanent arrangement and I do not feel quite sure he is the right man exactly,—he would be if he had more strength of character. Rec[d] a note from Miss Evans applauding Mackays 'suggestions'

99a. James M'Daniell was a newsvender of 1 Richmond Place, Park Road, Islington.

100. Orson Squire Fowler, *Physiology, Animal and Mental: Applied to the Preservation and Restoration of Health of Body, and Power of Mind*, New York, Fowler and Wells, 26th ed. [cp. 1847]. Chapter II (pp. 51–149) advocates a vegetable diet.

101. F. W. Newman had resigned his professorship at Bedford College 19 March 1851, in protest at the dismissal of the Rev. Thomas Wilson, whose theological opinions were disapproved by some members of the Council. On 2 April he agreed to retain his post till midsummer. A paragraph in the *Leader*, 5 April 1851, p. 321, said to have been inspired by Newman, whose "dignified conduct" in the Wilson affair it commended, stirred up the controversy anew; and in May he resigned both his professorship and his place in the Council. See M. J. Tuke, *A History of Bedford College for Women, 1849–1937*, London, 1939, pp. 69–76.

102. James Martineau, *Miscellanies: A Selection of Essays*, London, J. Chapman, 1852.

for the Catalogue and enclosing specimen critiques from her on Newman's books.

Went to Hampstead in the evening to call on Mrs Torrens, got back at 11.30. Beaty's canary (the male bird) was drowned today.

Tuesday 15 April 1851

Rec^d letter from Leighton in which he expresses his inclination to join me, and says that "the private relations most vital and sacred to me have been harmonized to this issue."

Went with Elisabeth to execute various commissions in the City, in the afternoon very busy at home. Received a letter from Woodfall rather upbraiding me about my calls upon him for help. Gave him a statement of my financial condition, and prospects for the coming month.

I HAVE NOT EATEN MEAT THIS LAST 2 DAYS, but do not feel well.

Wednesday 16 April 1851

6.20   12.0

Received a letter from Mr Lombe[103] of Florence proposing to bear the expense of a reprint of Parker or Hennell an abridgement of Strauss,[104] and in fact to assist me generally in such works, wishes me to get an essay written on "the incompatability of Christian Ethics with modern civilization," for which he will pay £50. Offers to assist in the establishment of a Quarterly that shall go far enough for him. He now pays £200 a year towards the Westminster.

Went with Elisabeth to Hullah's monthly Concert. Heard the "Passion" of Haydn, the "Sanctus" &c of Gounod, and Mendelsohn's "Praise Jehovah". I never enjoyed a Concert so much. I think my abstinence from meat the last 3 days had something to do with it.—

103. Edward Lombe (1800?–52). See pp. 54–55.

104. Theodore Parker, *Discourse of Matters Pertaining to Religion*, 1842, originally lectures delivered in Boston, 1841–42 by the American Unitarian; Charles C. Hennell, *Inquiry Concerning the Origin of Christianity*, 1838; David F. Strauss, *Life of Jesus*, translated from the fourth edition [by Marian Evans], 1846.

Thursday 17 April 1851

6.15

Leighton agrees to come 2 months on trial.

G. Woodfall & Son (result divided)	= 200. 0. 0.
Venables Wilson & C⁰ [105]	80. . 19. 6.

M[r] Eames of Nottingham called and detained me more than 2 hours. Visited M[rs] Hennell and consulted on the subject of M[r] Lombe's letter. She is quite willing that I should print a cheap edition of Hennell's "Inquiry", and thinks of reprinting the "Theism".[106] She concurs with me in thinking that an abridgement of Strauss would be better than a cheap reprint of the entire work, and that M. would do it better than anyone else. Thinks M[r] Grote[107] would be the best person to write an Essay as wished by M[r] Lombe on "The Incompatibility of Xtian ethics with the present state of Civilization."

Friday 18 April 1851

5.45.   27. 28.

Writing business letters until breakfast, and employed exclusively at business all day. Rec[d] a letter from M. in answer to my inquiry in which she expresses her willingness to abridge Strauss for £100.;—she is beginning to like the Catalogue work, and is now doing Miss Martineau's letters.—[108]

Elisabeth left the breakfast table this morning in tears, <caused by the sight of M's letter,>—we had without any reason a most painful and sorrowing morning, with some reaction in the afternoon.—

Rec[d] a letter from Greg[109] in which he says apropos of my re-

105. Wholesale stationers.
106. C. C. Hennell, op. cit., and Christian Theism, 1839. The latter was reprinted as number 5 in Chapman's Library for the People.
107. George Grote (1794–1871), reformer and historian, one of the founders of University College, London, where he endowed a professorship never to be held by any minister of religion.
108. H. G. Atkinson and H. Martineau, Letters on the Laws of Man's Nature and Development, 1851.
109. William Rathbone Greg (1809–81).

view scheme that Sir J. K. Shuttleworth[110] will help me if I make it moderately liberal and conventional, Foster[111] & Heywood[112] will if I make it thoroughly unshackled and free.

Saturday 19 April 1851

"He who has long known a deep and bitter Grief, need no longer strive after Happiness, but only after Peace, after inward composure and Forgetfulness; else he heaps up to himself Sorrow on Sorrow; and even if he should attain to what seems the Crown of Happiness, yet the jewel is wanting thereto, the ornamental Stone—in the Cross! Therefore lifelong Meekness must be the Portion of him whose Heart is broken! Also reverential Resignation to Him who has ordained it for him. In Piety alone is constant Satisfaction to be found."

Schefer[113]

Received a letter from Martineau approving in general terms my Catalogue scheme, a letter from his Sister[114] about her book, Comte, and C. Knight, a letter from Dr Hodgson strong in commendation of Leighton.

Had a long walk with Nixon in the Parks, we arranged that he should put a little money in my business, say £100 to start with.

110. James Phillips Kay-Shuttleworth (1804–77), founder of popular education in England, was interested in many social questions.

111. William Edward Forster (1818–86), woolen manufacturer at Bradford, married a daughter of Dr. Thomas Arnold. He wrote a number of reform articles for the *Westminster Review*, e.g., the one on "American Slavery," 59 (January 1853), 125–167. George Eliot describes him [1 February 1853] as "a very earnest, independent thinker, and worth a gross of literary hacks who have the 'trick' of writing." (J. W. Cross, *George Eliot's Life*, Edinburgh and London, 1885, I, 303.)

112. James Heywood (1810–97), reformer, was M.P. 1847–57. Debarred as a Unitarian from taking his degree at Cambridge, he worked vigorously for the abolition of religious tests. He was also interested in woman suffrage and was one of the earliest supporters of Girton College. See Barbara Stephen, *Emily Davies and Girton College*, London, 1927, p. 366.

113. Leopold Schefer, *The Artist's Married Life; Being That of Albert Dürer*, translated from the German by Mrs. J. R. Stodart, London, John Chapman, 1851. The quotation is from the penultimate chapter, "How Albert Bids Farewell to his Wife." In the American reprint, Boston, James Monroe and Co., it is found on pp. 162–163.

114. Harriet Martineau was considering an abridged translation of Auguste Comte's *Cours de philosophie positive*, 1830–42.

Mackay came and spent an hour with me, and then Cousin Marri-anne[115] came, reports herself not very well.—

Wrote long letters to Susanna <and Miss Evans, the latter was the consequent end with Elisabeth and the total loss of my evening so far as regards either peace or profit.> Had an animated conversation on Slavery in the Drawing Room, with Mr Hayward,[116] Mr Weeks, Mr Flaxon, and Mr Nixon.—

Sunday 20 April 1851

5.45   10.10

Passed the morning in reading "Albert Durer's Married Life" by Schefer, which delights me extremely, and exercises upon me a holy elevating influence.—

Took Anna Tilley[117] in a cab (it rained) to see the Crystal Palace. Felt weak and easily fatigued. Have pain in the kidneys, and rheumatic pains in the left hand and foot and in the right ear. Taking the mineral acids, and commenced to eat meat again at supper.—

Spent the afternoon and evening in writing a long letter to Mr Lombe, a good impression of which I got in the copy book.— Alarmed at Dinner by the servants room having taken fire, through their carelessness with a pot of brimstone. We succeeded in putting it out, but it was a very narrow escape.—

Monday 21 April 1851

5.30

William Sallis' Bill at 6 mo^s due =   27..2. 0

Rec^d from Miss E. a letter addressed to Susanna it was written in an able and excellent manner, and will I hope result in good. I forwarded it as she requested, as she did not know the address.

Susanna in her last letter says she thinks there is something in the Church system to be desired, that the most enlightened con-

115. Marianne Chapman.
116. The Haywards boarded at Chapman's until 13 June 1851.
117. Anna Tilley, a sister of Elisabeth, was at school in Greenwich, but occasionally visited at Chapman's.

sciences of the few should be the rule of the many. I wrote to say that I agreed with her and were it possible, I should be glad to contribute to such a result, but that I found so far as regards my

Tuesday 22 April 1851

6.0   12.0

own experience I need solitude chiefly. I find that *time* is as essential for me in the promotion of moral as intellectual culture. Alas I get little time for either at present. It is the order of nature that women should lean on men, but men have none to lean upon, and hence the necessity preeminently in them of SELF-culture and by a closer relation to nature so nourish and strengthen themselves by striking deep and extended roots in the spirit-world that they may stand strong alone. Few women understand or sympathize with this need, but rather oppose its fulfilment, and thus the spiritual nature of most men withers now.—

Wednesday 23 April 1851

6.0   10.0

Walter is 4 years old.[118]
Went to the Covent Garden Opera with Spencer last night to see Mario and Grisi in the "Hugenots" had good seats and were much gratified, and yet I am little moved by the splendid music.
Rec[d] a letter from Susanna giving a better account of Beatrice whom she wants to leave in Cornwall instead of Ernest. I feel inclined to think they had both better come home. <An interesting letter from Miss E. who is I am sorry to say still suffering.—>
Called on M[rs] Jackson[119] at Little Holland House, Kensington. She was dressed in black velvet, with exquisitely wrought satin slippers. She is a most intellectual beautiful and charming person. And her daughter is like a beautiful saint.

118. Mrs. Chapman's relatives the Brewitts had a deaf-and-dumb boy about this age, who sometimes came to London with them. See GE to the Brays, Monday [14 June 1852].
119. Mrs. Jackson, eldest sister of Mrs. Henry Thoby Prinsep of Little Holland House. Watts's drawings of her and her eldest daughter Adeline were in the Royal Academy Exhibition in 1850. See M. S. Watts, *George Frederic Watts*, 3 vols., New York [1919], I, 129–130.

Thursday 24 April 1851

5.45.   10.0

Received a long letter from Miss Martineau giving an interesting account of Mr Lombe who it appears is a gentleman of landed property in Norfolk.

Sent Miss Evans' letter last received to Susanna *at her request.*

Went to Greenwich with Elisabeth to take Anna to school, the weather was very beautiful and inspiriting.

Was much disappointed on my return to find a letter from Leighton virtually giving [up] the situation, for [one] he thinks more promising.—

Wrote to ask Susanna to bring both Bety and Ernest back with her.

Friday 25 April 1851

29. 30.   12.0

Had pleasant and large party. Johnson was annoyed because he did not get into conversation with Newman, the fault was mine in omitting to bring them together.

Mrs Torrens, her daughters, and Miss Barlund came to say goodbye, they leave for Paris on Sunday morning. I told her I had been to see Mrs Jackson who is going to Brussells in a few days. Her comments upon her, and her manner of speaking surprised me.—She proposes to return from Paris to London for a short time.

Saturday 26 April 1851

6.30   10.0

Wrote to my brother Thomas whom I have long neglected, and to Susanna whose letters to me are very unsatisfactory. Her remarks about Miss Evans are very unjust. Went with Mackay to call upon Mrs Jackson, had a gracious reception and were introduced to a Mr Watts[120] an artist.

I was astonished to learn from Mrs Jackson that she knows no ladies of her own rank, except her sisters who hold liberal opinions.

120. George Frederick Watts (1817–1904) lived with Mr. and Mrs. Henry Thoby Prinsep at Little Holland House, 1850–75.

The retrospect of each day I spend now makes me feel very hopeless. I accomplish so very little, and so far as any improvement of my moral and spiritual culture I seem to accomplish less.

Elisabeth gives me great concern from her continued weakness, —she is so quickly fatigued that her general health must be much depreciated.

Leighton has relinquished his engagement with me for a better as he conceives, hence I have advertized again,—in the "Athenæum"[121] and have all my work to do over again.

31–32.
Sunday 27 April 1851

5.30   11.0

Rewrote a Stanza.—walked with E in Hyde Park;—in the afternoon walked in Regents Park &c. with Spencer, then had tea with Mackay, we then all adjourned to a Miss Miller's house where we met Dr Brabant, Mrs Hennell, and a Miss James,—remarkable for her heresies.—

Was much interested in listening to Spencers conversation with Mrs Hennell, as I see in him in all his views, his zeal, his idealism and confidence that there is no absolute evil &c the mirror of what I was in 1843–4 & 5. Mrs Hennell quoted to me subsequently from Göthe a favorite passage of her husbands: "I slept and dreamed that life was beauty, I woke and found that life was DUTY."[122]

Monday 28 April 1851

7.0   11.0.

Bought a season ticket for the Exhibition. <I had a short simple note from M. this morning, which E. read and then flew into a great passion, and begged me not to speak to her. We separated all morning, she came to me after lunch, expressed her regret, and observed that I was so cruelly calm. I wrote a short proper note to

121. The advertisement appears in the *Athenæum*, 26 April, p. 441. The applicant was to be of superior intelligence and education, and have a sound judgment and a thorough knowledge of bookkeeping. Applications were to be addressed to X.Y.Z., care of Messrs. Woodfall & Son.

122. This is not from Goethe, but from a poem by Ellen Sturgis Hooper (1816–41), "Beauty and Duty."

M. which she did not see, in answer to her question I said I had written which caused another manifestation of excitement, from which however she soon recovered. Went with her to see her mother and aunt in the evening who arrived in Town yesterday. Her mother has £120[?] to depend upon!—>

Tuesday 29 April 1851

My cousin Mr Chapman[123] brought the 2 Parsees this morning, who are very intelligent fine men, they speak English admirably. They bought Mackay's book, and appointed to come and spend an evening to talk over books generally.—

Mackay came and staid a long time, also E's mother and Aunts so that I get nothing done.—

Sent Susanna my last letter before her return, enclosing one from Miss Evans for her, and hope they will become better friends now.—

Wednesday 30 April 1851

[No entry.]

Thursday 1 May 1851

The "Exhibition" opened this day,—it was an imposing spectacle, had a very good view of the procession.—Elisabeth very weak and poorly.—

Mr Hickson[124] called to ask if I am still disposed to purchase the

123. John Chapman (1801–54), son of a clockmaker in Loughborough, showed his mechanical genius in perfecting lace-making machinery and, according to *The Dictionary of National Biography*, "invented all the valuable improvements which have made the modern 'Hansom cab,'" on which he was granted a patent in 1836. He went to India in 1845 to promote the Great Indian Peninsular Railway, and on his return displayed a lively sympathy for the colonies. See Diary, 9 July 1851 and *Westminster Review*, 62 (October 1854), 473.

124. William Edward Hickson (1803–70) edited the *Westminster Review* 1840–51. Waterlow and Sons printed it from 1847 to 1851 (vols. 46–56). Chapman wanted the work to go to Woodfall, who financed many of the books Chapman published.

"Westminster Review". He asks £350 for it, I expressed my willingness to buy it but asked him to let the price be £300. He did not seem to object, the difficulty of closing lay in the fact that the present printer a relation of his desires to continue the printing. He cleared up in a satisfactory [way] my doubts in reference to his help from Mr Lombe, which it appears was accorded for special articles on special subjects. He told me that Mr Lombe's income is about £14000 a year. He is about 48 years old, and was not on speaking terms with his father for many years. He has not been in England for 25 years.—

Friday 2 May 1851

|| 33 || + E

My brother William was born 1819.

Had a long talk with Mr Kimber[125] about making a news room for the Americans, which he thinks would be a very desirable speculation.

Mr Dyer,[126] author of a Life of Calvin, called upon me in answer to my advertisement for a manager, but I do not think he would suit me.—

Susanna and Beatrice returned both looking better.

A letter from Nisbet, author of the "Siege of Damascus" stating he wants employment.—

A letter from Dr Hodgson urging me strongly to take Mr Hogg.—

Commenced (with a struggle) to sleep in Susanna's room.

Saturday 3 May 1851

Passed a profitless day of indecision as to whether I should take Mr Hogg as an assistant—Dr Hodgson recommends him so strongly—, and whether I should incur half the risk with Mr Hardie of printing a volume of Parkers Essays.[127]

125. An American boarder.

126. Thomas Henry Dyer published *The Life of John Calvin* in 1850.

127. This may mean Theodore Parker's *Discourse on Religious Matters*, 1852, or *Critical and Miscellaneous Writings*, 1853, both of which Chapman published.

My poor Elisabeth has been very sad and distant all day, she has scarcely spoken to me,—and went to Islington in the evening. I was delighted to hear an American visitor, Mr Kimber, speak very highly of her last night, and in a truly good and kind spirit. Her sadness imparts itself to me;—and yet I fear I am not as charitable forbearing and sympathizing with her as I ought to be.— Alas my love for her is no longer so dazzling as it once was, hence I discern her faults more (perhaps *too*) plainly.—I would that I could keep my own defects and sins more constantly in mind, so that I might be more intent on <my own> self improvement, and feel enabled to love her with that perfectness which will not permit her deficiencies to be any impediment to the full outflowing of my affection. She has a nature which eminently calls for this. But who has not when fully known?

I am ashamed of my own life and deeds and no one can tell but myself the many and deep reasons why I should feel thus. And yet alas, though I repine and lament, I do not feel that I become less selfish, purer or more earnest in my strivings after a nobler existence! God help me!

Sunday 4 May 1851

My Mother would have been 62 years old.—

Finished reading "Norica"[128] which I like much it is both instructive and elevating, and tends to inspire a true love of Art.

Had a walk with Susanna and Beatrice in Hyde Park,—took Elisabeth to Mrs Macdaniel's in the evening and then visited Mrs Hennell where I met Dr Brabant.

Monday 5 May 1851

Received a letter from Hickson making it almost certain I shall become proprietor of the "Westminster".

Received a cool letter from Miss Evans about the Catalogue, regret to learn she has been ill.

Relieved in regard to cash by remittances from America.

128. *Norica: Tales of Nurenberg*, translated from the German of [Ernst] August Hagen, London, J. Chapman, 1851. The original edition was published in 1829.

Tuesday 6 May 1851

Went to the Opera with Spencer. Saw "Robert the Devil"[129] in which Herr Formes acted ably.—

Wednesday 7 May 1851

Went to the Exhibition.—
Visited Mr Carter in the evening.

Thursday 8 May 1851

Accompanied some friends to the Waterloo Station where I met Mackay who expressed his willingness to help me in the matter of the Westminster Review. Saw Hickson and gave him the 'offer' in form; he promised to insert Miss Evans' article on Greg and Hennell[130] wrote to tell her so.—
Went with Greely[131] to the Cooperative Store in the evening, saw Maurice.—[132]

Friday 9 May 1851

Engaged in Business all day.
Mr Hogg came from Liverpool this evening, as my chief assistant. I hope now I shall get some relief. Had a long walk with him to Camden Town, Highbury & Islington.—

Saturday 10 May 1851
[No entry.]

129. Meyerbeer's *Roberto il Diavolo*, at Covent Garden.
130. The article was supplanted, however, by James Martineau's. It was finally published in the *Leader*, 20 September 1851, pp. 897–899. See Diary, 20 May and 2 July 1851. For Miss Evans's reply to Chapman see B. C. Williams, *George Eliot*, New York, 1936, pp. 71–72.
131. Horace Greeley (1811–72), editor of the New York *Tribune*, was boarding at Chapman's.
132. John Frederick Denison Maurice (1805–72) was at this time Professor of Divinity at King's College, London. He was interested in coöperatives and trade associations.

Sunday 11 May 1851

Took Elisabeth and Beatrice to the Zoological Gardens, where we staid until 3 o'clock, and came home quite exhausted. Unable to do anything during the evening.—
Mʳ Farrant came from Torquay.

Monday 12 May 1851

Took Elisabeth to the "Exhibition" and came home very tired. Were much delighted with Raffaelle Monti's Eve which is to me the most enchanting work of Art I ever witnessed.—
Mʳ Syme[133] came from Sunderland as a candidate for the situation of manager in my business,—he is a tall, striking and powerful man. Had a long conversation with him, and determined to engage him.—

Tuesday 13 May 1851

Went to the Exhibition with Mʳ Farrant, completely worn out, and came home with an intense headache,—found Mʳ Bray and Mʳˢ Hennell waiting for me. Lay on the Sofa all the evening unable to do anything.

Wednesday 14 May 1851

Had a long talk with Mʳ Syme, told him that I had determined to dismiss Mʳ Radley, to engage him to take his place in the front shop, and to retain Mʳ Hogg as Bookkeeper.—I shall then have three Scotchmen in my business, each at the head of a separate department! Gave Mʳ Syme several of my publications to write analyses of them.—
Mʳ Bray and Mʳˢ Hennell came, they have settled that Mʳˢ H. as-

133. Ebenezer Syme (1826–60), a former Unitarian minister, was a brother of the Reverend Alexander Syme of Nottingham. In 1853 he went to Australia, settling at Melbourne. The best account of him is found in Philip Mennell, *The Dictionary of Australasian Biography*, London, 1892, pp. 453–454. See also J. McCabe, *Life and Letters of G. J. Holyoake*, 2 vols., London, 1908, I, 224.

sumes the responsibility of the Child's School, with Mrs Bugden.—
Susanna will take Beatrice there as a pupil tomorrow.[134] Mackay
and young Constable called, they are going to Scotland.—

Thursday 15 May 1851

Told Elisabeth of Mr Bray's urgent invitation of me to Coventry, which I could not refuse without great difficulty, and that I
had promised almost to go. <She immediately became haughty
and indignant and left the room.> Susanna took my little pet to a
'boarding school' for the first time. Glad that the principal, M^rs
Bugden, pleases Susanna so much.—

Friday 16 May 1851

<Elisabeth still in the same state of sullen anger.>

Saturday 17 May 1851

Elisabeth's salutation of me this morning was in a changed and
subdued spirit, which promised some harmony. Alas, Susanna
presumed it attributable to efforts on my part, and that I petted
her just in proportion to her perversity, which excited her sense
of injustice, and jealousy;—hence my proposal to take E. to the
Exhibition annoyed S., but the feeling soon passed away. Before
going E. reproached me with several matters unjustly and which
in truth only evidenced her want of affectionate trust,—hence our
morning was embittered.—The objects of the Exhibition united
our interests, and thus reconciled us, whence we returned with
fatigue and headache.—

Went according to promise to see Beatrice, and was very sorry
to find myself too late to see her awake,—I looked upon her sleeping sweetly. Oh how much of my soul is concentrated in her!
And how intensely (alas too intensely) she returns my love! After

134. Mrs. Bugden's school was advertised in the *Leader*, 17 May 1851, p.
473: "Infant Education. An Educational Home near the Regent's-park for
children from Three to Seven years of age. Conducted on liberal principles.
Terms, £35 per annum—no extras. For particulars apply to John Chapman,
publisher, 142, Strand."

saying a little prayer, she asked Mrs Hennell if she thought I
should come tonight, she answered that she feared I was too busy
and could not; then two little tears came in silence, and in 10
minutes she fell asleep. God Bless her! Promised Mrs H. that I
would visit her tomorrow but found a note from Mr Parkes on
my return appointing me to meet him in the morning! I am very
sorry.

Sunday 18 May 1851

Susanna went and accompanied Beatrice in the Park, the little
pet was disappointed, bless her, at not seeing me.—
I spent the morning with Mr J. Parkes[135] discussing matters
connected with the "Westminster". He gave me a sketch of its
history, but seemed little inclined to accord any substantial aid.
He proposed that I should get up a list of £10 subscribers,—and
promised that when I supply him with the necessary papers to
make a prompt effort.—
I do not feel well, and half proposed to Susanna that I should
sleep on the spring Sofa in my room, my kidneys being inflamed
again, but the proposition pains her. The present plan, which
makes it uncertain when I can go to sleep in consequence of the
noise, and which exposes me to cold by sleeping in one room and
dressing in another, is attended with endless irregularity, discomfort, *and loss of time.*

Monday 19 May 1851

Had a long walk with Susanna in the City and to Islington. I
proposed to buy an Iron Safe for the business which was met by a
torrent of invective about my "reckless extravagance". She was
silenced by my remark that I thought she had better assume the
management of the business in order to ensure having matters ordered conformably to her views.—<I am [two words illegible]
sided.—Visited Mackay tonight.>

135. Joseph Parkes (1796–1865), solicitor and politician. He organized the
group of men who supplied funds to print Marian Evans's translation of
Strauss's *Das Leben Jesu* in 1846. His daughter Bessie Rayner Parkes Belloc
became acquainted with Miss Evans in 1850. See J. K. Buckley, *Joseph Parkes
of Birmingham,* London [1926] and *Contemporary Review,* 65 (1894), 208.

Tuesday 20 May 1851

On my way to Sir James Clarkes[136] to meet G. Combe[137] who has not reached Town I paid D[r] Gibson[138] a visit who examined my chest carefully, and found it flexible and sound.—He confirmed my practice of using nitrate of silver to my throat, and recommended me to take some Sulphate of Quinine.—

Called on Thornton Hunt who told me it has been a question whether it would not be better to suppress the religious side of the Leader, in consequence of the Chief Shareholder,—Larkin,[139] being a clergyman. He agreed with me to insert Miss E.['s] article on Greg and Hennell in the Leader.[140]

Wednesday 21 May 1851

Wrote to J. S. Mill, to ask him to accord me an interview,—I feel that my ideas are now assuming a definite shape in regard to the principles and arrangements of the Westminster.

I have determined to have about 11 sheets allotted to Articles for which the Editor shall be responsible, 5 where writers of diverse opinions may express themselves, and 4 for historical sketches of American and Continental Literature.

I should be glad to write an Article of Sociology for the first Number.—

My throat grows worse, it is now attended with a slight cough.

136. James Clark (1788–1870), court physician, had been unpopular for a time because of his connection with the case of Lady Flora Hastings in 1839. Combe often visited him at 22 Brook Street.

137. George Combe (1788–1858), son of an Edinburgh brewer, became a disciple of Spurzheim, whose theories of phrenology he promulgated and defended to the end of his life. He was a friend of Charles Bray, who had been convinced of the value of phrenology by reading Combe's book.

138. John Rowland Gibson at 115 Holborn Hill.

139. Edmund R. Larken, a Christian Socialist of the Maurice and Kingsley stamp, married a daughter of Lord Monson, who gave him the living at Burton-by-Lincoln. During April and May 1851 he was embroiled in a heated interchange of letters in the Leader, defending the clergy against charges of bigotry.

140. It appeared 20 September 1851, pp. 897–899.

Thursday 22 May 1851

Went to the Exhibition with Elisabeth, <met Miss Ebury[?] which gave occasion to some foolish remarks on the part of Elisabeth.>
I seem never to get any time for reading now.—

Friday 23 May 1851

George Combe came at 12 and stayed until 2,—with whom I had a long conversation respecting general principles, my intended plans in regard to the Westminster, Mr Lombe &c.—There was no point in which our opinions did not seem nearly if not quite coincident. He paid me the compliment of saying that he was very glad to learn that I intended to be the chief editor of the review myself. He admired my plan of allotting say 5 sheets to writers of diverse opinion (which Newman disapproves), and quite concurred with me in regarding Mr Lombe's proposed method of reform, or 'organic change' as impracticable and the announcement of it unwise.—He says he has received £125 from Mr Lombe in aid of his educational agitation in Scotland, and a request to be informed when more is needed.

Newman came at 3 and stayed until 5. Spent most of the time in discussing the principles by which the Review are to be conducted.

My throat is worse.—

Saturday 24 May 1851

Have been much interested and instructed by the perusal of 3 articles in the last Edinburg review, respectively on Victor Cousin, on Spain, and on our Colonies.—[141]

Rec^d a note from John S. Mill, expressing his willingness to *correspond* with me, about the "Westminster". Mrs Hennell says that the lady he has just married was a widow, her husband having been dead a year and a half, that during the life of her former

141. *Edinburgh Review*, 93 (April 1851), 429–498; the titles are "Cousin," "Spain, and Spanish Politics," and "Shall we retain our Colonies?"

husband a 'violent friendship' arose between her and him which caused him to think it desirable to go to the Continent whither she, it is said, followed him; and now (in consequence of these circumstances she presumes) Mrs Thornton Hunt declines to visit M^r and Mrs Mill.[142]

Went with Elisabeth to see Miss Wallace's[143] glassworks, which are absurdly overestimated. We had a long roundabout walk, going through Russell Square to Fitzroy Square! In my presence she asked Mrs Hill & Miss Wallace in something like tears whether they could recommend her a situation, and canvassed the subject of being employed by them in their ornamental glasswork! I was very angry. I took her in a cab with me to fetch Beatrice from Mrs Bugdens, the dear little pet was a charming contrast to E. of smiles and joy. She was in raptures at seeing me, and kissed E. most affectionately. $[144]

Sunday 25 May 1851

Wrote a long letter to Mr Lombe explanatory of my views about the Westminster, and stating that whatever relation I may sustain towards him it must be one of perfect independence.

Went to the Johnsons to call on Freiligrath and dined with them, returned early.—

Was gratified to find that Johnson entirely concurred in and admired my plans for the Review emphatically. I think so highly of his judgment that I am glad to have it on my side. On my return I found Mr Hogg, Mrs Hennell and Miss Susan Hughes,[145] read my letter to Mr Lombe to the 2 latter, Miss H. will help me somewhat with money I trust. My little pet is enjoying her visit home, she is very beautiful and charming in mind and body.—

142. John Stuart Mill (1806–73), the Utilitarian philosopher, had married Harriet Hardy Taylor, widow of John Taylor, at Weymouth, 21 April 1851.

143. Miss Eliza Wallace held a patent for decoration in glass, which in July 1851 she threw open to a Ladies' Guild organized as "an association of educated women . . . for remunerative employment." Miss Wallace was president, and Mrs. Hill vice-president; the headquarters were at 4 Russell Place, Fitzroy Square. See the *Leader*, 12 July 1851, p. 663.

144. This symbol refers to Susanna. Cf. Diary, 21 June, 19 July, and 13 September 1851.

145. Miss Susan Hughes was Mrs. R. H. Brabant's sister. See p. 24. Marian Evans wrote Sara Hennell, Monday [13 October 1851], that Miss Hughes was going to subscribe £20 to the *Westminster Review*.

Monday 26 May 1851

Accompanied Susanna to Mr Pilcher[146] with Beatrice to consult him about her throat and nostrils which are inflamed and swollen internally. She bore his examination beautifully; Mr Pilcher seemed to think she would certainly outgrow the malady which coincides with Dr Todds[147] opinion. I feel painfully responsible for her delicate health. No effort shall be wanting on my part to give her all the advantages of becoming stronger that I can command. Mama took her from Mr Pilcher to School;—I feel it a great priviledge to be able to put her under the superintendence of Mrs Hennell.—

Tuesday 27 May 1851

Had toothache several hours last night and could not sleep. Rose early in spite of taking 2 doses of laudanum. After dressing became faint, but soon recovered by aid of coffee (which was then just ready) and cogniac. There is dreadful insubordination among the servants just now,—disobeying Elisabeth especially. I gave Edward notice to leave (yesterday) in consequence.—

I reached Coventry tonight at 6 o'clock found at Rosehill Mrs Bray, Miss Evans and Mrs Thornton Hunt. Mr Bray and Miss Hennell came in later from Leamington, where he had been lecturing to young ladies!

<Found Miss Evans shy calm and affectionate[148]>

Wednesday 28 May 1851

Walked with M. before breakfast, and afterwards went with all the party to Allesly a village about 5 miles from Coventry in order to see Mr Bray's sister Mrs Pears,[149] but she was gone to London. Returned very tired.

146. George Pilcher, surgeon, 7 Great George Street, was a specialist in diseases of the nose and ear.

147. Robert Bentley Todd (1809-60).

148. Two concluding words, underlined and then deleted, are illegible.

149. Mrs. Pears was the wife of Abijah Hill Pears, Mayor of Coventry in 1842-43. When Miss Evans came to Coventry in 1841 she lived next door to Mrs. Pears and through her met the Brays.

In the evening we all went to a concert of amateur performers, most of the songs were sung in a very mediocre way but a few of the singers acquitted themselves well, I and Miss E. came out when it was half over and returned home when I began my Prospectus for the "Westminster".

Thursday 29 May 1851

E. +

Walked with M. before breakfast, told her the exact condition of things in regard to E. whom on every account I wish to stay at the Strand. She was much grieved and expressed herself prepared to atone in any way she could for the pain she has caused, and put herself in my hands prepared to accept any arrangement I may make either for her return to the Strand or to any house in London I may think suitable in October.—She agreed to write the article on foreign literature for each number of the Westminster which I am very glad of. Wrote the greater part of the Prospectus today, and then gave it to M. to finish.

Friday 30 May 1851

Received a kind note from Froude[150] congratulating me on the possession of the Westminster, and expressing his readiness to contribute to it either with or without payment. Accompanied M. to Leamington, and while she visited her sister[151] I went to the Dales,[152] Susanna['s] cousins; went to Kenilworth Castle on our way back, was somewhat disappointed with the ruin, but the effect from the Leamington side is very striking. As we rested on the grass, I remarked on the wonderful and mysterious embodiment of all the elements characteristics and beauties of nature which man and woman jointly present. I dwelt also on the incomprehensible mystery and witchery of beauty. My words jarred upon her and put an end to her enjoyment. Was it from a consciousness of her own want of beauty? She wept bitterly.

150. James Anthony Froude (1818–94), the historian, became a regular contributor.
151. Marian Evans's half-sister, Frances Lucy Evans, was the wife of Henry Houghton.
152. James Dale was a tailor and draper on the South Parade.

Saturday 31 May 1851

Wrote several business letters, and was much relieved this morning by a letter from Massie[153] of Manchester, agreeing to continue his loan with me for another year of his £200.

I find it a matter of great difficulty to determine what can be done in regard to M's return to Town. Both Susanna and Elisabeth oppose her return to the Strand, and I suspect they would be equally opposed to her residence elsewhere in London, and yet as an active cooperator with me in Editing the Westminster Review she must be in London much of her time. Oh how deeply I regret that any cause for distrust should ever have been given. I must and will recover the confidence I once possessed. I will act consistently with my own fairer thought and thus raise my own self respect and diffuse peace.—

[The next four and one-half lines have been so heavily deleted that only a few words are legible.]

For my own part I do not feel in raptures with any woman now, and my passionate moods are exceptional and transient and are rather *permitted* as a means of according the strongest evidence of *affection* than storms wh: I cannot controul. The benificent affection, and pleasure of social intercourse, which I experience, seems to be equally distributed towards Susanna E and M, but in regard to *passionate enthusiasm,* my 'first love' will I believe also be my last. I wish I could make her happy!

Sunday 1 June 1851

Read Mr Hogg's paper on "Ocean Routes" through, it contains much information, and has increased my respect for him considerably. I am suffering from Toothache. Went with all the Coventry party to Stonleigh Park[154] which is very beautiful, and the country through which we drove is very rich and charming.

Thornton Hunt added considerably to the pleasure of our afternoon at home, which we passed in the garden.—Hunt proposes to write an article for the Westminster on Sir Robt Peel.— Mr and Mrs H and M. sang exquisitely in the evening.—

153. Peter Massie's bill was due 30 June 1851.
154. Stonleigh Park, Lord Leigh's seat in Warwickshire.

Monday 2 June 1851

"Oh if thou didst but consider how much inward peace unto
thyself and joy unto others thou wouldest procure by demeaning
thyself well, I suppose thou wouldest be more careful of thy
spiritual progress."

Thomas à Kempis.[155]

Experienced intense suffering by the extraction of a tooth
which was pulled and broken 3 times by the forceps, and then
the Dentist made 3 *vain* efforts to extract the remainder which
gave me awful torture.—
M. is going without dinner in order to progress rapidly with
the Prospectus.—[156]

Tuesday 3 June 1851

Last night M finished and read the Prospectus. I liked it extremely as a whole and after some alterations at my suggestion I
sent it to press.—
Susanna's letter this morning say[s] Elisabeth is 'wasting away',
which makes me deeply anxious and sad. I would do anything
<in reason> to restore her, for I love her, and grieve over her
intensely.—Wrote to *her* and Susanna this evening, and offered to
defer to them the decision about Miss E's return to the Strand, or
to do anything they wish. Went with all the party to Ashow
Grove[157] which is extremely beautiful, but did not see it with a
bright spirit.—

Wednesday 4 June 1851

Last evening Miss Lynn's novel[158] gave rise to a discussion concerning the expediency of giving or withholding from girls, when

155. *De Imitatione Christi*, the final paragraph of Book I, Chapter XI. I
have no doubt that Marian Evans lent Chapman her copy (London, Williams
and Norgate, 1848) which she bought in February 1849. It was given to Sara
Hennell 20 January 1851, while she was visiting Miss Evans at Chapman's, and
is now in the Gulson Library, Coventry. This is the same volume from which
Maggie Tulliver learned renunciation. See *The Mill on the Floss*, Book IV,
Chapter III.
156. Chapman first wrote *Catalogue*, then canceled it and substituted *Prospectus*.
157. Ashow is a parish near Kenilworth.   158. Eliza Lynn, *Realities*, 1851.

the[y] reach puberty, a knowledge of the nature and consequences of the sexual function and its uses and abuses; comprehending of course careful instruction and guidance in respect to their relation with the male sex. Opinion preponderated in favor of giving such instruction. Had a long walk with M.

Enclosed proofs of Prospectus to Newman, Mill, Hickson, Froude, Martineau, Greg, Sir Wᵐ Molesworth,[159] Thornton Hunt, Lombe, Mackay & Dʳ Hodgson and wrote to each. Feel exhausted and not well.—Recᵈ kind letter from Geo. Combe approving mine to Mʳ Lombe.

Thursday 5 June 1851

Continuous rain today.

A Mʳ James Russell spent the day with us, who has come to Coventry to give Shakespear readings which no one will hear.— Recᵈ an unkind letter from Susanna regarding M. whom I told, and enquired of her whether she would prefer living her[e] or in Town. She became extremely excited and indignant, and finally calm and regretful.—Went with her to hear Mʳ Russel and found no audience. <During our walk we made a solemn and holy vow which henceforth will bind us to the right. She is a noble being. Wrote a chiding letter to Susanna.>

Friday 6 June 1851

Confined to the House by continuous rain. Russell dined with us, we all went to his 'reading' in the evening through the rain and found 4 auditors besides ourselves. The 'reading' was abandoned, he returned with us, and read Henry IV to us at home.—

A letter of objections to the Prospectus from Newman this morning.—They are not strong but pertinaciously maintained. Read Symes Article on Morell,[160] and wrote him a critical letter.

---

159. William Molesworth (1810–55), who had been educated in Germany, was expelled from Trinity College, Cambridge, for challenging his tutor to a duel. Four times member of Parliament, he supported such radical proposals as colonial self-government. As Chief Commissioner of Works, he opened Kew Gardens for the first time on Sunday. He founded the *London Review* in 1835 as an organ of philosophical radicalism, and amalgamated it with the *Westminster Review,* which he bought in 1836.

160. John Daniel Morell (1816–91).

Saturday 7 June 1851

Received cordial and approving letters from Froude and Greg containing valuable suggestions regarding the Prospectus. One from Hickson expressing annoyance that I should have done anything at present in the way of a Prospectus, and one from Susanna urging my return on Monday.—

Sunday 8 June 1851

Letter from Susanna evincing a changed and kinder tone <in regard to Marian> and some suggestions from Thornton Hunt.

Passed the morning in council determining what suggestions we should avail ourselves of from the letters rec^d and passed part of the afternoon in conversation with M.—

My last day at Coventry is warm and beautiful, with a strong and balmy breeze, and towards evening a beautiful clear sky.

Talked with Bray about the pecuniary arrangement with Marian E.

Monday 9 June 1851

$\overline{\underline{||\; 34\; ||}}$.

Left Coventry at 8 A.M. and reached London at 10.30. Elisabeth received me, and burst into tears, which frightened me, but I found they were tears of joy. I never saw her in such a rapture, which continued all day.

Susanna received me affectionately but soon got into disagreeable talk about M.

Rec^d a long half sarcastic letter from J. S. Mill containing severe animadversions on the Prospectus.—

Tuesday 10 June 1851

Received a half sneering cold letter from Martineau about the Prospectus. He says: "I am not so presumptuous as to offer any opinion. You probably aim, and do well to aim, at securing the support of the large and increasing class of men of thoughtful but not regularly disciplined or largely cultivated mind, the class who may perhaps be most influential in determining the next future. Otherwise,—if you aim at conciliating the attention of the intellectual and scholarly class who are the main supports of the 'Quarterly' and 'Edinburgh' I should doubt whether the Prospectus is quite the thing. It is very likely impossible to become the organ of the movement party in Politics as it now exists, without descending to a lower literary level. The course of the 'Westminster' for a long time past has seemed to imply this; and there may be commercial wisdom in acquiescing in it."

Received a kind suggestive letter from George Combe.—

Wednesday 11 June 1851

Spent the morning in conversation with Rev[d] J. J. Tayler[161] (who read the Prospectus and admired especially the 3rd paragraph on Progress) and Herbert Spencer who of course had many suggestions to give.

Took Elisabeth into the Parks, <she was wretched   [162]> Johnson and Freiligrath came at 5. Johnson thought the Prospectus good but tame, Freiligrath expressed his willingness to write the foreign article.

Thursday 12 June 1851

Dreadful headache all day.

Heard Thackeray lecture on Steele[163] and was much disappointed. The lecture was more like a long sermon than anything, and did not gain by being read. Hunt introduced me to him. He said he wanted to buy at the 'trade price' some of my 'atheistic' publications.

161. John James Tayler (1797–1869), Unitarian minister, was Professor of Theology at Manchester New College and one of the editors of the *Prospective Review*. Chapman had published his *Christian Aspects of Faith and Duty* in April.

162. About sixteen words in this deleted passage are illegible.

163. Thackeray read the third of his six lectures on the English Humourists at Willis's Rooms, King Street, St. James, at three o'clock.

Friday 13 June 1851

Our long inmates and friends Mr & Mrs Hayward left us this morning, which enables me to get the room they occupied as my study, and I mean to retain it now, and hope to turn it to profitable account. I sadly needed it, and shall henceforth work with more system and success.—

Putnam[164] arrived this afternoon.—

Had an interview with Hickson who is much annoyed that I should have taken any steps about the Prospectus; I find the chief reason is a personal and *small* one; to use his own words he does not like to be regarded for so long a time before he actually relinquishes the Review as the 'Setting Sun' and from whom therefore men anxious about the 'Westminster' may transfer their interest in order to give it to the 'rising man' before the time of actual change arrives!—I have consented to be quiet for the present.

Saturday 14 June 1851

5.30.

Mr Putnam spent some time with me this morning and told me of Mr Delf's[165] conduct towards him which has caused their separation:—he misappropriated money, rendered no accounts, and solicited Mr P's customers for himself.

Wrote to J. S. Mill, (see Copying Book), and M.—Thackeray called, I proposed to him to write an article on the Modern Novelists for the Westminster (Jany No); he declined, alleging that his writings were so much more valuable, pecuniarily, if published in other ways; that he, from his position, could not criticize his cotemporaries, and that the only person he could thoroughly well review and cut up would be himself! He complained of the ri-

164. George Palmer Putnam (1814–72), American publisher.

165. Thomas Delf was an American who had worked for Putnam in New York in 1842. In 1843 he went to London to be Appleton's agent. Later he was employed by Chapman in his American book-importing business until 30 June 1849, when that connection ceased because of Delf's actions. See R. L. Rusk, ed., *The Letters of R. W. Emerson*, IV, 159, 167. Delf appears in the *Post Office London Directory*, 1851, as importer of American books and agent for George P. Putnam, New York; his name does not appear in the 1852 edition.

valry and partizanship which is being fostered, I think chiefly Fo(r)ster'd, in respect to him and Dickins by foolish friends.[166]

I find that his religious views are perfectly *free,* but he does not mean to lessen his popularity by fully avowing them; he said he had debated the question with himself whether he was called upon to martyrize himself for the sake of his views and concluded in the negative. His chief object seems to be the making of money. He will go to America for that purpose. He impresses me as much abler than the lecture I heard, but I fear his success is spoiling him.

He recommended Miss Bronty[167] as likely to write an article for the Westminster.—

Sunday 15 June 1851

7.0.   11.

Rose late and unrefreshed, Susanna having kept me awake until 2 A.M. discussing and fretting about the removal of my table on Thursday from my old room to the one I now occupy. She used one drawer in the table for the custody of her letters which *alone* it appears she wished to retain, I did not understand her, but thought she wished to use 3 drawers in my study for her purposes, this I objected to as sure to result in constantly interrupting me, she became passionate, and burnt nearly all her letters in excitement and now regrets it.

Spent the evening at the house of Thornton Hunt at Hamersmith.—[168]

Monday 16 June 1851

My birthday, made wretched by Elisabeth's positive assurance that she will not live in the Strand after Miss Evans comes to London. This step would be fatal <to her peace and worldly ease and would be a source of lasting regret to me.—>

166. The allusion is to John Forster (1812–76), Dickens's friend and biographer.

167. Charlotte Brontë (1816–55) was in London at this time, visiting George Smith, her publisher.

168. "Good Mrs. Hunt has left behind a very pleasant impression. I think she is the most thoroughly unaffected being I ever saw." (GE to Chapman, 15 June 1851. See p. 36.)

Sent my letter after adding M's[169] emendations to J. S. Mill.

James Martineau and his wife and 3 children lunched with us, after which I and Susanna and Anna Tilley went with them to the Exhibition which was very crowded.—

Martineau spoke frankly and well about the <Catalogue.> 'Prospectus'.—

Tuesday 17 June 1851

6.   10.15.

Letter this morning from my assistant E. Radley, announcing his Father's death, and his sister was thrown from a horse and broke her thigh last Wednesday!—

Letter from Syme enclosing his analyses of "The Cotton & Commerce of India", and "Local Self Government" for my projected 'Catalogue raisonée'.[170]

Kind letter from R. W. Mackay dated Firth of Clyde, containing unimportant remarks about the Prospectus, and the following about his locality:—"I have discovered here a pleasant and pretty retirement, which being at a considerable distance from the nearest 'place of worship' is convenient for passing the Sabbath respectably."

Wednesday 18 June 1851

5.0—   ㉟

Spent the morning in writing to M—about the Prospectus chiefly.—

Elisabeth pained me by again repeating her assurance that she will leave me as soon as Miss E. comes to Town.—

Finished reading vol I of Dickens on America.—[171]

Commenced to take stock of the household furniture.

Susanna, and Anna Tilley gone to Hullah's last concert.—

Mr Sessions arrived.

169. See pp. 35–36.

170. *The Cotton and Commerce of India*, by John Chapman (1801–54). *Local Self Government and Centralization . . .*, by Joshua Toulmin Smith (1816–69). Both books were published by Chapman earlier in 1851.

171. Charles Dickens, *American Notes for General Circulation*, 2 vols., London, 1842.

Thursday 19 June 1851

Further discussions with Elisabeth about her leaving, read Dickens during the morning.

Agreed with Mr Hogg to give him a salary this year at the rate of £120 a year,—and that beginning with 1852 he shall receive 1 per cent on all *increase* of sales beyond what they prove to be in 1851.

Susanna went to see 'Ingomar' at Drury Lane.—[172]

Friday 20 June 1851

6.   11.0

Learnt today by a letter from W^m[173] that my father has married a third time.[174] His wife was a housekeeper, at or near Loughboro.—F. Chapman[175] came to spend the night.

Susanna fetched Beatrice home, she looks beautifully well. Mrs Hennell called while Susanna was gone. I agreed to accompany her to Walton on the Naze[176] with Beatrice and her son Frank. She said to Susanna she hoped she should have Beatrice and Ernest too at school in the Winter, Susanna said decidedly she intended to have them both at home, and that it would be wicked not to do so, and that she believes she could manage them best!

Saturday 21 June 1851

5.0   10.15

$

Worked at the Prospectus this morning and feel that I shall greatly improve it. Finished Dicken's "Notes on America" the object and spirit of wh: I admire exceedingly; and especially I re-

---

172. *Ingomar the Barbarian*. Lewes described it as a composite of "low comedy and traditional melodrame . . . written most likely by some fourth-rate German, whose views of life smack of the reveries which visit the soul in a *Wein Stube* dense with smoke. . . ." (*Leader*, 14 June 1851, p. 565.)

173. Chapman's brother William was born 2 May 1819.

174. Chapman's father was in his fifty-eighth year.

175. Perhaps Fanny Chapman. See 22 June 1851.

176. Walton is on the Essex coast near Harwich.

spect his moral courage for publishing his Chapter on Slavery; but that I am persuaded is the unpardonable sin, which has called up so much anger against him in America.—

Received a hearty letter from Lombe and a cold one from J. S. Mill in reference to the Westminster Review, one from the Hon. W. H. Seward[177] of Auburn, New York, which was sent to Groombridges,[178] agreeing to write the Article on Slavery, and one from M objecting to Miss Bronty as a writer of an article on the Modern Novelists.—[179] Shall ask M. to do the Article herself.

Rec^d long visits from Geo. Combe and Thornton Hunt, with the former I had a long rambling discussion about the affairs of the review generally; and Hunt brought me 2 copies of the Spectator to show me his notions about Peel;—says his fort is criticism of Art, and agreed with me, in admiring Monti's 'Eve'.

<Miss Evans' little note is inexpressibly charming, so quick, intelligent and overflowing with love and sweetness! I feel her to be the living torment to my soul.>[180]

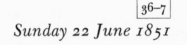

Sunday 22 June 1851

6.30.   12.0

My cousin Fanny Chapman will be 25 years old.

Spent the morning in rewriting the Prospectus.—Mrs Torrens came in the afternoon from Paris, I went with her to Poplar[181] to call upon friends, we returned and had tea, and then I accompanied her part of the way home, i.e. to 14 Norfolk St Park Lane, —her brother in law's[182] house. She is looking exceedingly well and gives a good account of her children.

Elisabeth distressed me much by looking very poorly tonight.

177. William Henry Seward (1801–72), one of the earliest political opponents of slavery, was at this time a Senator from New York. The article was not forthcoming, however; the one that appeared in the Westminster, 59 (January 1853), 125–167, was by W. E. Forster.

178. Richard Groombridge and Sons were the publishers of the Westminster Review, 54–57 (October 1850–April 1852).

179. See p. 38.

180. Since nothing in her letter warrants the tenderness Chapman feels, this must refer to a "little note" that was enclosed with it. See pp. 37–38.

181. A part of London east of Limehouse.

182. Capt. Frederick Torrens.

Monday 23 June 1851

6.45.

Found E. in my room very low and sad, and she burst into tears, lamenting her position &c. &c., and hence a wretched morning, and partly so the evening. When Susanna returned with Mr Sessions from Richmond she said she had heard of a situation for E. in Lancashire, of a kind which she had expressed a wish to have; <but I trust her and wish[183] . . . would trust E & me.> It has cast a sad gloom over me.—

I & Susanna took Beatrice to a Dentist where she bore the extraction of several Stumps admirably. I had one stopped. He says my teeth are in a dreadful state.

E +

Tuesday 24 June 1851

6.30   12.0

Elisabeth and Susanna had a long conversation about the proposed situation, which I believe has ended in nothing so far,—but it must be settled. <The wretchedness which Elisabeth diffuses by her intense and morbid egoism is quite unjustifiable and shall be withstood. I have suffered much and long for the sake of being her tenderest friend and securing her a real home for life, motives which I am sure influenced me far more strongly than all others.—But my patience is becoming exhausted, and I fear that I neither can nor must afford the time henceforth>[184]

Wednesday 25 June 1851

Poor Sissie[185] is suffering very much physically today,—quite faint and exhausted, oh how much her maidenhood costs!—Nature exacts such a terrible revenge for the nonfulfilment of her claims.

Went into the City and saw Johnson and Freiligrath, the former said that if the latter wrote the Article on Foreign Literature

183. Two or three words are illegible here.
184. Ten or twelve words concluding this passage are illegible.
185. Elisabeth Tilley.

for the Westminster he would undertake that it should be in good english. Leut. Tilley[186] called and was much affected by seeing E. looking so ill.

Woodfall called and promised to take Susanna to Walton. Spent a miserable useless evening through indigestion.—

Thursday 26 June 1851

6.0.

Wrote to the Hon. Wm Seward in Auburn U. S. about the Article on Slavery, and gave him a sketch of my notions of the *line* of treatment which would be desirable. Left home at 8.20. to meet Mrs Hennell & party including Beatrice Frank[187] and servant at Blackwall whence we proceeded[188] to Walton on the Naze which proves to be a very nice quiet place. Had much interesting conversation with Mrs H. on a great variety of topics. She thinks that before we can make any great moral progress there must be some restraint on the number of children born, which I think impossible absurd and unnecessary. She thinks our sexual relations are very conventional, and that though pure monogamy is the ideal, it will only be reached thro' a previous age of general licence! I don't agree with her that such a mud bath is at all necessary.

Friday 27 June 1851

Bathed in the Sea this morning and enjoyed it much.—
Passed the day with Mrs Hennell and the children.—

Walton on the Naze
June 27, 1851[189]

Mrs Hennell told me the following yesterday, that Mrs Bray is and has been for years decidedly in love with Mr Noel, and that Mr Bray promotes her wish that Mr Noel should visit Rosehill as

186. Gwavas Speedwell Tilly, second lieutenant 19 December 1844, first lieutenant 1 April 1846, was probably Elisabeth's brother. The name is spelled *Tilly* in *Hart's Army List*.

187. Mrs. Hennell's son.   188. By steamboat.

189. This long entry is written on three blank pages at the beginning of the Diary.

much as possible, and that she in return trys to promote his happiness in any way that his wishes tend. That Miss Mary Hennell[190] used to live with the Brays, and that she was the especial object of his affections and shared his literary interests when writing his book, and his wife who was reasoned into the marriage and became a wife from a feeling of duty was a secondary person and far from happy; but has been much happier lately.—

Her attachment for Mr Noel[191] would seem to have arisen when his wife was dying of consumption, as she then went into Devonshire to nurse her. Mrs H. says that she doubts if the feeling is reciprocated. All this was beautifully confirmed to me at Coventry when speaking of Mr Noels procrastination in writing she quietly said she did not think frequent writing a test of deep feeling, that in her opinion many evaporate what feeling they have in writing and that if Mr Noel were not to write for a hundred years she should feel equally sure his *friendly* feeling (I think she said) would continue unchanged. Here a delicate blush spread over her. (Bless her! I admire her extremely, she is very near heaven, and is quite an angel.)

Mrs Hennell repeated exactly what Miss Evans had told me previously as a great secret (as was the case with the preceeding page) that in 1843 Miss Evans was invited by Dr Brabant (she being then only 22)[192] to visit his house and to fill the place of his

190. Mary Hennell was a sister of Mrs. Bray, Charles C. Hennell, and Sara Hennell. In 1841 Charles Bray's *The Philosophy of Necessity* was published with an appendix by Mary Hennell, reprinted separately in 1844 as *An Outline of the Various Social Systems and Communities which Have Been Founded on the Principle of Co-operation,* with an introduction by Bray.

191. Edward Noel's father, the Rev. Thomas Noel, was an illegitimate son of Lady Byron's grandfather, Lord Wentworth. As he would have succeeded to the Wentworth estate had his parents been married, Lady Byron felt it her duty to provide for him. She gave him the living at Kirkby, educated his four sons, and established them in life. For Edward, the youngest, she bought an estate on the island of Eubœa, Greece. He was married 18 June 1838 to Frances Isabella, daughter of Col. Carlo Joseph Doyle, Lieutenant-Governor of Granada. According to her death certificate, Mrs. Noel died of "phthisis" 5 November 1845 at Atholl Lodge, Parish of Tormoham, Torquay, Devonshire, aged twenty-six. See E. C. Mayne, *The Life and Letters of . . . Lady Noel Byron,* 2d ed., London, 1929, pp. 275, 295, 330, *et passim; Gentleman's Magazine,* 164 (August 1838), 207; entry of death at Somerset House. Mrs. Bray was expecting word from Noel while Chapman was at Rosehill early in June 1851. See p. 36.

192. Marian Evans was a bridesmaid at Rufa Brabant's marriage to Charles C. Hennell in London, 1 November 1843. She was not twenty-two, but within a few days of her twenty-fourth birthday. She arrived at Devizes to visit the Brabants 14 November and returned to Coventry 4 December 1843.

daughter (then just married) she went, the Doctor liked her extremely, and said that so long as she had no home she must consider his house as her permanent home. She in the simplicity of her heart and her ignorance of (or incapability of practicing) the required conventionalisms gave the Doctor the utmost attention; they became very intimate, his Sister in law Miss S. Hughes became alarmed, made a great stir, excited the jealousy of Mrs Brabant, <who insisted> Miss Evans left. Mrs B. vowed she should never enter the house again, or that if she did, she Mrs Brabant would instantly leave it. Mrs Hennell says Dr B. acted ungenerously and worse, towards Miss E. for though he was the chief cause of all that passed, he acted towards her as though <she> the fault lay with her alone. His unmanliness in the affair was condemned more by Mrs Hennell than by Miss E. herself when she (a year ago) related the circumstances to me.[193]

I inquired of Mrs Hennell whether the fact that Mr Hennell wrote the "Inquiry" caused their intimacy to which she answered "Yes, my father bought it as soon as published, we read it with great pleasure, my father concluded it was written by an old man as his last confession before leaving the world, he went to London found Mr Hennell's address invited him to his house, and said he had a daughter who he thought would interest him. He came down, staid 10 days, made me an offer when he had been there a week,—Dr Brabant found his lungs unsound, opposed the match, acceptance deferred.—Medical examinations instituted, desease in the lungs certified, and advised not to marry. Agreed not to see each other for a time. Met again at Coventry, and then in Oxfordshire, and settled the matter by mutual promises to marry, father still opposed, could not marry for want of means, at length I had a little money left me and we then married 5 years after we first met, and I feel abundantly thankful to have been his wife for only the 7 years that he lived.[194] We never had a quarrel during our married life, and but one misunderstanding before it."

She has the additional compensation of a most magnificent boy.

193. This effectually disposes of the preposterous fiction invented by E. and G. Romieu in *La Vie de George Eliot*, Paris, 1930, and repeated by Simon Dewes in *Marian: The Life of George Eliot*, London, 1939, that Miss Evans fell in love with Charles Hennell in 1842, but was jilted when Rufa Brabant appeared. Rufa was engaged to him four years before Miss Evans met him. It was she who sent Emerson the translation of a German review of Hennell's *Inquiry;* Emerson assumed that E. R. Brabant was a man. See R. L. Rusk, ed., *The Letters of Ralph Waldo Emerson*, 6 vols., 1939, III, 70–71.

194. He died 2 September 1850.

Saturday 28 June 1851

Weather still clear and beautiful, and enjoy it much.—Regret that I find my heart palpitate extremely in bathing. Herbert Brabant[195] joined us in the evening.

Sunday 29 June 1851

Passed the greater part of our time in discussing the best course to be pursued by H. Brabant who has already raised £3000 on his 'expectations'.

Monday 30 June 1851

11.0—

Peter Massie's Bill due =   £208.. o.. o.

Had a drive by H. B. in his 'Dog Cart' and left Walton about 11.30 A.M. my dear little pet kissed her hands to me as the boat left the Pier, and could not restrain the tears.

Reached home at 8.30.—Affectionately received by Susanna and Elisabeth, the latter having hastened from Islington to meet me. Went to bed with headache.

Tuesday 1 July 1851

5.0   38–41.

Went to a meeting on the American Copyright Question, intended to get a reversion of Lord Campbell's decision that a foreigner may obtain copyright here by priority of publication, which thus enables American Authors to obtain a copyright here without the necessity of their according to Englishmen a reciprocal right.[196] Heard Bulwer speak, he being in the chair. He spoke

195. Rufa's brother.
196. The meeting was held at the Hanover Square Rooms, with Sir Edward Bulwer Lytton as chairman, and Henry G. Bohn the publisher, vice-chairman, to protest the reversal by the Court of Error of the previous decision of the Court of Exchequer that foreign authors could obtain copyright only if their countries accept the International Copyright Act. Mr. Bohn moved the resolution, which was adopted after a nullifying amendment had been rejected. See the *Leader*, 5 July 1851, p. 624.

of Bohn as one of those publishers whose names will be immortal, whereupon Mr B. put on such an exquisitely saintlike Pecksniffian aspect as to seem nearly in heaven.—The blessed man!—

Wednesday 2 July 1851

7.0

Finished a long letter to Mr Lombe explanatory of my plans respecting the Westminster Review. I fear he will entail much laborious correspondence upon me.—
Read Martineau's Article in this Month's Westminster on Greg.[197] It is very clever but abounds too much with finely spun metaphysics, and I think a certain want of sincerity in regard to the resurrection is discernible.—

Thursday 3 July 1851

Conversed with Mr Radley about his prospects, found that Washbourne[198] had offered to sell him his business. He states that the returns at £13000, and the capital needed £6000.
Went with Susanna to the 'Royal Exhibition of paintings', thought that on the whole there are few striking pictures. Maclise's picture of Caxton showing his printing to the King, and Barker's hunting scene, where Rufus is saved by his Mistress are good. Foley's "Mother" is I think the best piece of Sculpture. 'The Rejected Cupbearer' and "Psyche discovering Cupid" are also beautiful works.—[199]

Friday 4 July 1851

42.

Bill granted to Spalding & Hodge due =   117..14..7.

Sent long letter to M. Went to the Dentist and was operated

197. "The Creed of Christendom," *Westminster Review*, 55 (July 1851), 429–453.
198. Henry Washbourne, bookseller, 18 New Bridge Street, Blackfriars.
199. At the Royal Academy. Daniel Maclise, "Caxton's Printing Office," (67); Thomas Jones Barker, "An Incident in the Life of William Rufus" (640); John Henry Foley, "The Mother" (1260); William Calder Marshall, "Hebe Rejected" (1254); E[phraim?] Ambrose, "Psyche Discovering Cupid" (1277).

upon for about 2 hours, having had 3 teeth stopped with gold, and 2 with Amalgam.—

Miss Martineau and Mr Atkinson called to enquire of me whether I should be disposed to publish at my own risk 'dividing the profits' an abridgment of Compte's Philosophie Positive, in one or two vols.—[200]

She looks exceedingly well,—and is a perfect zealot in her new negative faith.[201]

Finished "Paul Clifford".[202]

Saturday 5 July 1851

Rose early, and started from Blackwall at 9.30 with Elisabeth whom I took to Walton, where we arrived about 3.30. We spent the evening in walking and conversation with Mrs Hennell.—My dear little pet[203] is thoroughly enjoying herself and looks much more healthy than she did some time ago.—

Read the Articles in the Westminster Review on the Enfranchisement of Women, and on the Extinction of Slavery; neither of which are striking. The former is said to be by J. S. Mill.[204]

Sunday 6 July 1851

Spent the morning with E. and Mrs H. each reading beneath the shade in a field. Mrs Hennell gave her views of what the relation of the sexes ought to be.—

She seems to think that the attitude of woman towards man i.e. of wife towards husband, should be unquestioning faith and worship.—There is much that is beautiful in such a relation, but I do not think it the true one.—

E. is strangely susceptible.—Her eyes filled with tears 3 times today.

200. Auguste Comte (1798–1857) had published his *Cours de philosophie positive*, 1830–42; it had not been translated into English.
201. The "new negative faith" was the form of "atheism" professed in the *Letters on the Laws of Man's Nature and Development*. Douglas Jerrold proposed as a motto for the title page: "There is no God, and Harriet Martineau is his prophet."
202. By E. Bulwer Lytton, 1830.   203. Beatrice.
204. "Enfranchisement of Women," *Westminster Review*, 55 (July 1851), 289–311, was Mill's; "Extinction of Slavery," pp. 329–345, is signed W. E.

Monday 7 July 1851

43.

Left Walton at 11.30, and reached London at 7.30.—
Accompanied Susanna to see a private performance of the
'Critic' and other pieces at Miss Kelly's Theatre.[205] Mr and Mrs
Lewes, Thornton Hunt and others played.—Were much pleased,—
and especially with the beauty of the audience. There was one ex-
quisitely beautiful being. Had a long talk with Leigh Hunt.[206]

Tuesday 8 July 1851

Spent the day altogether in business. Miss Penington sung beautifully in the evening.

Wednesday 9 July 1851

W. R. Greg called, we conversed on a variety of topics connected with the Review and I was glad to find we agreed generally, but especially about Lord Palmerston's[207] Policy, the character
of Sir Robt Peel,[208] the needfull government of our Colonies,[209]
the Relative Claims of local self government, and Centralization,[210] and the difficult question of Competition or Cooperation.
I proposed to him to write an Article on the Relation between

205. Frances Maria Kelley (1790–1882), actress and friend of Charles Lamb,
conducted a dramatic school after her retirement from the stage. Her theater
in Dean Street was called the Soho after 1852. See the *Critic*, 1 February 1851,
p. 69, and George Hodder, *Memories of My Time*, London, 1870, 151–155.
There is no mention of this performance in the *Leader,* for which Lewes wrote
the dramatic criticisms.

206. James Henry Leigh Hunt (1784–1859), essayist and poet, was Thornton
Hunt's father.

207. Henry John Temple, third Viscount Palmerston (1784–1865). An article
"Lord Palmerston and his Policy" [by T. C. Grattan] appeared in 57 (April
1852), 555–592.

208. Robert Peel, second baronet (1788–1850). An article "Sir Robert Peel
and his Policy" [by W. R. Greg] appeared in 58 (July 1852), 205–246.

209. "The Government of India," 57 (April 1852), 357–405, "Our Colonial
Empire," 58 (October 1852), 398–435, and "India and its Finance," 60 (July
1853), 177–199 [all by John Chapman (1801–54). See Diary, 29 April 1851].

210. "The Latest Continental Theory of Legislation" [by F. W. Newman],
57 (January 1852), 143–161.

employers and employed,[211] which he seems inclined to do.—He said if I could get an able Article on Lord Palmerston, "it would be a fortune for the Review," but like myself he cannot think of the man to do it.

A brother of the late David Scott called, he seems an able man.—[212]

The Queen went to a Ball at Guildhall tonight, through the Strand, the crowd was immense, and our American visitors much gratified.[213]

Thursday 10 July 1851

10.45.

Rose late, discovered the errors in the Banking account, but disabled all day nearly by acute headache. Spencer gave me a ticket for the Opera[214] to which her Majesty went 'in state', was in good time and might have had an excellent place but for the vexing regulation that 'press tickets' must be exchanged which destroyed my chance of admittance. I never saw such a crowd.

Brought down my Sofa into my own room, Susanna reluctantly acquiescing, and now I hope I may go to bed with some regularity and rise early, otherwise I have no chance of reading.—

Friday 11 July 1851

6.20.

Had a long visit from W. R. Greg who agreed to write the Article I proposed to him on employers and employed.

Consumed the evening in a painful conversation with Susanna upon a number of topics, all of which received their animus from the fact that I had determined to sleep in my own room. I did not get to bed till 11.30.

211. "The Relation between Employers and Employed" [by W. R. Greg], 57 (January 1852), 61–95.

212. William Bell Scott (1811–90), brother of David Scott (1806–49). Both were painters.

213. The way was elaborately decorated and lighted from Temple Bar to Guildhall. For a rather satirical description of the affair see the *Leader,* 12 July 1851, p. 648.

214. A command performance of *Il Flauto Magico* at Covent Garden.

Saturday 12 July 1851

Richard Kinder[215] Bill due =   80. . 11. 2

Left the Strand at 8.45 for Walton, had a pleasant passage and recognized Goodwyn Barmby[216] on board.—

On the way read the papers on Peel by Hunt and Greg, and admire the latter most.

After my arrival when I found my child and all well, I took a walk with Elisabeth, who fully expressed to me her willingness to remain with me constantly. As an earnest of her intention she consented to meet Miss Evans as a visitor to the Strand.—I hereby vow that so far as lies in my power she shall never regret her decision.—

Mr Howell, one of Mr Hennell's executors, came down in the boat with me, (accompanied by his son) his object being to court Mrs Hennell, who will accept him if after more consideration and trial she finds she cannot do better. She wants a younger man, and has set her affections on Dr Travis![217]

Enjoyed a bath in the Sea at 8.30. P.M.

43—4—5
Sunday 13 July 1851

Passed the morning with Elisabeth in the fields;—bathed and walked, but can get no reading done.

Monday 14 July 1851

46. 60 minutes

Had a bath but did not enjoy it much as the tide was low.

215. See Diary, 8 August 1851.

216. John Goodwyn Barmby (1820–81), Unitarian minister, Christian Socialist, and author of religious works.

217. There is no further mention of either Mr. Howell or Dr. Travis. In 1857 Mrs. Hennell married Wathen Mark Wilks Call. See Diary, 13 September 1851.

Tuesday 15 July 1851

Wrote to invite M^r and Mrs Bray, and Miss Evans and Miss Hennell to spend a week with us in August.

Had a beautiful swim today in sight of Elisabeth and Mrs Hennell.

Had a late walk on the sands.—

47.

Wednesday 16 July 1851

Had a long swim this morning and then started with Elisabeth and Herbert Brabant for Town.—

Thursday 17 July 1851

Found an order from a new foreign house in Madras, which is encouraging.

No money having arrived from America by the last mail, I am much straitened. I wonder how long this pecuniary difficulty will continue from time to time to press upon me! I must give more heed to the monster and conquer it for until I have I cannot go about my work in peace.—

A misunderstanding between me and E. about Miss Evans' return to the Strand caused some suffering this evening.—

Friday 18 July 1851

5.50.

Saturday 19 July 1851

Took Susanna to Walton, and Mr Woodfall accompanied us. The latter part of the journey very wet, and Susanna sick, she recovered however immediately on landing, and we all had a pleasant walk in the evening, my darling Beatrice not being the least delighted of the party.—   S. +

Sunday 20 July 1851

Troubled with Diarrhea all day, but able to go out.

Monday 21 July 1851

Rose at 3 with Susanna to see the Sun rise, still unwell, left Walton at 5, and reach[ed] London by train at 11.15. and found my brother Thomas waiting for me.—
Dr Brabant gave me permission to supply his son with money at my discretion.

Tuesday 22 July 1851

Went with my brother to the Exhibition.

Wednesday 23 July 1851

E. +

Had a long interview with Mr Foster[218] of Rawdon.
Took Cousin Marian[219] to the Boulogne Steamboat, in the morning, and Susanna and Beaty arrived in the evening escorted by Herbert Brabant.
Elisabeth is suffering awfully, much more than usual at similar periods.—

Thursday 24 July 1851

[No entry.]

Friday 25 July 1851

Had headache all day.
Took Susanna and Beatrice to the Exhibition, the latter not so much delighted as I hope you [hoped she] would be.—

218. William Edward Forster. See 18 April 1851.
219. Marian (usually Marianne or Marrianne) Chapman.

Took Thomas, Elisabeth and Mrs Hennell to the Olympic theatre, to see Miss Faucit in Rosalind,[220] we were all pleased.

Saturday 26 July 1851

Dr Hodgson passed the day with me, in discussing the various matters that interest us.

We went to Hampton Court in the afternoon and took with us Elisabeth and Anna Tilley. Elisabeth is dreadfully weak, and has lost 8 lbs. this last year in weight;—she is now   9s^t. 2 lbs.[221]

I am 11 " 9 " [222]

Susanna sat talking a long time with me this evening partly about M. but chiefly about Elisabeth. She is decidedly of opinion that M. ought to live with us when in Town; and that medical aid might relieve E's sufferings.—

Sunday 27 July 1851

Dr Hodgson called, accompanied him to the Railway and agreed with him to write an Article on the Use of the Bible in Public Schools.

Went with my brother to dine at Mrs Johnsons, met Freiligrath and a Herr Merks,[223] another exile.—

E. seemed quite excited when I returned.—

Monday 28 July 1851

Elisabeth's Thirty-first Birthday.[224]

Greeley finally left London.—

Saw the Eclipse with Elisabeth from the top of the house. It was a noble keeping of her birthday, which I feel especially desirous of remembering as the beginning of a new epoch, and which

220. In *As You Like It* with J. W. Wallack, Jr., as Jaques.
221. 128 pounds.   222. 163 pounds.
223. Karl Marx, who was living at 28 Dean Street, Soho, was in especially embarrassing financial straits at this time. See *Karl Marx, Chronik seines Lebens*, Moscow, 1934, and *Marx-Engels Briefwechsel*, Berlin, 1929, I, *passim.*
224. Chapman originally wrote *thirtieth.*

I have marked by presenting her with a ring.—But alas the evening was gloomy!—

Rec^d considerable cash from America today which is a much needed and effectual relief.

Tuesday 29 July 1851
48.

Nearly finished my revised Prospectus. Went with Thomas to buy a Barometer for me, and to look at Bookshelves which I purchased, and which has annoyed Susanna exceedingly.—She teazed me, and occupied my time till 11 P.M. about it. Read 2 first Articles in the Edinburgh Review which seem to me dull.[225]

Wednesday 30 July 1851

Went to Lion House[226] with Susanna and my brother and his wife. We parted with them to return, and they went to Kew Gardens. Susanna and I had a serious altercation about going on Sundays,—an old subject:—She said how much she should like to spend the whole of the Sundays out, I said "yes so should I, but you prevented it" meaning that she would not recognize my right to take her or E. as I might think best something like alternately. Her remarks were one tissue of exaggeration misrepresentation prevarication and passion, I bore it calmly, with one or two exceptions, when I could not help stopping her by saying she was a liar, for which I afterwards apologized. Passed the evening with Spencer, and Dr Hodgson.

Thursday 31 July 1851

Had a renewal of the discussion of yesterday, until at length in view of the painfulness of my position and prospects domestically I burst into tears.—Susanna's excitement was then allayed.—

Occupied all day on the Prospectus and never went out,—retired quite exhausted.—

225. *Edinburgh Review*, 94 (July 1851), "The Greek Text of the New Testament" and "Johnston's *Notes on North America*."
226. At the Zoological Gardens in Regent's Park.

Friday 1 August 1851

Visited by Maccall who seemed poorly,—says he cannot sleep.—
Accompanied Lewes to the French Play,[227]—could not understand all, but sufficient to enjoy it. M. Buffé was the chief actor.—
Returned at 12,—when Susanna kept me awake until one by renewal of the theme of yesterday but with kind intent.

Saturday 2 August 1851

Went to Exhibition with Elisabeth, did not enjoy it much, having headache and a constant consciousness of her feebleness and
fatigue.

Susanna went with Sofia Tilley[228] to the Olympic.—[229]   49.

Sunday 3 August 1851

A party of us,—my brother Thomas, his wife, Mr and Mrs Hunt
& Son, E. and her sister, a french visitor and his wife, and myself
all went to Hampton Court and spent the day which was beautifully fine.

We were 5 hours going up by the River, and returned by rail.

Monday 4 August 1851

Spent the day chiefly at business accounts,—and wrote a long
letter to Perry in the evening.—My little pet Beatrice amused me
in the evening by saying to me as a very serious affair "Papa I
have quite made up my mind not to take my new doll to school,
for you know when we play in the garden the boys would soon
spoil it"!

50.

227. *Michel Perrin* at the St. James's theater.

228. Sofia Tilley was described by Marian Evans as a "younger sister of Miss
Tilley's—a poor girl quite dependent on her own labour as a milliner." (GE
to Charles Bray, Friday [18 March 1853].) In April 1853 she sailed with Mr.
Syme and his family for Australia, where two of her brothers were settled.

229. The program consisted of *The Farmer's Story, The Fire Eater,* and
Diogenes and His Lantern.

Tuesday 5 August 1851

My brother Thomas, and his wife Hannah, returned to Glasgow this evening, both having well enjoyed their visit. They feel the residence in Scotland as a kind of exile, and long to be located in London. My Brother's position in a pecuniary point of view is far from satisfactory unable to calculate on more than £300 a year with a capital of £1100 besides borrowed money, and giving all his time laboriously to the business. I have striven hard to rouse him to make an effort to improve his prospects,— either by engaging himself in some other business where there would be more scope for his energies and talent (as for instance in a business in America in connexion with me) or by concentrating his studies with a view of obtaining a Professorship in some department of Natural History.[230]

Wednesday 6 August 1851

[No entry.]

Thursday 7 August 1851

Visited Sir Joshua Walmsley[231] with whom I had a long walk,— and talk of various topics and on the Westminster Review in particular. He is interested in the work and will I doubt not aid it indirectly by recommending it, and by supplying me with articles written by Dr Hodgson, but I fear he will contribute no cash, having been much drained by the Daily News. He does not strike me as likely to set the Thames on fire.

Attended a Summons at Bow S^t by Panittzi[232] on the part of the Brit. Museum and paid £3. 14. 0.

230. In 1871 Thomas Chapman was still in business at the same address, 56 Buchanan Street, Glasgow.

231. Joshua Walmsley had been mayor of Liverpool and agitated against the Corn Laws. He was M.P. for Bolton 1849–52. In 1863 his daughter became Dr. Hodgson's second wife.

232. Anthony Panizzi (1797–1879) was Keeper of Printed Books at the British Museum. The summons was no doubt in connection with some violation of the law requiring publishers to deposit books in the Library. For the report of a similar case in which James Gilbert was fined £4. 10 see the *Critic*, 15 March 1851, p. 142. The *Leader* 10 July 1852, p. 661, in an article called "The Book Wolf," attacked Panizzi's methods. "The practice of reminding men of their civil duties through a police court is not a very English proceeding, and it reminds the publishers that the gentleman who pursues it with such zest is not an Englishman."

Friday 8 August 1851

51.

Kinder[233] called upon me and explained to me the condition of the "Inquirer". It circulates 1000 copies and pays expenses of paper, print, at cost price, subeditor and all miscellaneous charges, but the Editor, Mr Lalor has been paid out of a special fund. He has resigned, and the fund founders are in despair. Kinder is inclined to let me have the paper for £50, and to charge the printing at cost until the circulation reaches paying point. I am *inclined* to take it, if I can see my way clearly.

Visited Northumberland House,[234] and delighted with the copies of Raphael.—

Saturday 9 August 1851

Rec^d a letter from Mr Lombe in answer to my letter enquiring if he would assist in the publication of an abridgment of Comte's "Philosophie positive" and in which I enclosed a letter on the project addressed to me by Miss Martineau. M^r L's letter is as follows:—

"Florence August one 1851, My dear Sir, Yours of the 24th ult.
"was received this day annexed is my answer to the enclosure it
"contained. On other matters another time. Yours very sincerely
                                                EDWARD LOMBE"
"John Chapman".—

                                        Florence Aug^st one 1851.
"Gentlemen,
    "On receipt of this letter I request you will do me the very
"great honour of transferring Five Hundred Pounds say £500. to

233. Richard Kinder was a printer at 2 Green Arbour Court, which was also the address of the *Inquirer*. He was later a member of Woodfall's firm. The *Inquirer* was started 9 July 1842 "as the organ of the Unitarian body." (H. R. F. Bourne, *English Newspapers*, 2 vols., London, 1887, II, 131.)

234. Northumberland House, on the southeast side of Trafalgar Square, was removed in 1874 to make way for Northumberland Avenue. It belonged at this time to Sir Algernon Percy, fourth Duke of Northumberland (1792–1865).

"the credit of Miss Harriet Martineau in support of a great Lit-
"erary work.

Your very obliged servant
EDWARD LOMBE

"Messrs Barclay, Bevan, Tritton & Co
London."

I acknowledged the receipt of the Draft but proposed to him
(Mr L) that he should only contribute what may prove to be needful in the case, in order that he may help in other works, and proposed Parker's Discourse for cheap reprint. (See the copy of the
letter).

Sunday 10 August 1851
52

Took Susanna to Richmond where we spent some hours. Passed
the evening in writing 6 letters of Introduction for Herbert Brabant.

Susanna's incapability of walking far or fast, and general debility presses upon me how much she has aged latterly, and makes
the future look sad.—

Monday 11 August 1851

Herbert Brabant called prior to his departure to Philadelphie,
whither he sails in a Screw Steamer on Wednesday next. His
father commissioned me to let him have money to the extent of
£100 *if I thought proper*. I told him I was empowered to let him
have £50. and his sister[235] compromised me by telling him the extent of his father's liberality, which has caused him to distrust me.

Went in a cab with Mrs H. to see him at his lodgings for a last
conversation.[236]

Syme thinks I ought to print my own books.

Tuesday 12 August 1851

Elisabeth is much distressed this morning by a letter from her
brother Wm in Australia stating that he has been 5 months suffer-

235. Mrs. Charles C. Hennell, the *Mrs. H.* of this entry.
236. He was back in London by April 1852.

ing from Rhematism, that he now walks on crutches, expects to
be a cripple for life, and has already paid his medical attendant
£200!—

I immediately wrote him an encouraging letter of advice, and
urged him not to despear getting the use of his limbs again, and
told him I will send out by his brother Todd's book on Gout and
Rhematism which may help him.[237]

Wednesday 13 August 1851

Miss Evans and Mrs Bray arrived from Devonshire,[238] I met
them and Mr Bray at the Railway Station, and spent the evening
with them at Miss Marshalls where I read my amended Prospectus, and had a long discussion about the Prospective Review.[239]

Thursday 14 August 1851

Elisabeth acquiesced in Miss Evan's return to the Strand for
residence during the winter which at once cuts a difficulty in two,
and increases my respect for her.—

Went over the Royal Academy and Northumberland House
with Mr Bray and Miss E.

Accompanied Susanna to call in the evening on the whole
party, but especially to see Mrs Bray, who is very poorly.[240] Decided with Miss E. that Martineau had better write the Article on
Christian Ethics and Modern Civilization.[241]

Friday 15 August 1851

Spent most of the day at the Exhibition with Miss E. Miss Hennell, and Mr Bray. The ladies came home with me in order that
Miss E. might "make a call" on Susanna, and afford the oppor-

237. Robert Bentley Todd (1809–60), *Practical Remarks on Gout, Rheumatic Fever, and Chronic Rheumatism of the Joints*, London, 1843.
238. Since the end of July they had been visiting Mrs. Bray's friends, the
Noels, at Bishop's Teignton.
239. See p. 7.
240. Mrs. Bray had been ill in Devonshire.
241. "The Ethics of Christendom," *Westminster Review*, 57 (January 1852),
182–226.

tunity of a long Editorial Conference, in which after coffee we accomplished much. Susanna is very poorly with bad headache,— and Elisabeth is far from well. She was sad and in tears this evening.

Saturday 16 August 1851

Elisabeth has been sad and low again this morning, I begin to fear she must make a long visit into the country for her restoration.

Spent 3 hours at the Exhibition with the Coventry party, and after they left E met me by appointment, when we staid until 5, both returning very tired.—Did nothing in the evening but read the Leader.—

Elisabeth in Tears again.

Cousins Marian and Millie Chapman arrived.—

After I went to bed Susanna seemed to wish to discuss Elisabeth &c, but being thoroughly tired of all this continued talk of feeling and personality, I begged her to desist.

Read this week an able article in the Quarterly on Sanatory Consolidation by a Mr Ward,[242] and Gladstone Pamphlet on Naples,[243] which contains horrible disclosures.

Sunday 17 [27] August 1851

It is now August 27th 10 days thus elapsing without my having made any record of my proceedings.

Mr Mackay returned from Scotland on the 16th and consented somewhat indistinctly to write an Article in compliance with my request which I propose to entitle:—"The essence and results of Protestantism".[244] His fancy about the bad air of St John's Wood (where he nominally resides)[245] will not let him stay at home so

---

242. [Frederick Oldfield Ward], "Sanitary Consolidation," *Quarterly Review*, 88 (March 1851), 435–492.

243. William Ward Ewart Gladstone (1809–98), *Two Letters to the Earl of Aberdeen on the State Prosecutions of the Neapolitan Government*. The preface is dated 14 July 1851. The conservative Gladstone had been shocked by the atrocities that followed King Ferdinand's suppression of the reform movement in Naples.

244. The article did not materialize.   245. 41 Hamilton Terrace.

he started for the Isle of Skie last Thursday. I regret his absence for his discussion and counsel I found of much use.

Monday 18 [27] August 1851

E. +

I have labored considerably to close the balance sheet of my business which required much examination and correction in consequence of my clerk, Mr Hogg, having had no experience in the business, It has been an anxious time, but I rejoice to find the result somewhat more satisfactory than I hoped for.

The Business has paid the whole of the Rent & Taxes, £500, and has made a profit of £375 in spite of deducting £55 for depreciation of Fixtures &c, and of losing about £400, more or less,

Tuesday 19 [27] August 1851

in selling off by Auction a number of my unsuccessful publications and old books.

Proposed to and agreed with Lewes to write an Article on the Modern Novelists for the Jany N° of the Westminster. He seems to have no idea of treating the subject which shall exhibit a definite purpose in the Article and since conversing with him about it, it has occurred to me that Froude would be a much more appropriate man, I suggested that he should give the characteristics

Wednesday 20 [27] August 1851

of each of the leading Novelists, describe their relative and intrinsic merits, erect a standard of Criticism whereby to judge them with a view of elevating the productions of the Novelists as works of Art and as refining and moral influences. If more were claimed from the Novelist the best of them would accord more. But Lewes is a 'bread scholar' and lacks that enthusiasm of thought and earnest purpose which I must alone seek for in Contributors to the Westminster.[246]

246. No such article appeared. Lewes contributed "Julia von Krüdener, as Coquette and Mystic," 57 (January 1852), 161–182.

Thursday 21 [27] August 1851

Wrote to James Martineau and requested him to write an Article on "Christian Ethics and Modern Civilization" leaving to him to determine the scope of it, and the mode of treatment. Rec^d from him a kindly written and discriminating letter in reply expressing doubt whether he could write the Article but asking for some indications of the mode of treatment we wish to be adopted. I went to Coventry on Saturday and fully discussed the subject with Miss Evans, after which I noted down the topics and mode of treatment to be adopted in the Article, which she embodied in

Friday 22 [27] August 1851

a sketch for a letter with such modifications as she thought necessary, and from this material I shall write him our views on the subject, but I fear they will not be acceptable.—(See copy book).

Spent much of my time at Coventry in determining on the final form of the Prospectus (which is now much improved on the first Draft), and on the contents of the January N°.

Reached home at 11 on Monday night 25th inst.

Saturday 23 [27] August 1851

Dr Carlyle[247] called upon me and said he thought his brother would be glad to write for the Review, and expressed a warm interest in it generally. He gave me to read a letter from Emerson to his brother which describes a long journey he has been making in the Western and Southern States, and I am sorry to say gives as a reason for his infrequent writing to his friends here that he is suffering from some affection of the eyes.[248]

Dr C. said Browning is in Town and as he knows Lombe, and would likely be interested in the Westminster seconded my idea of seeing him. I accordingly wrote to him, and he called upon me on Tuesday when we had a very cordial and pleasant interview.—[249] I read to him a letter just rec^d from Lombe in reference

247. John Aitken Carlyle (1801–79), Thomas Carlyle's younger brother, had published a prose translation of Dante's *Inferno* in 1849.

248. For Emerson's letter to Carlyle, 28 July 1851, see *The Correspondence of Thomas Carlyle and Ralph Waldo Emerson, 1834–1872*, 2 vols., Boston, 1883, II, 200–204.

249. For Browning's account see pp. 41–42.

to the course I pursued about the cheque for Miss Martineau; he said he thought I had acted rightly and that Mr Lombe's letter was quite uncalled for.

Sunday 24 [27] *August 1851*

Read again Martineau's Article in the Westminster on Greg's "Creed of Christendom",—it is very ingenious, masterly and eloquent, but pervaded it seems to me by some fundamentally erroneous views.

Monday 25 [27] *August 1851*

Read Greg's Chapter on "Christian Eclecticism"[250] which I admire for its moral earnestness, plain straightforwardness and courage.

Tuesday 26 [27] *August 1851*

53-4.

Susanna's Birthday.
Spent the morning in making final corrections in the Prospectus which I today sent to press again.—
Susanna was [in] an unhappy excitable mood, and made Miss Evans the subject on which she gave vent to it, and hence I had a miserable morning, <supplemental to Elisabeth's upbraidings before breakfast that I was not kind to her and that every time last night I met her coldly the dear!>

Wednesday 27 August 1851

Spencer and Johnson read the proofs of the Prospectus this afternoon and suggested some valuable verbal corrections.—
Wrote an independent letter to Lombe tonight rebutting his reproofs &c &c. (See copy book).
Poor Sissie's health is diminishing which is now my chief concern and cause of sadness. Prompt means must be taken to recover it.

250. Chapter 14, Christian *Eclecticism*.

Thursday 28 August 1851

Miss Martineau called when I communicated to her Mʳ Lombe's intentions which delighted her extremely. I took [tea] with her and her cousin, and staid until 12 o'clock. She talks extremely well. I proposed she should appropriate £150 as remuneration for the abridgement of Comte, and should devote the remainder to its publication. She assented.[251]

I told her the nature of my correspondence with Mʳ Lombe,— she observed that I was quite right. She wanted me to publish Deerbrook[252] in the Cheap Series, but I did not encourage the idea.—

Friday 29 August—Monday 1 September 1851

[No entry.]

Tuesday 2 September 1851
55

Received a long and characteristic letter from James Martineau in answer to mine requesting him to write an Article on Xtian Ethics. Answered it Sepᵗ 6ᵗʰ (See copy Book).

Wednesday 3 September—Friday 5 September 1851

[No entry.]

Saturday 6 September 1851

Called upon Mʳ Ward the author of an Article in the Quarterly on Sanatory Consolidation &c, and it seems a writer in the Times. I found him a young handsome man, complaining of feeble health and exhaustion the result of his labors. He rather evaded the question of writing for the Westminster, observing that he

251. In her account of the transaction Harriet Martineau says "taking £200 for my own remuneration." (M. W. Chapman, ed., *Harriet Martineau's Autobiography*, 2 vols., Boston, 1877, II, 66.)
252. Her novel, first published in 1839.

had now more calls upon him than he could answer. By invitation I dined with him at 6, met Lewes, passed an agreeable hour but nothing more passed in reference to my object. Ward impressed me as being superior to the average of literary men as much in his moral tone as he is in literary power.—

Susanna called for me in a Cab whence we went and had tea with M^r & Mrs George Combe. We had a very interesting evening, he is venerable and full of wisdom, and the calm earnestness of his conversation is at once impressive and suggestive of the apostolic character which he seems to be conscious of as the teacher of a new science which he believes all important to the welfare of the race. He takes great interest in the Review, desired me to put him down as a subscriber for £20. (He is the first one) and will do all he can for me. We were delighted with Mrs Combe, so handsome, ladylike, and so completely a Siddons.[253]

Sunday 7 September 1851

Went with Susanna at 8, Morning, to Blackwall with a view of finding the Mercury Screw Steamer due from Falmouth and in which we expected Earnest.—[254] We could gain no intelligence of her anywhere. We wandered about in a boat for some hours, when Susanna went home, and I went to Blackwall and waited on the Pier until dark, was very cold, went home for an extra Coat and refreshment, and when I got back found the vessel arrived, and Earnest already gone to the Strand; and thus passed a weary day for nothing. Earnest is looking exceeding well, but changed.

Monday 8 September 1851

56.

Much disappointed this morning by the non arrival of remittances from America. Had it not been for the loan of £90 from the boarding house I could not have met the £200 due on Saturday. This ever recurring monetary difficulty is a painful addition to my many other anxieties, and I see no immediate prospect of deliverance from it. It must be so so long as my capital sustains

253. Mrs. Combe was Cecilia, daughter of the famous actress Mrs. Sarah Siddons (1755-1831).

254. Earnest had been at Truro; see Diary, 13 March 1851. Chapman spells his son's name this way several times.

such a relation to the sales effected as it does now. I have only £3000 nearly the half of which is locked up in "Goodwill & Fixtures" so that with £1500 available, I have turned over £6700 in the half year.—

Suffered from indigestion all night.

Tuesday 9 September 1851

Rec^d a letter from Martineau consenting to write the Article on "Xtian Ethics" but skillfully evading my question as to the meaning he attaches to the words "divine and permanent" in Xty. I wish I could nail him to an unequivocal confession of faith.

G. Combe called to recommend Mr Grattan[255] to write the Article on Lord Palmerston.—

Went with Mr Ireland & Dr Hodgson to the Zoological Gardens, and saw the Ourang outang for the first time.

Susanna took Earnest to see Beatrice after their long separation. Elisabeth's health becomes more impaired, she alarmed me today by 2 sudden screams from spasms in the head.

Wednesday 10 September 1851

57–8.

Spent a large part of today in addition to much time already in collecting facts and arriving at a decision in reference to a gas cooking stove.—

What with business, studies, an Editor's duties, the claims of my family, and the attention needed by the boarders and the means of carrying on the boarding house heaven knows I have my hands full.—However I have I think discovered a plan whereby we can use gas in a satisfactory way.—

Thursday 11 September 1851

Went with Mr Ireland and Dr Hodgson to dine with M^r & Mrs Wills, where we met Miss Glyn[256] the actress, who I fear is suffer-

255. Thomas Colley Grattan (1792–1864) was the author of a number of historical works. The Palmerston article appeared in the *Westminster Review*, 57 (April 1852), 555–592.
256. Isabella Dallas Glyn (1823–89) was playing at Drury Lane in 1851. Amaurosis is "decay of sight occurring without perceptible external change."

ing from the first stage of Amaurosis, and Mrs Harvey[257] the wife of the Editor of the Athenæum.—I discovered that Mrs Wills[258] is sister to the Messrs Chambers. Learnt from Wills that Dickins walks 12 miles a day.—

Had a long interview with Mr G. Combe this morning who manifests a very warm interest in the Review. Elisabeth surprised and pained me by reproaching me with want of hospitality to her friends—the Farrants!—

Friday 12 September 1851

Mr Woodfall returned from the Continent, and kindly offered monetary help if needed, as a facility for my going out for a fortnight, as I could not leave home with my present small balance in the bank.—But I fear the necessity of my presence to launch the first N^o of my "Library for the People"[259] will keep me at home.

<Elisabeth in tears again tonight, distrusting my affection. I was occupied with my book   indifferent   in despair.>[260]

$

Saturday 13 September 1851

Rec^d a letter from Call[261] saying that he has already made an abridged translation of the half of Compte, and that he intends to compress the whole into 2 volumes,—precisely what Miss Martineau proposed to do. I forwarded to her a copy of his letter

257. Eleanor Louisa Montagu Hervey, wife of Thomas Kibble Hervey (1799–1858).

258. Mrs. W. H. Wills was Janet, youngest sister of Robert Chambers (1802–71), the Edinburgh publisher and author. Wills had been Dickens's secretary since 1849.

259. The first number was William Ware's *Sketches of European Capitals*. Fifteen numbers were published in all, 1851–54.

260. About seven words in this deleted passage are illegible.

261. Wathen Mark Wilks Call (1817–90), of St. John's College Cambridge, A.B. 1843, was a clergyman of the Church of England 1847–57. "After a struggle which left lasting marks upon him, he renounced a sphere for which he had seemed exceptionally qualified." (*Athenæum*, 30 August 1890, pp. 288–289.) Call married Rufa Brabant Hennell in 1857. He contributed many articles to the *Westminster Review*, among them the ones on Carlyle and George Eliot in 1881. Chapman published his *Reverberations and Other Poems* in 1849.

which I fear will cause her great regret; but I hope she has too much good sense to wish to proceed under the circumstances.

A final letter from James Martineau fully confirming his former one—that he will write the Article on "Christian Ethics and Modern Civilization."

Went with Susanna to call upon the Combes before their departure for the North,[262]—found them both at home. He called up[on] me in the Morning, and left an advertizement for the Jany N^o of the "Westminster". He is therefore the first subscriber and first advertizer to the Review.

The 2 Neubergs and Miss Neuberg[263] arrived, Joseph will be a valuable aid in regard to giving an a/c of German literature.

E +
Sunday 14 September 1851

| 4. A.M.   59 ⊙ | From this day henceforth I desire to abstain totally from all alcoholic liquors, except when taken medicinally, and to limit this exception as stringently as possible. May this and another resolve I have formed today be firmly kept!

I left London Bridge this morning with Hodgson and Ireland at 8 for Brighton, where we had a most beautiful day, and seabath, after which I had a row. Had a long conversation with Ireland at his request on the subject of Women, Prostitution, Marriage and the relation of the sexes generally.

Monday 15 September 1851

Poorly all morning from indigestion. Took E. in a Cab. for a little air, she being very weak, and made some enquiries about a ship for her brother to proceed to Australia.

Rec^d a letter from Mr Combe written by Mr Clarke (son of Sir

262. The George Combes lived at 45 Melville Street, Edinburgh.

263. Joseph Neuberg (1806–67), born in Germany, made a fortune in Nottingham and then retired to become secretary to Carlyle, to whom Emerson had introduced him. He boarded at Chapman's house for long periods. Miss Neuberg, his sister, had lived with him since his wife died. The other Neuberg was probably a brother, come to London to see the Exhibition. In 1855 Joseph was a suitor of Barbara Leigh Smith. See Chapman's letters to her 8 and 15 August 1855.

James)[264] containing some valued hints about writers on our foreign policy.

My Brother Henry[265] who has come to see the Exhibition called upon me, he seems as clownish and non-progressive as ever, and weak from some affection in the throat.

Tuesday 16 September 1851

Rose unrefreshed as is now usually the case, having had excited dreams. I will try such discipline of myself as will tend to allay them.

Prof. Newman passed the afternoon with me, he seems very bitter against Lord Palmerston, and alleged some things which *if true* are much to his discredit. I asked him *generally* to become a contributor to the Review but no subject[266] suggests itself to him at present. He seems to be in a hopeless chaotic state on political topics. Recᵈ a letter from Miss Martineau about Call's version of Comte,—she does not like to relinquish the task.—

Wednesday 17 September 1851

Rose at 5.30.

Wrote to ask Froude to supply a light article for the January Nᵒ, and to ask Miss E.'s opinion about the Comte affair.

Took Susanna and Ernest to Hyde Park and Rowed them on the Serpentine and overfatigue[d] myself—curiously Ernest became sick.

Ordered a gas cooking stove,—fitting and all complete £42.. 0.. 0.

<Elisabeth took offence at an expression, "I count the days until friday week" in my letter addressed to Miss Evans.—>

Thursday 18 September 1851

Rose at 5.30 feeling headache, worked all morning at the Suffrage Question.[267] Walked to the Exhibition and back and saw a

264. See Diary, 20 May 1851.
265. The only other mention of Henry Chapman is the record of his birthday, 27 December 1823.
266. The words *but no subject* are inadvertently repeated.
267. See Diary, 4 October 1851.

new "Eve and the Serpent" by Van der Ven.[268] Very beautiful but not equal to Monti's.

Susanna was out of temper and anxious for a scene, in reference to E. and Miss Evans coming.—Then E. came to me and complained that Susanna tried to lay her troubles at her door,— she cried also, of course,—what a life it is!

Nixon vested £85 in my business making the total of his loan £150.

Friday 19 September 1851

5.45.

Reading on the Suffrage.—

Had a letter from Newman about the Article on "Sanatory Consolidation" in the Quarterly, very characteristic of his present phasis.

My brother Tho⁵ sent me a dressing case which he had made for me,[269]—I showed it to Susanna, when it became the occasion of a long and most painful altercation or conversation arising out of her condemnation of what she chooses to designate my extravagance.

Went to see Beatrice who was very happy tho' affected by the chickin pox. Met Owen,[270] Travis and Dʳ Brabant.

Saturday 20 September 1851

Resolved to go to Birmingham by way of Coventry, stopping at the latter place until Monday.

When I communicated my intention to Susanna she reproached me for not inviting her to accompany me; which I avoided doing having reflected about it and concluded that as there would be no time to give the Bray's notice it would not be prudent. However I was constrained to ask her to accompany me, and just when starting it occurred to me that Mʳ Noel[271] and his family would possibly be visiting the Brays. We found them expected tonight, Mʳˢ Bray very ill, and all painfully concerned by our arrival. We

268. Jean Antoine van der Ven (1800–66), Dutch sculptor.
269. Thomas Chapman was a cutler and dressing-case maker in Glasgow.
270. Robert Owen (1771–1858), socialist and philanthropist, shared Dr. Travis's enthusiasm for spiritualism and coöperatives.
271. Edward Noel.

tried to go to an Hotel but Miss H.[272] would not let us, and finally as the Noels did not come we slept at Mr Bray's House.—

Sunday 21 September 1851

A most lovely day, which we all enjoyed fairly, but with the heavy drawback of Mrs Bray's illness, and the consciousness that we ought not to have troubled our friends with our presence at such a time.

Miss Evans thinks I should lose power and influence by becoming a writer in the Westminster Review, and could not then maintain that dignified relation with the various contributors that she thinks I may do otherwise.

Monday 22 September 1851

Susanna returned to Town, and I went to Birmingham at 11.40.—dined with Mrs Dawson at Edgbaston (her husband having gone to London),[273] then called at Mr Robt Martineaus,[274] had a long conversation with Miss Martineau who gave me the history of J. S. Mill's relation with Mrs Taylor, now his wife. Walked to Town (Birmingham) called on the Booksellers with a view of establishing an agency for my books,—went to a concert at the Town Hall, where by appointment I met the Martineaus with whom I returned and supped. Left them at 11.15. and Birmingham by the midnight train at 12.15.

Tuesday 23 September 1851

60–1

Reached home at 5.30 A.M.

Lewes called in the afternoon to express his high opinion of Miss Evans' Article in the Leader.[275]

272. Sara Hennell, Mrs. Bray's sister.
273. George Dawson (1821–76), popular lecturer and preacher, was pastor of the Undenominational Church of the Saviour in Birmingham from 1847 till his death. Chapman published Mrs. Dawson's *Stories for Sunday Afternoons*.
274. Robert Martineau was a brother of James and Harriet.
275. The review of Greg's *The Creed of Christendom*, 20 September 1851, pp. 897–899.

Wednesday 24 September 1851

A letter from Call expressing a willingness to put the 3 vols. (abridged) which he has done of Comte into the hands of my "correspondent" (i.e. Miss Martineau) to use as part of the abridgment to be published by me. Sent a copy of the proposition to her.

A letter from Newman expressing his willingness to write one of 3 Articles which he names.—

Walked home with Syme who says he is not enjoying good health. I half fear he may not be able to do the American Article after all.—

Thursday 25 September 1851

62.

Wrote to Froude about the Article on Mary Queen of Scots.[276]
Proposed to Neuberg to give some help in the way of supplying German literary intelligence which he agreed to do.—
Attended Limbirds[277] sale.—
Received another design for the cover of the "Library for the People" but am not yet quite satisfied.

Friday 26 September 1851

Went to the Exhibition with Elisabeth and Ernest,[278] the pleasure was destroyed by E's sensitiveness. I expressed an opinion differing from hers on the subject of the Children and their education perhaps rather brusquely, when she reproached me with unkindness.

In the afternoon I expressed my wish decisively respecting some pens she was giving Mr Hogg instructions about when she complained that I commanded her, and went into tears again.

It seems to me that in proximity with women a man cannot command his own peace!

276. "Mary Stuart," *Westminster Review*, 57 (January 1852), 96–142.
277. John Limbird, printer and publisher, 344 Strand.
278. Chapman wrote *Earnest* and deleted the *a*.

Saturday 27 September 1851
63.

Busied with preparing the design for the cover of the "Library for the People". It costs me so much time and labor, that I fear the speculation will not be a profitable one.—

Rec^d the first book *gratis,* on a/c of the Westminster Review, viz, "Letters of Mary Queen of Scots" from Colburn.—[279]

Went to meet Susanna and M^{rs} and Miss Hardmeet[280] at the Exhibition, and found Beatrice and Mrs Hennell at home on our return.

Beatrice seems to improve in health, and is remarkably intelligent.

Consulted Mrs Hennell about Call's translation of Comte,—we are both of opinion his ought to be proceeded with and that Miss Martineau should leave the field open to him.

<Spencer spent the evening with us when we had of course abundant discussion.>

Sunday 28 September 1851

Took E. to Regents Park, thence to call on Mackay whom we found as 'odd' as ever.

Spencer took tea and passed the evening with us.—

I am becoming more and more impressed with the importance of rousing the attention of the public to the condition of our Colonial empire with a view to such legislation as shall secure its integrity, and propose if I can find the right man to commence a series of Articles on the subject in the Jany N^o of the Review.[281]

Monday 29 September 1851

Miss Evans and D^r & Mrs Hodgson arrived.—

279. Agnes Strickland, ed., *Letters of Mary, Queen of Scots,* new edition, 2 vols., London, Henry Colburn, 1850, was one of the books reviewed in the "Mary Stuart" article.
280. Cf. Diary, 20 February 1851, where the name is spelled *Hardmett.*
281. See Diary, 9 July 1851.

Tuesday 30 September—Thursday 2 October 1851
[No entry.]

Friday 3 October 1851

64.

Accompanied R. W. Mackay on his first visit to the Exhibition. Dr Brabant Mr Bray, and Elisabeth also went with us.—

Saturday 4 October 1851

Spalding and Hodge's[282] Bill due =   117..14. 6.

I and Dr Hodgson called on W. J. Fox and had a long conversation with him on the educational movement. He read the Westminster Prospectus and expressed his admiration of it, and agreed to write the article on "National representation," I providing the facts.—[283]

We then went to call on Ward, and took him to Hyde Park, where we had a Row on the Serpentine. He nearly agreed to write the Article on the Peerage. The Dr and he got into a long discussion in reference to life in general and the design of creation in regard especially to the enormous cruelty evinced.—We were delighted with the spirit and tone of his remarks.—

Sunday 5 October 1851

Took Elisabeth to Camden Town with me to see the Children, who were truly delighted with our visit, and I the same, especially with Ernest's manifestation of affection for me.—

Dr & Mrs Hodgson, Miss Evans, and I went to dine with the Ellises[284] where we enjoyed ourselves very well.—

Walked home with Miss Evans.

282. Wholesale stationers.

283. William Johnson Fox (1786–1864), preacher, politician, and man of letters, had written the initial article for the *Westminster Review* in 1824. Fox's article, "Representative Reform," was placed at the beginning of Chapman's first number of the *Westminster*, 57 (January 1852), 1–41.

284. William Ellis (1800–81), economist, Utilitarian philosopher, and founder of the Birkbeck schools, lived at Champion Hill.

Monday 6 October 1851

65

Had a long walk with Miss Evans in Hyde Park, called on Jeffes[285] the french-Bookseller who agreed to lend us books for the purpose of Review.

Tuesday 7 October 1851

66.   5 a.m.

Called on Ward and proposed to him to write an Article on the Peerage to meet Mr Lombe's wishes;—he declined on the ground of differing from Mr Lombe in toto, and that he wishes to devote his energies to the Sanatory Question.—Had a long conversation with him and was much gratified.—

Took Elisabeth early this morning to the Railway Station to accompany her brother into Berkshire.—This evening determined on the writers for the foreign section of the Review.—

Wednesday 8 October 1851

Completed my purchase of the Westminster Review by the payment of £300, to Mr Hickson, and our mutual signature of the deed of agreement.

The non-arrival from America of remittances is embarrassing me extremely.—

Had a large party this evening on a/c of Miss Bremer,[286] including Sir David Brewster[287] & Daughter, Mr Ellis and family, Mr Kay,[288] Dr Hodgson, Dr Booth, & others. The Unitarian element

285. This call at William Jeffs's shop in the Burlington Arcade was the occasion of Marian Evans's first meeting with George Henry Lewes.

286. Frederika Bremer (1801–65), Swedish novelist, had gone to America in 1849, and was stopping in England on her way home. Her books were well known through English translations by Mrs. Howitt.

287. David Brewster (1781–1868), scientist and author of many works on optics, is famous for his discovery of the polarization of light. He was a leader in the Scottish Free Church movement.

288. Joseph Kay (1821–78), economist and writer on social and educational reform, was a brother of Sir James Phillips Kay-Shuttleworth.

represented by Mr R. Martineau & Wife, and Mr Shaen[289] and Wife was becomingly rigid and cold. Miss Seton is a delightful girl.

Thursday 9 October 1851

Called on the Secretary of the Chemical Society[290] for the £63 rent due from the Soc: he promises it in a few days, wh: in the meantime alas is no relief to me. I have desired the assistants to postpone the execution of foreign orders for the present, wh: is a very painful step to me.—I have consumed £220 lent me by Woodfall, and am yet in the same pressing difficulty.

Had severe headache this evening, took a long walk with Dr Hodgson, and returned quite exhausted.—

Mackay read my financial circular of the Westminster, in a hopeful spirit.—

Friday 10 October 1851

E +

Walked to Chelsea with Miss Evans, and left her while I called on Carlyle to request him to write an Article on the Peerage, which he declined to do.[291] He talked a long time to little purpose, and seems to be angry with most things and especially with the Exhibition and "that blockhead, Cole."[292]

In the afternoon I called on Harwood[293] requesting him to

289. William Shaen was a London solicitor with progressive sympathies.

290. The Chemical Society rented two rooms at 142 Strand, 3 November 1849, at £55 a year. The arrangement proved unsatisfactory, and 7 April 1851 the Society moved to 5 Cavendish Square, which the 1852 Report refers to as "a locality more worthy of its high position. . . . The advantages of the present abode need not indeed be particularised in addressing Members, upon whom the deficiencies of our former locality must be vividly impressed." See *The Jubilee of the Chemical Society of London,* London, 1896, pp. 157–158. Robert Warington was Secretary.

291. For Carlyle's account of the visit see p. 41.

292. Henry Cole (1808–82) was a leading member of the committee for the Exhibition. He had helped Hickson buy the *Westminster Review* from Mill in 1840. See Carlyle to Sterling, 11 April 1840, in *Letters of Thomas Carlyle to Mill, Sterling, and Browning,* London [1923], p. 233.

293. Philip Harwood (1809–87), journalist, at this time on the *Morning Chronicle.* He was formerly a Unitarian minister.

write the Article referred to he declined, because he has not time. Afterwards I visited the Children at school;—when Ernest came into the room and found it was I, he said "Oh is that all!"

[Two leaves containing entries for *Saturday 11 October—Friday 17 October 1851* have been cut from the Diary.]

Saturday 18 October—Tuesday 28 October 1851
[No entry.]

Wednesday 29 October 1851
My mother died this day—1824.

Thursday 30 October—Friday 14 November 1851
[No entry.]

[Two leaves containing entries for *Saturday 15 November—Friday 21 November 1851* have been cut from the Diary.]

Saturday 22 November 1851
Miss Evan's Thirty-first birthday.—294

Sunday 23 November—Friday 28 November 1851
[No entry.]

Saturday 29 November 1851
My Father will be 59 years old.—

294. Chapman began to write *thirtieth*. It was really her thirty-second.

Sunday 30 November—Friday 26 December 1851

[No entry.]

Saturday 27 December 1851

My brother Henry was born 1823.—

Sunday 28 December 1851

Beatrice will be 7 years old.

Monday 29 December—Wednesday 31 December 1851

[No entry.]

"The Harmony of the Comprehensible World" (promised me) by Sir Richard Vyvyan Bart.[295]
L'origine des tous les culte" par Depuis.[296]

295. These notes are written at the end of the Diary, on the page for January accounts.
Richard Rawlinson Vyvyan, Bart. (1800–79), printed the book anonymously in 2 vols., 1842, and in 1 vol., 1845. See *The Dictionary of National Biography*, London, 1899, LVIII, 400.
296. Charles François Dupuis (1742–1809), *L'Origine de tous les cultes, ou la religion universelle*, 1795.

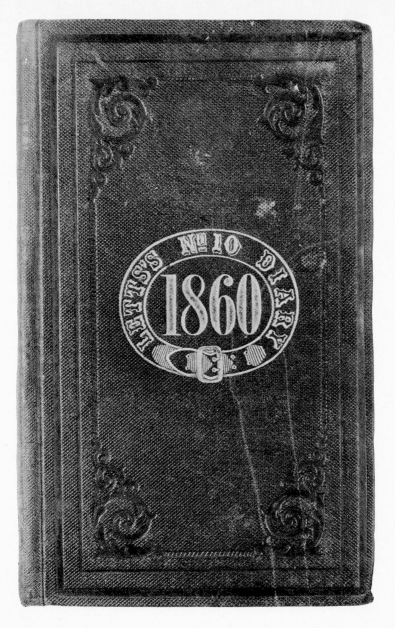

COVER OF CHAPMAN'S DIARY FOR 1860

CHAPMAN'S DIARY FOR 1860

√ Biography of Manin[1]
√ The Ethics of War[1]
√ Plutarch[1]
√ Japan[1]
√ Political State of Hungary[1]
√ The Study of Languages[1]
  Reform of Parliament (Spenser)[1]
  Philosophy of Religion[1]
√ Religions of India[1]
√ Rawlinson on the Evidences of Xtian Religion[2]
√ Latham on Darwin and Antiquity of Human Race.[3]
√ On teaching Latin to the Working classes.

The Study of Latin by the Working classes
Rawlinson on Evidences of Xtian Religion[2]
Plutarch[1]

    There are two Mills on the cooperative plan at Rippenden near Hallifax.

M[r] Bridges[4] commends Clairant's Geometry, and Algebra, in French.—

To Sundry a/cs due, viz.—

Rob[t] Hogg[5]	5.. 13.. 11
Berrall & C[o] [6]	5.. 1.. 0
Pope & Son[7]	10.. 10

1. These notes are suggestions for articles in the *Westminster Review*, 73 (April 1860).

2. "Rawlinson's Bampton Lectures for 1859," *Westminster Review*, 74 (July 1860), 33–49.

3. "Darwin on the Origin of Species," *Westminster Review*, 73 (April 1860), 541–570, [by Robert Gordon Latham (1812–88)].

4. John Henry Bridges. See 3 January 1860.

5. Robert Hogg, pharmaceutical chemist, 9 Albion Place. Chapman lived at 1 Albion Street.

6. Boot and shoe manufacturers, and importers of French shoes, 60–61 Marylebone Lane.

7. Furnishing ironmongers, 80–81 Edgeware Road.

Winckworth & Price[8] *say*	3..	3..	0
Smethurst[9]	2..	1..	3
Gillatt & Son[10]	2..	17..	0
H. B. Fearon & Son[11]	18..	4..	0
W. C. Cartwright	20..	0..	0

Paid
Dec. 20th

W. M. W. Call	22..	12..	0

Paid
Dec. 20th

Harrison[12]	15..	0..	0
Savill & Edwards[13] Jan[y] 25	78..	16..	2
Spalding & Hodge[14] "	57..	17..	4
F. M. D. Davis[15]	10..	0..	0
Authorship of Jan[y] W. R.[16]	77..	14..	0
	319..	10.. 6	

1860
Dec[r] 20

By Cash in Bank		371..	10..	2
" Manwaring's acceptance[17]		100..	0..	0
" Cash per M. in Jan[y]		190..	0..	0
	661..	10.. 2		

Sunday 1 January 1860

Headache all day: an ominous beginning of the New Year. Did nothing all day except call on the Mackays who came and spent the evening with us. Spencer who also came gave a qualified assent to act as a shareholder in the Westminster Publishing Comp[y] on behalf of M[r] Smith.[18]

8. Wine and spirit merchants, 80 Marylebone Road.
9. Lamp and oil merchants, 139 New Bond Street.
10. Wine and spirit merchants, 16 Jermyn Street.
11. Wine and spirit merchants, 145 New Bond Street.
12. Frederic Harrison, see Diary, 22 January 1860. This, like the payments to Cartwright and Call, was for an article in the *Westminster Review*.
13. Printers of the *Westminster Review*.   14. Wholesale stationers.
15. Frederick Maurice Drummond-Davies, for the article on Ceylon.
16. i.e., for the other articles.   17. See Diary, 1 April 1860.
18. Octavius Henry Smith, owner of the great distilling business bearing his name, was a son of William Smith, M.P. (1756–1835) and an uncle of Florence Nightingale and Barbara Leigh Smith Bodichon, George Eliot's friend. He shared Spencer's disapproval of "government meddling" in business affairs. See Herbert Spencer, *An Autobiography*, London, 1904, I, 375; II, 33, *et passim*.

Monday 2 January 1860

Rejected and returned articles as follows:
On Japan By Rev[d] A. J. Ross—[19] badly constructed and a failure as regards description.
On Gothic Architecture, by L. J. Trotter—clever, smart and effective but very onesided and full of bad taste.
On Bain & Ferrier,[20] by J. O'Connell, acute and logical but shallow, unconscientious & sarcastic.

Tuesday 3 January 1860

M[r] J. H. Bridges[21] writes that my "Christian Revivals"[22] article "is the boldest assertion of spiritual freedom that the Review has contained for a long time", and that he prefers the *style* much to any article he has seen of mine. M[r] W. B. Donne[23] writes,—"The Christian Revivals is an admirable and most useful article—I suppose by "Adam Bede"[24] from the intimate knowledge displayed of the religious emotions of the lower classes". Wrote to M[r] Hippisley[25] Beatrice[26] and Elisabeth.[27]

Wednesday 4 January 1860

Received a letter from T. C. Sandars—[28] a "Saturday Review" writer—very characteristic of "Saturday Review" principles. He

19. Alexander Johnstone Ross.
20. Alexander Bain (1818–1903), psychologist and logician, published *The Emotions and the Will* in 1859. James F. Ferrier (1808–64), metaphysician, was Professor of Moral Philosophy and Political Economy at St. Andrews. His *Institutes of Metaphysics* was published in 1854, second edition 1856.
21. John Henry Bridges (1832–1906), Positivist philosopher. He was a disciple of Richard Congreve, at whose house he had Christmas dinner with Lewes and George Eliot in 1859, when he told them that Chapman's publishing business was to be turned into a Limited Liability Company. See GE to Sara Hennell, Friday [30 December 1859].
22. "Christian Revivals," *Westminster Review*, 73 (January 1860), 167–217.
23. William Bodham Donne (1807–82), Librarian of the London Library, 1852–57, was Examiner of Plays in the Lord Chamberlain's Office, 1857–74.
24. The identity of Marian Evans and George Eliot had become generally known in the summer of 1859.
25. J. H. Hippisley, a gentleman of independent means, lived at Cox's Hotel, 55 Jermyn Street.
26. Beatrice Chapman. See Diary, 12 January 1860.   27. Elisabeth Tilley?
28. Thomas Collett Sandars (1825–94), London barrister and editor of Justinian's *Institutes* (1853).

says,—"I do not see what the Saturday can say on the Revivals article which is excellent and very instructive. But the writer goes to the root of the matter and there the Saturday cannot follow her." Again the writer is thought to be *a woman*, and in Sandars' case certainly Mrs Lewes.

Thursday 5 January 1860

Resumed my German readings with Johanna—[29] beginning with "Don Carlos",[30] and my exercises in writing German.

How difficult is self-culture—of the *whole* man! Among my many faults I desire to struggle separately with the following: 1st my unduly strong love of approbation and praise; 2nd my unduly

Friday 6 January 1860

frequent consultation of others before deciding in each case needing decision instead of quietly deciding at once for myself; 3rd my desultoriness and expansiveness in study; 4th my restless unhappiness unless basking in the smiles of Johanna, who though in respect to beauty of form and voice and certain mental qualities is a glorious & fascinating creature, is nevertheless very capricious and often both ungenerous and unjust; 5th my habit of letting all my time pass in common secular work—giving none to spiritual culture and self-elevation. How few moments of aspiration how few hallowed hours I now experience!

Saturday 7 January 1860

Prepared statements as a basis for determining the price at which my business shall be bought by the shareholders of the W. R. Comp^y and the amount of the shares to be allotted to the capital creditors fixed.

Letter from Johnson admiring my article. Went with S. to the Rowans to meet a few friends. Mr Woodfall expressed strong commendation of the Review and said my article was only too short.

29. Johanna von Heyligenstaedt. See pp. 106–110.
30. Schiller's play.

Sunday 8 January 1860

Spent the morning with Mr Grote,[31] who expressed himself delighted with the Revival article. Had much physiological conversation with him. Asked him to authorize me to act as his representative-shareholder in the W. R. Comp^y. He agreed to do so with Lord S——'s[32] consent.

Visited David Power, Q. C.,[33] and his wife at Wimbledon with whom I stayed all night.

Monday 9 January 1860

They praised the Revival article strongly. They asked me to become M^{rs} P's physician. Left them at 1 p.m., having enjoyed my visit much.

Agreed with Mr Drummond-Davies[34] to write an article on Japan.

Letter from Mr Sandars inviting me to dine on Wednesday with me [him] and congratulating me as the author of Christian Revivals. Ernest out until 11.40 p.m! Lord Macauley[35] buried.

Tuesday 10 January 1860

On Sunday morning[36] I said a few words simply by way of suggestion that the various kinds of food &c for the house might be bought in larger quantities and at less frequent intervals. These remarks irritated Susanna and have by successive waves direct and reflex involving Johanna risen into a complete storm.

31. George Grote (1794–1871), historian, was one of the original founders of London University, of which he became Treasurer in 1860, and President in 1868. He persuaded J. S. Mill to write for the *Westminster Review* after Chapman bought it in 1851, and was one of the group who saved it from bankruptcy in 1854.

32. Edward Henry Stanley, fifteenth Earl of Derby (1826–93), was M.P. for Kings Lynn 1848–69 and Indian Secretary 1858–59. He was the author of *The Church Rate Question Considered*, 1853, and other liberal pamphlets. See p. 103.

33. David Power, Queen's Counsel on the Norfolk Circuit and Recorder of Ipswich.

34. Frederick Maurice Drummond-Davies. *Westminster Review*, 73 (April 1860), 508–540.

35. Thomas Babington Macaulay, first Baron Macaulay (1800–59) died 28 December. He was buried in Westminster Abbey.

36. 8 January.

Wednesday 11 January 1860

Went to dine at Southgate[37] with M[r] T. C. Sandars who had two of the Village ladies besides his wife and sister to form the party. Had a long chat alone with him until midnight. It *was* Miss Evans to whom he ascribed "Christian Revivals"; he thought the style and thought hers and agrees with it wholly. He thinks the Westminster original but *crude*.

Thursday 12 January 1860

Completed my private accounts for 1859, during which I have expended £550. I cannot afford to continue this scale of expense.
Yesterday Madame Wartel[38] came to board with us at 30/– a week. She has a sitting-room and piano in the next house.

I feel extremely anxious about dear Beatrice who is alone with Mme de Pontés, and who attending to her in the night has insufficient rest.[39]

Friday 13 January 1860

Occupied all morning in preparing statements as bases of conversation with Lord Stanley tomorrow.

Had a pleasant walk with Johanna in Kensington Gardens talking chiefly German in order to exercise myself. Susanna and Ernest are gone to visit M[r] and Mrs Keymer.—

Saturday 14 January 1860

Went to the Hospital again after a long absence and heard Bence Jones[40] lecture. At Mrs Malleson's party in the evening. Had an interview this morning of about an hour with Lord Stan-

37. In Middlesex, about five miles north of London.
38. Alda Thérèse Annette Wartel (1814–65), French pianist.
39. In September 1859 Beatrice went to stay at 23 Rue du Château, Neuilly, Paris, with Madame de Pontés, who taught her German in return for her services as companion. See Chapman to Johanna von Heyligenstaedt, 26 September 1859.
40. Henry Bence Jones (1814–73) was on the staff of St. George's Hospital 1846–72.

ley. He wrote a formal note to me making the £600 he advanced to me in Novr 1858 a free gift. Without making any proposal he evinced a disposition to help me as he intended to have done by a yearly sum before the advance of £600 had been advanced to pay Mr Courtauld.[41] He expressed great satisfaction with the Review and said he agreed with every word of my article. He also told me that he was in the society of several clergymen who quoted the article with approval.[42]

Sunday 15 January 1860

Mr Malleson[43] came to fetch me to attend his little girl.
C Johanna whose singing has now been interrupted several days at length became unwell.
This irregularity is a terrible trial in her profession.

Monday 16 January 1860

During a discussion on the Book of Genesis yesterday Susanna took offence at a remark of mine and began to cry. Just as I went out to Mr Malleson's I put a paper into her hand saying I did not intend to hurt her feelings, I was sorry if I had unintentionally done so, and begged her to think and *say* no more of it. Still she reverted to the subject at night, and as I forbad further discussion she began again today!

Tuesday 17 January 1860

Wrote to Mrs Lewes asking her consent to my republication of her articles which appeared in the Westminster;[44] and to Mr O. H. Smith & to Mr Spencer urging a final decision as to their position in the Westminster Comp^y.
Visited Miss Mabel Malleson again, and obtained a new subscriber to the Westminster.

41. Samuel Courtauld. See p. 64.
42. In 1858 Lord Stanley had expressed to Chapman his approval of Spencer's articles in the *Westminster Review*. See Herbert Spencer, *An Autobiography*, 2 vols., 1904, II, 39-40.
43. William Taylor Malleson.   44. See p. 102.

Wednesday 18 January 1860

Had a slight attack of Erysipelas around the right ear last night —the pain preventing sleep almost entirely. At 10 p.m. took Tinct. Ferri Sesqui. Chlorid. m. XX, and as the pulse and inflammatory symptoms increased took Pil. Cal. C⁰ g. V at 2 a.m: Some hours afterward felt sufficiently well to go out. Called on Mr Grote who wrote me a formal authorization to act as his representative shareholder in the Westminster Compy.

Thursday 19 January 1860

Called on Mr O. H. Smith and was disappointed and surprised to find him draw back from the assent he gave Dec. 30 to commute his claim into shares. His ground being that unless more influential names can be obtained the Compy will fail. Dr Carpenter[45] expressed much sympathy with my object, and promised, if he had Mr Grote's approval to join. Prof. Huxley[46] gave such a promise absolutely.

Friday 20 January 1860

Addressed to Mr Grote the letter which is copied at the beginning of this diary.
Copy of a letter to Geo. Grote 20 Jany 1860.

"Dear Sir, I beg to apologize for my inattentiveness which caused me to misunderstand what you said, and you to have the trouble of correcting my error respecting the time when convenient to you to see Mr Smith. I have written to him to rectify my mistake.

"I regret exceedingly that your valuable time has been so much drawn upon by reason of the trust which you were good enough to undertake, and which could I have foreseen the trouble it has involved, I should not have ventured to ask you to take charge of; for I well know how precious your hours are. Unfortunately I can only express my gratitude for your very important aid in an affair both difficult and delicate, and one which I could not have rightly managed myself.

45. William Benjamin Carpenter. See Diary, 6 January 1851.
46. Thomas Henry Huxley (1825–95).

"When Lord S—— advanced the £600, which at that time he desired me to regard as 'a debt of honour', he entrusted it to me to use it only on condition of being able by means of it so to free myself from my business and creditors as would ensure the safety of the Westminster Review.

The terms of the advance and the duty implicitly imposed on me to take care that the money should be used only to purchase Mr Courtauld's claim, and not to advantage other creditors, seemed to me to necessitate extremely circumspect action, and I hope that under the circumstances, you do not think me to have been unduly guarded in my communications on the subject with Mr O. H. Smith.

"I told you yesterday that I believed Mr Smith was informed at the time when Mr Courtauld's claim was bought who advanced the money: on reference to my Diary today I find that my memory was not accurate, and that it was a few weeks afterwards, viz., on the 17th of Jany 1859, that I told Mr Smith, in strict confidence, the precise nature of the transaction."

"I am, dear Sir
Very truly yours
JOHN CHAPMAN"

"George Grote Esq."

Saturday 21 January 1860

Am suffering so severely from Cold that I am unable to go out.

Sunday 22 January 1860

Cold becomes worse. Johanna in the same condition. M^m Wartel also affected, but not so bad.

Mr Bridges, Mr Beasley[47] and Mr Harrison[48] came & spent the evening with us. Mme Wartel played magnificently a magnificent piece from Beethoven.

47. Edward Spencer Beesly (1831–1915), Positivist, had been appointed Professor of History at University College, London, in 1859.
48. Frederic Harrison (1831–1923), jurist and man of letters. Like Beesly and Bridges, Harrison came under Richard Congreve's influence at Wadham College and remained a Positivist all the rest of his life.

Monday 23 January 1860

Mr Smith called. He was much pleased with the prospect of gaining scientific adherents to the Comp^y. Intimated that he should probably be willing ultimately to give his name.

Letter from Beatrice.

Tuesday 24 January 1860

Wrote to Prof. Newman and the Countess Teleki[49] about their articles, as well as sundry other letters.

Feel better but far from well. Received from Mr Grote a reply to my letter addressed to him on the 20th ins^t. It is all that I could wish, and sets my doubts entirely at rest. Heaven knows that in the matters to which my letter to him refers I have carefully striven to do the exact right, but distrusting myself as I do, it is a great satisfaction to have Mr Grotes cordial approval. Have copied his reply.—

Copy of Mr Grote's reply to the above [20 January 1860]:—

"Barrow Green—Oxted—Surrey   Jany 24. 1860

Dear Sir

"It was quite unnecessary for you to excuse yourself for taking up so much of my time: which is undoubtedly very precious to me, but which I am glad in being able to employ so as to serve both a cause and a person whom I very much esteem.

I saw Dr Carpenter on Friday, and talked with him on the matters which I learned from you. I gave him my *own* opinion very decidedly: but that after all is only an individual opinion; and he seemed determined to take the step of consulting the Vice Chancellor: which is, in his position, the most prudent course of proceeding.

"I think the only common ground upon which you can take your stand, is to secure perfect freedom for the promulgation of all varieties of individual conviction."

Yours very truly

GEO. GROTE"

"Dr Chapman"

49. Countess Teleki von Szék had come to England from Transylvania with her husband, who became a British subject 18 November 1856. For an account of the family see *Historisch-Heraldisches Handbuch*, 1855, pp. 991–994. Her article is perhaps that on "Austria, and the Government of Hungary," *Westminster Review*, 73 (April 1860), 457–485.

Wednesday 25 January 1860

Called on Prof. Huxley. Spencer came in immediately afterwards, and though he saw he was an interruption had not the politeness to go. Silence having lasted some minutes after he had done his business with Huxley he boldly asked if I had come to talk over the Comp^y scheme. He then helped Prof. Huxley to the conviction that such a Comp^y is needless. Huxley wants to make it a condition of his adhesion (already conditionally offered) that the Comp^y shall have controul of the Rev.

Thursday 26 January 1860

Prof. Huxley breakfasts with O. H. Smith this morning to discuss the subject. Dr Carpenter assured me today that if the Vice-Chancellor of the Lond. University[50] approves his joining the Comp^y he will do so however Huxley may decide; and added that he thinks Huxley has no right to attempt to dictate to me what I shall do with the Review.

Johanna's cough & my cold still persist.

Friday 27 January 1860

Mr Smith called and echoed the views of Spencer & Huxley as to the formation of the Company.

I therefore put three plans before him one of which he must authorize me to carry about: 1. To allow me to form the Comp^y with the elements now available. 2. To place the business in Mr Manwaring's[51] hands, Mr S. and I being his capital creditors. Or (3) to wind up the business forthwith. He promises to give me a final answer.

Saturday 28 January 1860

Mr Morton (introduced by Thos Cholmondeley[52]) spent the evening with me.

50. William Benjamin Carpenter was Registrar of London University, 1856–79. Sir John George Shaw-Lefevre (1797–1879) was Vice-Chancellor 1842–62.

51. George Manwaring. See p. 104.

52. In 1854 Chapman published *Ultima Thule: or, Thoughts Suggested by a Residence in New Zealand,* by Thomas Cholmondeley.

Sunday 29 January 1860

Feel somewhat better and had a walk with Johanna in Kensington Gardens.

Mr Crawford and Mr Morton spent the evening with us.

Monday 30 January 1860

My cold considerably worse. Did not go out.

Mr Church, who dined with us, says that Harriet Martineau is reporting injurious things of me in the hope of preventing me from forming the Comp^y.!

Tuesday 31 January 1860

Rose at 7 and did a German exercise before breakfast.

The Review is selling excellently. Only 10 copies now left out of 1620.

Ernest is suffering from Diarrhœa. Finished reading an able article on Trades-Unions by a carpet weaver J. Michie of Kendal.

Wednesday 1 February 1860

Rose at 6.30. Shocked by learning that England's greatest Physician—Dr Todd, died suddenly on Monday last! What a loss!

Mr Bridges called to say Farewell. He marries on Tuesday next, and leaves Plymouth for Australia on the 10th proximo. Wrote to C. Tenant, Miss Lipscomb, J. Michie, Prof. Newman, and J. H. Hippisley. Asked the latter for his annual contribution to the *Westminster* of £100.

Thursday 2 February 1860

[No entry.]

Friday 3 February 1860

Called with Johanna on Mrs Malleson who, however, was not at home. Wrote and sent off 8 letters. Feel much better today.

Saturday 4 February 1860

Called on Dr Carpenter who told me that the Vice Chancellor of the Lond. University did not object to his joining the Comp^y but that unless other scientific men joined it he should prefer not to be the only one. He, Huxley, Major Noel[53] & others had dined together and they had all adopted the same opinion as to the desirableness of identifying the Review with the Comp^y. Called on Huxley, while I was there, Sir C. Lyell[54] came in. I mentioned the Comp^y scheme to him. He was quite indisposed to consider the subject, and told me that I am the most sanguine man he knows. Had a long talk with Huxley afterwards, but he persists in his opinion. Ernest got up early for the first time and began latin again.

Sunday 5 February 1860

Feel very poorly this morning; pulse 56 only and very feeble; urine turbid; headache. Went with Johanna to Hampstead where we walked and then had Bread Cheese & Beer, and this evening— we both feel much better.—Asked Ernest to go but he declined.

Monday 6 February 1860

Called on Mr O. H. Smith for his decision concerning the business. We talked 3 hours, and he then finally said he should wish to see Mr Grote before deciding. He said that if the business be wound up Mr Manwaring must of course be paid his £180, and the publications should be placed with someone for sale on commission.

Received £100 from Mr Hippisley. A letter from Beatrice.

Tuesday 7 February 1860

Made a present to James Michie, a poor carpet weaver at Kendal, of a set of the Review. Wrote to Mr Hippisley. Proposed to

53. Robert R. Noel, the second son of the Rev. Thomas Noel, was an elder brother of Edward Noel. See Diary, 27 June 1851; E. C. Mayne, *Life of Lady Byron*, pp. 373–381; Gerardine MacPherson, ed., *Memoirs of the Life of Anna Jameson*, Boston, 1878, and Mrs. S. Erskine, ed., *Anna Jameson: Letters and Friendships*, London [1915], *passim*.
54. Charles Lyell (1797–1875), geologist.

Mr Wilson[55] to write an article on the Papal Question. Called on
Mr C. Tenant who wants to write an article on Direct Taxation.
He is a religious bigot. Ernest who has been suffering from Diar-
rhœa is now much better.

Wednesday 8 February 1860

I easily form and easily break my resolutions; from this time
forward I will strive to be more inflexible.
Rose at 6.20. Wrote to Beatrice.
Cards came this morning, addressed to me, announcing Dr
Bridges' marriage. Mrs C. was vexed because they were not addressed to her. Later in the day she made this circumstance an
introduction to one of the usual useless and odious conversations.
She afterwards spoke with Earnest on the subject and then having
given me an open note by Ernest, who says he did not read it,
telling me her resolution was taken she went to Mrs Bell.—

A new Patient—Miss Sidebottom of Hallifax.

Thursday 9 February 1860

The mental excitement of yesterday has made me poorly and
capable of little work. S's "resolution" to leave me has already
vanished! She tells me that Beatrice writes enquiringly to her
(and Ernest privately) asking for information about me and the
Fräulein. She tells Ernest to remember that whenever anything
goes wrong in the house I always scold Mama!

Friday 10 February 1860

Wrote for Mr Bridges letters of introduction to Mr C. H. Watts
and Mr Syme[56] of Melbourne Victoria. How happy Mr B's seem-

55. Thomas Wilson (b. 1811), Corpus Christi College, Cambridge, A.B. 1833,
A.M. 1838. He was curate of St. Peter's Mancroft, Norwich 1845–47, when he
resigned and left the Church. He was the author of *Catholicity, Spiritual and
Intellectual*, published by Chapman in 1850, the unorthodox character of
which caused the loss of his professorship at Bedford College. See M. J. Tuke,
A History of Bedford College, London, 1939, pp. 69–76, 315.

56. Ebenezer Syme. See Diary, 12 May 1851. He went to Australia in April
1853.

ing prospects and destiny are![57] Called on Lord Stanley. He did not approve of the scheme, I am happy to say, of identifying the property of the Review with that of the proposed Comp^y. Took S. to Huxley's lecture on Darwin.[58] Was disappointed.

Saturday 11 February 1860

Spent the morning discussing about the business with O. H. Smith. He authorizes me to propose to Mr Manwaring to carry on the business on his own a/c, Mr S. and I being his creditors. Made the proposal to Mr M. who will consider it. S. & Ernest ill with Diarrhœa. Find I can now read a German Medical book freely.

Read Darwin's Chapter on geological periods,[59] and Lewes's Introduction to his new edition of the Biographical Hist. of Philosophy.[60]

Sunday 12 February 1860

Worked until 11 a.m. and then my energy was wholly exhausted. Had a pleasant walk in Kensington Gardens with J. We met Mr Corbauld, Major Noel, and M^r & Mrs Whitehead.

I hope the removal of the Duty on Paper will benefit me to the extent of about £60 a year.—[61]

Monday 13 February 1860

Mr Manwaring expressed his willingness to conduct the business on his own name and on his own account. The feeling of coming freedom from business makes me feel unusually well today.

Mr Garcia and Mr Church spent the evening with us, and kept me up very late. J. ☽ tonight, two days too early.

57. It is ironical to note that Mrs. Bridges died soon after their arrival in Australia. Bridges returned to England, practising medicine at Bradford.
58. "On Species and Races, and their Origin," at the Royal Institution.
59. *On the Origin of Species,* Chapter IX, "On the Imperfection of the Geological Record."
60. There were editions in 1845–46, 1852, 1857, 1867, 1871, 1880, and 1891. This one is unrecorded.
61. The expected repeal of the Paper Duty was rejected by the House of Lords. Gladstone finally succeeded in forcing its acceptance 12 June 1861. See G. M. Trevelyan, *British History in the Nineteenth Century,* London, 1930, p. 329.

Tuesday 14 February 1860

Called and informed Mr O. H. Smith of Mr Manwaring's acceptance of the proposition made to him. M^r S's reply was—"What proposition was that Dr Chapman?" (!) He now urges that I should endorse Mr Manwaring's promissary note to him, in order that he may avail himself of Lord Stanley's aid to me! I have appealed to him in writing (see Copy Book) to reconsider his decision. Feel poorly and cannot work this evening.—

Wednesday 15 February 1860

[No entry.]

Thursday 16 February 1860

Called on Mr O. H. Smith again in great anxiety concerning his decision. He was in bed, from cold; I was taken to his room, and found him very cordial. My letter had evidently made an impression on him. His impulse was to wind the business up as the simplest way of terminating the whole tiresome affair. I offered, if he choose to let the business go on to transfer securities now held by Mr Grote to the extent of £100 to him so as to increase his share of the ultimately available assets. I think he was pleased with this offer, but said he did not feel inclined to avail himself of it. Finally he suggested that the publications might be made over to him by way of paying his debt. Called on Mr Mackay, Mrs Malleson, and heard Dr Perfitt[62] lecture in the evening.—

Friday 17 February 1860

[No entry.]

Saturday 18 February 1860

[No entry.]

62. Philip William Perfitt, Ph.D., was pastor of the Independent Free Church.

Sunday 19 February 1860

The Fräulein passed the morning in crying with vexation at the insult which she has just discovered herself to have received in the fact of the disappearance from her room of the key which locks the door between her room and mine. She says that she knows it to have been in the door some days ago, and misses it this morning.

Monday 20 February 1860

Yesterday afternoon Susanna confessed to having taken it out of the door on Saturday. I requested her to return it which she has done. After I went to bed last night Johanna began a discussion with her on the subject when words ran high. This I am very sorry for, and consider Johanna greatly to blame after I had undertaken to speak in order to save her from needless excitement—so injurious to her voice. Thus have passed two days of useless and uncalled for misery.

Tuesday 21 February 1860

Finished reading Darwin's book "On the origin of species by natural selection". It impresses me as one of the most important books of this century, and as likely to effect an immense mental revolution. The sagacity, knowledge and candour displayed in the work are unusually great and wonderful.—

Wednesday 22 February 1860

Called again on M[r] Smith who has not yet seen his lawyer and can say nothing decisive. Ernest still continues very poorly. Took him a walk into the Park and tried to cheer him up. Took Susanna to the Richardsons in the evening to meet D[r] Barker[63] of Bedford in order to get information of the schools of that town with a view to Ernest going there.—

63. Thomas Herbert Barker, M.R.C.S. 1842, M.D. London University, 1847, was vice-president of the Bedford Literary Institution, fellow of Queen's College, Birmingham, and a member of many professional and scientific societies.

Thursday 23 February 1860

Had very little sleep last night, and consequently quite energy-less this morning.

Spoke to Johanna in strong but general terms of condemnation of dresses which sweep the street. She was greatly offended & pained and thus our walk to Golden Square⁶⁴ was anything but a pleasant one. Settled the Business Bank a/c which shows a balance of only £116.

Mr Smith called at King Wm Stᵗ⁶⁵ to tell me that his solicitor says a plan may be devised which he can approve for placing the publications in his hands by way of payment of my debt.

Friday 24 February 1860—Sunday 4 March 1860
[No entries.]

Monday 5 March 1860

This evening Susanna and Ernest started to Paris via Dieppe. The position of Beatrice with Mᵐᵉ de Pontés since her husband's death has given me much anxiety. Madame's monomania that she might have saved him has in no degree lessened, and poor [Beatrice] is at length getting out of heart, and wrote for Mama to come to her.

Accompanied Johanna and Mᵐᵉ Wartel to an evening party at the Smiths (O. H.) Sir George & Lady Grey⁶⁶ and *Ben*. Smith (!) were there. Of course I never spoke with the latter.⁶⁷

Tuesday 6 March 1860—Friday 9 March 1860
[No entries.]

64. Adolphe Ganz, Johanna's singing teacher, lived at 37 Golden Square.
65. The office of the *Westminster Review* was transferred to 8 King William Street, Strand, in 1854, when Chapman moved to Blandford Square.
66. George Grey (1812-98), Governor of New Zealand 1845-53 and 1861-67.
67. Benjamin Leigh Smith, brother of Madame Bodichon. See p. 91.

Saturday 10 March 1860

J. H. Bridges sailed for Melbourne with his young wife.[68] His friend Harrison tells me that she is 1 or 2 years older than he; plain but possessing a vigorous intellect and excellent heart. Though the daughter of a clergyman and living in a secluded village she has quite freed herself from the popular Christian superstition!

Sunday 11 March 1860—Wednesday 28 March 1860

[No entries.]

Thursday 29 March 1860

This morning at about 10 a provisional agreement by which I transfer my business to Mr Manwaring was at length signed. This is an immense relief to me! I was prepared after all the difficulties and delays of the negociation to find Mr Manwaring break it off at the 11th hour. The signature was just in time to permit of announcing the transfer in the new W. R.[69]

Friday 30 March 1860

Susanna and Ernest returned from Paris yesterday afternoon after a long & rough passage via Havre. Ernest looks much better. At Beatrice's urgent request, at Mme's earnest wish and by my permission Beatrice is to remain with Madame 3 mo^s longer at any rate. Madame seems to get worse rather than better, and I feel very anxious about dear B.

Saturday 31 March 1860

The Review advertisements are good this time—there have rarely been so many. Mr Manwaring looks more cheerful than he

68. Susan Torlesse, fifth daughter of the Rev. Charles Martin Torlesse, vicar of Stoke-by-Nayland, was a cousin of Bridges.
69. See p. 104.

did when about to sign the agreement.—He tells me that the large houses have taken as many copies of the Review as they did of the January N⁰—

Wrote yesterday to Mʳ Darbishire, Mʳ Courtauld, & Lord Stanley. The latter sent me a very kind reply today.

Sunday 1 April 1860

Engaged all morning with the Review and domestic accounts. There is £126 in my private Bank, and exclusive of the April N⁰ there is about £100 due to me on account of the Review. But I fear Mʳ Manwaring will not be able to pay it at once. I greatly need a little more money to enable me to move freely. Johanna, Ernest & I caught in a storm in the Park.—

Monday 2 April 1860

Ich schreibe in der deutsche Sprache weil ich keine andere Uebung im deutschen Schrift habe.—Es ist nicht Geld genug im Bank die verschiedene Rechnungen zu bezahlen. Wenn Mʳ Manwaring fünf hundert omstatt drei hundert Pfund hätte wurde seine Pflicht viel leichter sein. Schriebe an Mʳ Hippisley, Mʳ Wilson Mʳ Pulszky⁷⁰ und andere. Ich habe Magen-Krankheit diesen Abend.

Tuesday 3 April 1860

Extremely annoyed today to learn that Mʳ Manwaring thinks I have altered a part of the Draft deeds of agreement in my own favour concerning the renewal of certain Bills! After a considerable talk he at length withdrew the odious imputation.

Wednesday 4 April 1860

Called on my lawyers but find no progress made. Mʳ Chorley⁷¹ has not communicated with them.

70. Francis A. Pulszky was the author of *Tales and Traditions of Hungary*, 3 vols., 1851. He may have written "Grievances of Hungarian Catholics," *Westminster Review*, 74 (July 1860), 178–193.

71. Thomas Fearncombe Chorley, Manwaring's solicitor.

A letter from Mr Courtauld declining to receive Manwaring's Bill in payment of my debt. The tone of the Letter is detestable.

The Michigan Central Dividend (24. 7. o) and £50 from Scott & Co came to hand.

Thursday 5 April 1860

Went with Mr Torr[72] to Mr Chorley and settled all the points in dispute in the agreements which are now fixed to be signed at 12 a.m. Saturday next.

Herbert Spencer & Drummond Davies dined with me.

Went at 9 p.m. with Johanna to meet her Mother & Sister[73] expected at the Lond. Bridge Station from Berlin at 10 p.m.: they did not arrive until 2 a.m. Friday so that we had to wait 4 hours at the Station.—

Friday 6 April 1860

Rose at 9. I have thought a great deal about Susanna with much compassion lately: precisely because her temper is so incontroulable, her domestic management such hopeless inefficiency and confusion and her incapacity of being cheerful or of allowing others near her to be so. I feel extremely sorry for her, try to be friendly & kind to her and frequently reprove Johanna for her least want of considerateness toward her. But alas! it is all in vain. She *determined* to have a scene with me this morning.

Saturday 7 April 1860

This morning the formal agreement for the transfer of my business was signed by us both; but to my surprise the bills as security for the purchase money were not forthcoming! Hence a short provisional agreement was again necessary until the bond and bills are prepared to be delivered next Thursday. Johanna very poorly, and her Mother very anxious this morning but well this evening.—

72. Joseph Hooley Torr, Chapman's solicitor.
73. Idalie von Heyligenstaedt.

Sunday 8 April 1860

Accompanied Frau v. Heyligenstaedt and her two daughters to Richmond where we spent the day. Madame—pondering over the causes of Johanna's depression and impaired health—asked Idalie whether it were possible that Johanna liebt den Doctor?!

The day was cold and damp, and the leaves not being out yet we profited by more than we enjoyed our excursion.

Mr Wise spent the evening with us. He says he believes that his novel[74] does not sell. Alas! poor man!

Monday 9 April 1860—Thursday 12 April 1860

[No entries.]

Friday 13 April 1860

J. v. H. ☽ 8 p.m.

Saturday 14 April 1860—Friday 11 May 1860

[No entries.]

Saturday 12 May 1860

Savill & Edwards (Jany West. Rev.)   79..0..0

Sunday 13 May 1860—Friday 22 June 1860

[No entries.]

74. John R. Wise, *The Cousin's Courtship*, London, Smith, Elder & Co., 2 vols., 1860.

Saturday 23 June 1860

Instructed Messrs Sudlow & Co 75 to deliver to Geo. Manwaring a written demand signed by me for the West. Rev. a/c.—

Witnessed the Review of the Volunteers76 in Hyde Park in company with Johanna v. Heyligenstaedt.

Spent the morning and evening with O. H. Smith discussing Mr Manwaring's affairs.

Sunday 24 June 1860

Went to Brighton; but obliged to pass the day reading Westminster Rev. proofs. Had a painful talk with Ernest.

The Fräulein wrote him a letter which annoyed him and his mother too. He willfully forgets now that he called out her free speaking by his former confidences to her about himself. Idalie returned to Town with me.

Monday 25 June 1860

Sent the last M.S. for the July Review to press only this morning.—

Spent the evening with Mr O. H. Smith. Helped him to compose and wrote from his dictation a letter to Mr Manwaring expressing his interpretation of the meaning of the Westminster Review agreement and his recommendation of what should be done respecting the bill which I have retained and which Manwaring claims.

Tuesday 26 June 1860

Mr S. wrote that he endorsed my interpretation of the agreement; recommended that I should retain the bill and should lend Manwaring £65 out of it; and that we should assent to his decision in writing. Manwaring refused to give me a written assurance of submission until I told him that unless I had it I should not advance any money. This brought him to terms. I then lent him £75.—taking his acceptance for £40 at 5 mos and for £35 at 8 mos.—

75. John James Joseph Sudlow & Co., solicitors.
76. The Volunteers were organized in 1859.

Wednesday 27 June 1860

The settlement as above effected yesterday with M[r] Manwaring is a great relief to me; as it obviates the necessity of legal proceedings: but I am very anxious as to the payment of the amounts falling due successively on account of the Westminster. I fear he will not pay me and that I shall be compelled to remove the Review from him.—

Thursday 28 June 1860

[No entry.]

Friday 29 June 1860

Returned the last proofs of the Review to press today.
Accompanied Johanna and her Mama to M[r] Ganz's[77] concert at S[t] James's Hall.—

Saturday 30 June 1860

Went with Johanna and Idalie to the Crystal Palace to hear the French Orpheonistes.[78] Their singing was very good, the effect was excellent, and general delight was the result; but I must confess that I was not stirred in the least. There was no grand and soul-raising sentiment in any of the things sung:—battle songs, and the glory of France were the highest peaks attained. The fountains, the whole of which played, were supremely beautiful.

Sunday 1 July 1860

The whether has at length begun to be fine. Spent part of the day in Kensington Gardens, the rest in working at my Cash account.

77. Adolphe Ganz, Johanna's teacher, had been musical director of the German Opera Company in London since 1845.
78. A chorus of 3,000 French singers at Sydenham. See the *Critic*, 30 June 1860, pp. 808–809.

Two things I ardently wish to accomplish:—1st to acquire a habit of reticence; 2nd to become more polite—treating even those most near to me with more outward and formal respect.—

Monday 2 July 1860—Monday 23 July 1860

[No entries.]

Tuesday 24 July 1860[79]

I am greatly embarrassed to decide which of the following courses I shall adopt: 1st To go on editing the Review, living in the same house and waiting for practice as now and endeavouring to secure what subsidies for the Review I can; 2nd To try to get a government situation continuing on as in Nº 1 meanwhile; 3rd To continue on as in Nº 1 but to endeavour to cultivate a practice among insane patients; or 4th While still editing the Review to avoid writing and to qualify myself for medical practice generally so as to be able to take a country practice hereafter.

Domestic difficulties are equally great: the longer I live the more painful to me is residence in the same house with my wife. Whether the change is chiefly in me or equally in both of us I cannot tell: it has certainly been very gradually effected. Now the gulf is too wide ever to close again. If her personal unattractiveness were the only fact I had to deplore we might at least live together in a friendly and even affectionate relationship; but alas there are almost no elements of satisfaction: As a housekeeper she is utterly inefficient; under her rule disorder reigns everywhere, —in every room, every drawer, box, basket and cupboard; the servants are prevented from doing their work regularly which seems therefore to be double its necessary amount; she can never rise early enough to secure that the breakfast shall be ready at the appointed hour; punctuality at meals is impossible; many of my most precious evening hours are lost because tea can never be had at the proper time; the domestic accounts, when she keeps them, are always in confusion; and notwithstanding all her *busi*-ness as housekeeper the cost per head of the family is either as little or is less when I am my own housekeeper as it is when she undertakes

79. This entry is written on the pages provided for the entries of 2–13 July.

it. Moreover while the fuss and bustle of her management is a continual disturbance, all is orderly and quiet in her absence. Though making pretensions to literary judgment, and the discussion of theological and social questions, she simply puts forth her crude opinions with a confidence as if they were really sustained by evidence or careful reasoning, and attempts to silence objectors by the most intolerant and unjust denunciations: on social topics especially all are immoral who dissent from her doctrines. Her chief reading is novels. Real study of any kind she has never applied herself to since her marriage. She has almost always had the children, i.e., Beatrice and Ernest with her and ought to have given them a good education. The chief thing she has done for Beatrice is to habituate her prematurely to read novels—her knowledge of French and Italian having been got elsewhere. Ernest is only now beginning to read easily and can scarcely write at all. Anything like real discipline,—the inculcation of habits of self-controul, good manners, studious application during a fixed time each day, has never been effected. For years I have steadily protested against her practice of giving [the] children tea and coffee each day: she has found it easiest and pleasantest to do so and therefore has persisted; and has thus contributed as I believe to induce puberty in both of them earlier than it would otherwise have come. In Ernest the morbid consequences are inflicting great injury on him and great anxiety on me. It was inevitable that my intimacy with J. v. H. should not escape the observation of the children, but the painfulness of my whole position has been greatly and needlessly increased by Mrs C's unjustifiable discussion of all matters with them.

My pecuniary difficulties still continue: Mr Manwaring owes me £175 on account of the July No of the Review, which ought to have been paid July 1st; meanwhile I cannot pay the contributors to the last West. and have only sufficient to subsist on.—

I believe I shall resolve to abstain from writing during the next 12 mos and shall devote most of my time to professional study. If the Review promised to be alone sufficient to support me I would throw myself wholly on it; as I much prefer to work at it.

Wednesday 25 July 1860—Tuesday 31 July 1860

[No entries.]

Wednesday 1 August 1860[80]

Took Idalie to the Isle of Wight. We reached Sandown the same night, and stayed at the Hotel there. The bay is 8 miles across, the bathing excellent but the village is not beautiful. The moon shone over the sea magnificently. We thoroughly enjoyed a walk on the beach, and the evening in the room where we supped with the window opening on the sea.

Thursday 2 August 1860

Having risen and breakfasted early we set off to walk along the edge of the cliff to Shanklin. The morning was lovely as the pre-ceeding day. We there found a beautiful spot—Gatten Villa—where we got rooms. The Landlady, Mrs Quinton, agreed to pro-vide board for Idalie at 15/— per week—the rooms being 25/—. She is enchanted with the place and arrangement. I left at 5 and reached home at 10.30 p.m.

Mme v. Heyligenstaedt was perfectly satisfied with the arrange-ment but Johanna was extremely angry because I had not gone on to Ventnor as originally intended, and because I had left Idalie alone in private lodgings.

Friday 3 August 1860—Friday 10 August 1860

[No entries.]

Saturday 11 August 1860

Rendered my account to Madame showing a balance due of £80. She was taken by surprise. Much more money has been spent than she counted on. She therefore got into a towering passion which she vented on Johanna who resented it very ill temperedly, and at last burst out crying. In fact the last night of their stay in the house was made wretched by this occurrence.

Mr Mayall[81] photographed Johanna and me; I fear the like-nesses will not be good.

---

80. The entries for 1–11 August are written on the pages provided for the entries of 13–17 July.
81. John Edwin Mayall, photographer, 224–226 Regent Street.

Sunday 12 August 1860

Left Waterloo Station by Excursion Train at 7.45. with Johanna and her mother and reached Shanklin at 2.30. Found Idalie looking very well. She gave me a very cordial greeting, and had had an excellent dinner prepared for us. The day was beautiful, and Gatten Villa was charming.

I left Shanklin at 4 and reached Albion S[t] at 12 p.m.

Monday 13 August 1860

A beautiful letter from Idaly.

The house seems a desert in gloom. Oh what a prospect the future now presents!

Called on Mayall. He has not succeeded well in photographing either me or Johanna. Sent his proofs to her.

Arranged with M[r] Call and M[r] Pattison[82] for Articles. M[r] D. Davies with me from 3 to 11 p.m.

Tuesday 14 August 1860

Mess[rs] Savill & Edwards' Bill on M[r] Manwaring falls due this day = £94. . 6. 4 guaranteed by J. C.

M[r] Mayall photographed me again yesterday—I believe successfully.

Wednesday 15 August 1860

Engaged all last night and nearly all today in making an analysis of the Heyligenstaedt's accounts. From January 1. 1859 to 7th 1860 Johanna's expenditure amounted to £296—nearly a third of the am[t] being for lessons.

Ernest returned at 6.30 from Brighton by Coach. He has a boil on his neck and his eyes are not well.

A letter came from Coulthard[83] who is expecting to become a Papa.

82. Mark Pattison (1813–84), writer on educational subjects, was elected Rector of Lincoln College in 1861.

83. Joseph Coulthard, Jun., translated William von Humboldt's *The Sphere and Duties of Government*, which Chapman published in 1854.

Thursday 16 August 1860

Called on Dr Carpenter about his article on Scientific Education. Promised to write him within 6 *days* if I should want it for October. He spoke slightingly of the National Review.[84] Mr Martineau is writing for its next N^o. Susanna and Beatrice returned from Brighton. They are both looking well. Wrote to Johanna, and sent Cash Book. Read Call['s] corrected article on Wit. Dont think it much improved.—

Friday 17 August 1860

Sent M^r C's article to Johnson for his opinion which [he] has written to me, and which confirms mine. Spent the morning in reading midwifery, and in the evening resumed my studies—for the book on Prostitution.[85]

Wrote to Idaly. Tried Beatrice in German-reading. She knows a good deal of German and shall read with me daily for improvement.

Saturday 18 August 1860

Sent advertisement to the Times (2 insertions) of Frau Bessels school.[86] Had a long discussion with Ernest about his future.

Johanna's letter which came today was not very agreeable in tone.

Read German with Beatrice, and continued my reading of Wilson, but was too tired to continue longer than 9 p.m. Learn that Mr Manwaring has gone out for 14 days; he leaves me without any intimation of a settlement of the amount he owes me.

84. The *National Review* was founded in 1855 by James Martineau and his friends after their disagreement with Chapman. See pp. 76–79.

85. The book was never finished. An article, "Prostitution in Relation to the National Health," appeared in the *Westminster Review*, 92 (July 1869), 179–234, and was reprinted as *Prostitution: Governmental Experiments in Controlling It*, London, 1870.

86. "Education in Germany. The principal of a boarding school for young ladies situate in the healthiest part of Heidelberg, desires to increase the number of her pupils. The instruction comprises the usual branches of a liberal education, particular attention being given to the German and French languages. For full particulars and terms, which are very moderate, apply to John Chapman, M.D., 1, Albion-street, Hyde Park, W." (London *Times*, 22 and 23 August 1860, p. 3.)

Sunday *19 August 1860*

Went to Beckenham, Kent, to visit Mr F. Harrison in order to hear his article on "Essays and Reviews". The scope tone and style are alike excellent. I shall let it stand as N° 1 in the next Westminster. During my walk to the house a lady met me and turned and stood several times to look at me. I found from Mr Harrison that she is Miss Shore—a lady I know!

Monday 20 August 1860

A letter from Mr Call expressing strong dissent from Johnson's criticism on his article, and evidently extreme vexation at my decision. Poor fellow he may well be vexed: he has written the article three times over!—
A long letter from Johanna.—

Tuesday 21 August 1860—Thursday 23 August 1860

[No entries.]

(Idaly
Friday 24 August 1860[87]

No letter has come yet from Manwaring. His conduct is as extraordinary as it is indefensible. Fears have crossed me that he designs starting for America with the money which I know he has at present in the bank. He owes me including his acceptances £240 besides the am^t of the purchase money of the business which is £900. I am liable for an acceptance of his for £35, and for the Rent of the business premises due at Midsummer; probably also for various accounts contracted before last April and which he may not have paid, as he is bound to do. The worst of it is I cannot take summary measures to make him pay by proceeding to remove the Review from him without lessening my prospect of

87. This entry is written on the pages provided for the entries of 21–24 August.

getting a release from O. H. Smith, which he has now twice promised me.—He called upon me on Wednesday, and then promised
he would return my acceptances forthwith; but he has not done
so. He also promised to send me a release from all claims as soon
as I send him a letter from Manwaring acknowledging that he
holds Mr Smith's stock on certain agreed upon conditions.

Since M^rs C's return home this time we have persistently avoided
all reference to painful topics, and by being cold, distant but respectful I have secured more peace during the last few days than
I have experienced in the same length of time with her in previous years.—

Saturday 25 August 1860—Wednesday 28 November 1860

[No entries.]

Thursday 29 November 1860

Bill due by Geo. Manwaring 40..16. 8

Friday 30 November 1860—Sunday 30 December 1860

[No entries.]

Monday 31 December 1860

Bill due by G. Manwaring March 1, 1860	36.	3. 4
Acceptance Sep^t 22. 1860 drawn by Savill & Edwards for	78.	16. 2
becomes due 25 Jany 1860.		
Acceptance drawn by Savill & Edwards Jany 1, 1861 at 4 mo^s and due 4th May 1861	73.	8. 6

[Two leaves containing the February accounts have been cut from
the Diary.]

NOTE ON CHAPMAN'S DIARY FOR 1863

A third Diary, dated 1863 on the cover, found with the others at Nottingham, was in the hands of Clement Shorter about 1915. Mr. Gabriel Wells, through whom the Yale University Library acquired the Diaries for 1851 and 1860, never had the later one in his possession. I have been unable to learn its present whereabouts. According to a note left by Mr. Shorter it contained no literary references, but only records of Chapman's medical practice.

Three articles by S.Y.E. in the *Nottingham Guardian* describe the Diaries in some detail. I have abstracted here the passages about that for 1863:

The third [Diary] has entries from January to March, 1863—then further entries dated 1866, 1867, 1877, and 1878, and the last entry dated Paris, December 14th, 1878. It is fair to conjecture that this was the last diary kept by John Chapman, and that after March, 1863 he kept no consecutive record of his affairs.

Nottingham Guardian, 4 May 1915.

In the last of his diaries, Chapman makes frequent mention of the books on medical subjects which he was writing—"Chloroform" was one, on which he had also contributed an article to the *Westminster*. . . . In his diary for 1863 he notes with all an editor's pride that in travelling by train he observed one of his neighbours reading the review. . . .

On January 21st, 1863, Chapman's diary contained a note that this was the last night he would sleep at the Albion-street house, and then he moved to No. 25, Somerset-street, Portman-square, where he remained until he left for Paris in 1875.

In this last of his diaries, the bulk of the entries, which are of a very interesting personal character, refer to his resumption of medical practice, among his patients whose names he records being Georgina Wilton, "the sister of Marie Wilton, the actress," who is better known to the present generation as Lady Bancroft. Chapman notes calls on Henry Morley, of the *Examiner*, R. H. Hutton, of the *Spectator*, and Edwin Arnold, who "offered to do something for me in the *Telegraph*" [to advertise his medical pamphlets?], but there are practically no entries relating to his friends of former years. . . . In 1866 he hears Dr. Bell Taylor lecture before one of the medical societies.

Nottingham Guardian, 1 June 1915.

INDEX

GE = George Eliot
JC = John Chapman
WR = Westminster Review

B ELIOT, G.
Haight, Gordon Sherman.
George Eliot & John
Chapman, with Chapman's
Diaries,